Europe
from A to Z
Guide to European integration

Werner Weidenfeld
Wolfgang Wessels

Institut für
Europäische Politik

**European
Commission**

European Documentation

Europe from A to Z
Guide to European integration

by Werner Weidenfeld and Wolfgang Wessels
Institut für Europäische Politik
Manuscript completed in November 1996
Drawings: Gelsomino D'Ambrosio
Cover and layout: Segno Associati, Italy

Contents

Foreword

The last few years of the 20th century are full of challenges for the European Union: at the top of the agenda is an institutional reform in 1997, followed by the final stages of economic and monetary union, and lastly the planned enlargement of the Union to include the new Central and East European democracies and Cyprus. At the same time many European Union citizens are facing high unemployment and other serious threats. The globalization of the economy seems to call into question the European Community model. Consequently, many people are viewing the future with pessimism and scepticism.

These challenges have given rise to debates in many countries about the purpose and objectives of the European Union in the run-up to the year 2000. The end of the millenium can be seen as the signal for a new beginning, leaving behind what is probably Europe's bloodiest and darkest century, to emerge into a new age, which, following the historic turning point of 1989, seems to hold out the promise of unification rather than division of the continent and peace instead of war. However, peace and prosperity cannot be achieved merely by a change of date, however symbolic, but only if the people themselves play an active part in shaping society and in living together. The European Union has been created with this in view, step by step over the five decades since the Second World War. For the next stages, if not a complete new beginning, the people of Europe are being called upon to mould European integration according to their wishes. Democratic forms have their beginnings in opinion-forming and discussion.

With this book the European Commission, together with independent experts on European affairs, aims to shed light on the tasks, organization and policies of the EU as seen from various viewpoints. The authors were asked to write about their respective areas of specialization in as concise, readable and factual a way as possible, to provide the reader with a reference work offering a quick but accurate overview of the EU. Following the articles in the 'Guide to Europe', there is an ABC of Europe containing brief definitions to help with the Community vocabulary. Readers of *Europe from A to Z* can therefore choose between a short statement of the facts or a more detailed outline. For example, should you wish to know what Socrates stands for, the answer is to be found in the list of abbreviations; the ABC of Europe contains a short description of this Union-wide university exchange programme, and anyone who wants to know more can find out from the article on education and youth exactly why the EU offers a programme of this type and what the other priorities of this policy area are. In each case, cross references guide the reader to further reading. The chronology sets out key events of European integration from 1946 to 1996.

Balanced information is a vital element of opinion-forming on the basic questions of European policy outlined here. We invite you to take this opportunity of finding out about and discussing Europe. At the end of the book is a supplement giving references to other sources of information produced by the Commission to explain its point of view to the public. You can also find up-to-date information which expands on the contents of this book on the Internet under http:\\europa.eu.int. The European Commission and the European Parliament also have contact points in every Member State, and you will find their addresses at the end of this book. This edition of *Europe from A to Z* has its origins in a highly successful book published several years ago by the Institut für Europäische Politik in Bonn. We would like to thank the publishers of that book, Dr Werner Weidenfeld, Director of the Centrum für angewandte Politikforschung, Munich, Dr Wolfgang Wessels, Director of the Institut für Europäische Politik, Dr Mathias Jopp, Mr Gerhard Eickhorn, Managing Director of the Europa Union Verlag, and the editor, Ms Nicole Schley of the research group on Europe at the University of Munich, headed by Mr Josef Janning.

Upheaval in Europe

For some years now Europeans have been living history in quick motion, going through a period full of conflict but without any clear defining pattern – in some respects an era with no name. Integration and disintegration, internationalization and provincialization, balance of power and struggle for power – all have been occurring at the same time, giving Europe a unique shape with new risks and uncertain constellations. There is no 'other side' to help us define ourselves any more. Europe has to constitute itself, positively and from within. Why should the nations and peoples of Europe bind themselves together in a common political system? And how is that system to be organized in such a way that it fulfils its citizens' expectations?

The current state of integration is simply the result of the gradual Community-building process begun by the Six in the 1950s. There may be more angles to it, but the thinking remains the same. This old thinking has exacted a high price, first from the Twelve and now from the Fifteen: the capacity for action has been greatly weakened. The Intergovernmental Conference on Maastricht in 1996-97 will have to provide a blueprint for a 20-nation and, in the medium term, a 30-nation European Union.

The situation after the Second World War In Europe's darkest hour, amidst the ruins of the Second World War, the most creative answer was offered to the question of what was to become of Europe. That answer was integration.

In his Zurich speech of 19 September 1946, shortly after the war, Churchill was already mapping out the way forward with his vision of a 'United States of Europe', the first step towards which was to be the establishment of a Council of Europe. Churchill spoke of a union, under the leadership of France and Germany, of all States wishing to join. Against a background of the worsening East-West conflict, the European movement, in the process of organizing itself in 1948, received a lasting impetus from the founding of the Organization for European Economic Cooperation (OEEC). The OEEC, set up to coordinate the implementation of the Marshall Plan, also demonstrated clearly that the international order could exercise a great deal of pressure to push along the process of European unification. As the eastern bloc became increasingly solid, there was the perceived threat of communism. In the meantime the Americans were lending their support to the European unification project, hoping to ease the burden that weighed upon them as world power and looking forward to the opening up of large, new markets. At the same time, the Western European countries wanted to join together to remove the risk of individual national States making new and dangerous attempts to go it alone.

This shared basic attitude did not, however, prevent differing tendencies from emerging on the question of integration after the founding of the Council of Europe on 5 May 1949: the confederation of States and the federal State.

At no time in the immediate post-war years, therefore, was the idea of European unification linked to one political concept or a single model of integration. Not being blindly fixed to a closed model of Europe, the unification process was able to take its impetus from completely different political events depending on the situation. From that starting point fresh progress could be made. In this way, the main feature of the wrangling over the unification of Europe over the years can be seen as a matter of pure pragmatism.

The Council of Europe In 1948, the Hague Congress demanded that a Council of Europe be set up. This was the moment when the European movement was born. The birth was marked by the dispute between federalists and unionists who were mainly in disagreement over the question of nations surrendering sovereignty to Europe. A political declaration demanded the political and economic union of European States involving the transfer of a limited portion of sovereignty. At this point there was mention neither of a federal European State nor of a European constitution. Nevertheless, several of the points made in the Hague resolution were later to acquire importance when they were implemented by the Council of Europe.

The European Coal and Steel Community On 18 April 1951, at the prompting of French Foreign Minister Robert Schuman (the Schuman Plan of 9 May 1950), the Treaty establishing the European Coal and Steel Community (ECSC) was signed. The original idea came from the Head of the French National Planning Institute, Jean Monnet. The ECSC was designed to create a common market for coal and steel, allowing common control, planning and exploitation of these raw materials and products. The motives underlying this proposal were ideas on how to overcome the traditional enmity between France and Germany and the desire to lay a foundation stone for a European federation. The Treaty establishing the ECSC came into effect on 23 July 1952 and, for the first time, one of the central areas of policy, until then a matter exclusively for the nation State, passed into the hands of a supranational organization. This comprehensive economic integration of the coal and steel industries was intended to lead eventually to political union.

The European Defence Community and European Political Community On 27 May 1952, representatives of the ECSC Member States signed the Treaty establishing the European Defence Community (EDC). It was the

idea of René Pleven, the then French Prime Minister, who was looking to establish a common European army under a European Defence Minister. This initiative had very far-reaching implications for the notion of national rights as the armed forces are an essential aspect of the sovereignty of the nation State.

At the same time, and as a response to the partial success represented by the integration of the ECSC and the attempts to set up the EDC, efforts were being made to achieve a complementary political agreement: the constitutional model. On 10 September 1952, at their first meeting as Council of the ECSC, the six Foreign Ministers decided to extend the assembly on an *ad hoc* basis with a view to drawing up the constitution of a European Political Community. This new Community was to have responsibility for coal and steel and matters regarding defence. It was also intended to guarantee the coordination of Member States' foreign policies. Further objectives for EPC were to be the development of a common market in the Member States, the raising of the standard of living and growth of employment. The existing ECSC and the planned EDC were to be integrated into the Political Community within two years.

However, at subsequent negotiations the Foreign Ministers failed to reach agreement on the extent to which nations were to cede sovereignty and in August 1954 the EPC was defeated in the French National Assembly. This meant there was no longer any basis for the constitution and the idea of a Political Community was abandoned.

1957

25 March 1957
The treaties of Rome establish the European Economic Community/EEC between Germany, France, BeNeLux and Italy

The Treaties of Rome At the conference of Foreign Ministers in Messina on 1-2 June 1955 it was decided to begin negotiations on integration in two further areas. The basic idea behind this move came from the Spaak Report, named after the Belgian politician Paul-Henri Spaak. The outcome of these negotiations was

the signing on 25 March 1957 of the Treaties of Rome which established the European Economic Community (EEC) and the European Atomic Energy Community (Euratom). Within the framework of the EEC, the six founder States of the ECSC wanted to set up a customs union. Another aim was formulated, namely the creation of a common market to allow the free movement of persons, services and capital. Euratom was designed to encourage the development of the nuclear industry in the six Member States. It obliged the Member States to use atomic fission exclusively for peaceful ends and also ensured supplies of the necessary raw materials. The Merger Treaty of 8 April 1965, which came into force on 1 July 1967, amalgamated the institutions of the ECSC, the EEC and Euratom.

The Friendship Treaty between France and Germany After the failure of the Fouchet Plan, which advocated a loose form of political harmonization between the Member States, the Franco-German Friendship Treaty of 1963 was the next major step forward in terms of integration. The Treaty was concluded by Adenauer and De Gaulle with a view to establishing close political cooperation which would inevitably attract the other Member States in the long term. Joined together in this way, Germany and France were to become the driving force behind European political union.

In the 1960s the difficulties involved in implementing the Treaties of Rome became evident. Since various aspects of economic policy had not been taken into consideration in the Treaties, calls were heard for economic and monetary union in order to avoid further crises being caused by national policies.

The Luxembourg compromise After the series of successes regarding European integration, the 1966 Luxembourg compromise represented a setback. During the period of transition provided for in the Treaty from 1 January 1966 the Council of Ministers would have been able to take decisions in important areas by qualified-majority vote. From 1 July 1965 France had been refusing to participate in EEC meetings, seeking through its 'empty chair policy' to prevent the transition from taking place. In response, the Luxembourg compromise of 27 January 1966 stated that consensus should be sought in areas of disagreement. France assumed that if it proved impossible to obtain this consensus, each Member State possessed a right of veto should its vital interests be affected. As a consequence, many promising lines along which a dynamic integration policy could have developed were cut off in the Council of Ministers.

1973

1 January 1973
Denmark, Ireland and United
Kingdom join the EEC following
accession treaties signed in Brussels
on 22 January 1972

Enlargement to the north The Hague summit of 1–2 December 1969 gave
fresh impetus to the integration process. Not only was the Community to be
enlarged to bring in northern European countries, it was also decided to introduce
economic and monetary union (EMU) by 1980, to reform the institutions, to hold
direct elections for the European Parliament and grant it additional powers. The
accession negotiations with Denmark, Ireland, Norway and the United Kingdom
that had started on 30 June 1970 were concluded with the signing of the
accession treaties on 22 January 1972. On 20 October 1971 the House of
Commons had voted in favour of joining the EC, and referendums in Ireland and
Denmark produced majorities in favour of accession. Only the Norwegians rejected
membership. The conclusions of the Hague summit also pointed to the need for
reform in important areas of the European Community and for greater integration.

Reform reports The crises and stagnation of the Community during the 1960s
prompted certain ideas of an intergovernmental approach. European Political
Cooperation (EPC) was established, providing the main instrument for
coordinating EC Member States' foreign policy, and on 27 October 1970 the
Foreign Ministers agreed on the principles and procedures of closer political
cooperation, as had already been set out in the Davignon Report. In its quest for
'European Union', uncertainties as to objectives caused the European Community
to formulate a general framework, the detailed content of which was supplied by
the Tindemans Report. The Report assigned the European Council, the successor
to the Conference of Heads of State or Government, the role of decision-making
body and emphasized the need for European integration, at 'two speeds' if
necessary.

The first attempt at Economic and Monetary Union The Hague summit and two Council resolutions, in March 1971 and March 1972, made clear the desire to add to the common market a common economic and monetary policy, the aim being to establish economic and monetary union (EMU) by 1980. This was intended to bring about the freedom of movement prescribed in the Treaties of Rome and to create a fixed exchange rate structure with unlimited currency convertibility. Moreover, Member States were to transfer central economic and monetary powers to the Community institutions. The plan was to be put into operation in several stages. The Werner Plan of October 1970, named after the then Luxembourg Prime Minister and Finance Minister, detailed these steps towards EMU. However, fundamentally different views of economy and integration, and the crises which the Member States had had to contend with, ruled out any possibility of coordinating economic and monetary policy, and thus of setting up a Community exchange rate system.

The fight against inflation which most of the EC States had been engaged in since the mid-1970s later resulted in a convergence of economic and monetary policies, greatly assisting a Franco-German initiative proposed by Helmut Schmidt and Giscard d'Estaing to establish a European Monetary System (EMS) centred around a common exchange rate mechanism. On 13 March 1979 the EMS came into force retrospectively from 1 January 1979. Exchange rates were to be stabilized for the good of economic development in the EC States. Every effort would also be made to lower inflation rates.

Interim results at the end of the 1970s A dispassionate stocktaking of the process of European integration at the end of the 1970s would have had to record omissions and flaws as well as successes and achievements.

- There was no doubt that the EC had gone a long way to achieving the basic freedoms laid down in the Treaties of Rome. Important obstacles to the free movement of goods had been surmounted and a common customs tariff had been introduced. It was also a feature of the common market that laws had been harmonized to dismantle barriers to trade and to taking up occupations. Yet despite this positive trend, some objectives had not been or had only been partially achieved. There were still, for example, customs formalities, freedom of movement was still limited and there were different tax rates. These failings made further progress on a common market essential.

- However much the details could be criticized, it could not be overlooked that crucial political spheres had been brought under the control of the Community and that this had played a not insignificant part in improving the economic welfare and democratic stability of western Europe.

- A common foreign trade policy had also been successfully introduced alongside the common market.

- The network of international preferential agreements and association agreements developed by the Community had increased its international standing and enabled it to pursue an active development policy.

On the other hand, it could not be ignored that the breakthrough to EMU had not been achieved. It was, however, clear that the Community was quite prepared to move into policy areas beyond those laid down in the Treaties if the tasks to be accomplished appeared to require it. This applied particularly to the development of new instruments which were in one sense outside the Community but were closely linked to it politically (e.g. EPC, the European Council and the EMS). It was also true of the reform of the Community finances, of the shifting of power within the Community through the transfer of budgetary powers to the European Parliament or the passing of the Act on elections to the European Parliament. Any move beyond the key areas laid down in the Treaties of Rome created new problems regarding integration, however, for national policies needed to be coordinated if areas in which the EC had not originally been given powers were to be absorbed into the Community sphere. Within the spectrum of strategies there were two competing views: supranational decision-making and international coordination. There was a growing danger that the strategy of international coordination might carry the day against the supranational strategy.

The catalogue of problems at the beginning of the 1980s The crisis afflicting the economies of the EC Member States since the mid-1970s produced a trend towards protectionism and nation States going it alone. Unfavourable developments in the world economy and economic problems within the EC made Community interests increasingly incompatible with those of the nation States. It was clear that solidarity was on the wane. Action by the Community was further hampered by problems regarding its institutional structure. Every single Community institution was facing enormous problems. In the years that had gone by the Commission had lost a great deal of its political weight. By applying the principle of unanimity, the Council of Ministers had greatly undermined the political logic behind the Commission's right of initiative. The work of the Council of Ministers, the Community's central decision-making institution, was characterized by ineffectiveness, its activities shrouded in the secretive mists of the decision-making procedure. The limited powers of the European Parliament were most relevant in the budgetary procedure, while the parliamentary element remained underdeveloped.

Another problem in the 1980s was posed by the difficult negotiations regarding enlargement to include the southern European countries. Growing resistance within the Member States – particularly France – delayed the admission of new members. While it was clearly tempting to expand the common market and strengthen the Community on the international stage, the attraction was offset by concrete drawbacks, such as increased expenditure on agricultural policy, on the Structural Funds and alterations to fisheries policy. The Community once again faced the question of the efficiency of decision-making procedures that had been developed for a Community of Six.

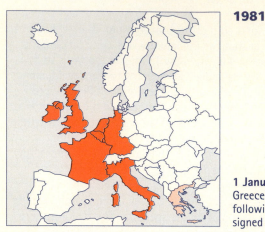

1981

1 January 1981
Greece joins the Community following the treaty of accession signed in Athens on 28 May 1979

Enlargement to the south Having overthrown the military regime and embraced democracy, Greece joined the European Community in the second enlargement on 1 January 1981. In the case of the Spanish and Portuguese dictatorships too, the European Community had always indicated that accession was possible as soon as the countries became democracies. The two countries of the Iberian peninsula explicitly gave their democratic processes a European dimension and the Community now had to keep its word.

In spite of the worries and fears, there was an air of celebration when the Spanish and Portuguese accession treaties were signed on 29 March 1985 and came into force on 1 January 1986, the accessions being viewed as a success, something of a rarity in European policy at the time. These two enlargements, which should be taken together, changed the political architecture of the EC. The common trend of development towards political union in Europe was displaced by a more economics-oriented approach. The contours of the integration process altered as the arrival of new southern European members shifted the political emphasis to the Mediterranean.

1986

1 January 1986
Portugal and Spain join the
Community following accession
treaties signed in Lisbon and
Madrid on 12 June 1985

Completion of the single European market One of the cornerstones
of continued integration was the Single European Act (SEA), which, after being
adopted by the Heads of State or Government at the Luxembourg summit in 1985,
came into effect at the same time as the accessions of Spain and Portugal. The
principal aim of the SEA was the completion of the common market as laid down
in the Treaties establishing the Communities. There were important reasons for
reiterating this aim and to set a date for completion – 31 December 1992.

- The EC was growing noticeably weaker on world markets and the times when
  the Community had recorded the highest growth rates worldwide were long
  gone.

- Resources were clearly being wasted in the field of research and the application
  of research results.

- Ten years of high unemployment with what were initially rapidly rising rates of
  increase prompted reflections on how to make the European economy more
  effective.
- It was also gradually becoming clear how expensive it was just to maintain
  cumbersome market segmentation.

The decision to create a market without barriers was the long overdue response.
The completion of the single market saw a dramatic expansion in the number of
areas where decisions were taken at European level. Once largely the preserve of
the individual States, the political framework of the market was increasingly
handed over to the Community political system. This made the question of
capacity for action one of the burning issues in Europe in the 1990s.

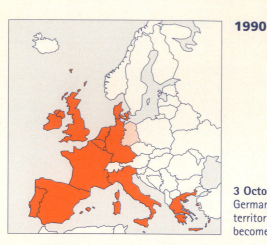

1990

3 October 1990
Germany is reunited and the
territories of the former GDR
become part of the Union

The development of the Community into the European Union

The consequences of the single market, both for internal and for foreign policy,
have greatly increased the need for effective decision-making. The Community
must respond to this: monetary union, powers with regard to the environment,
foreign policy, internal and external security. Community institutions must also
adapt. There needs to be efficient political leadership, a transparent, controlling
parliamentary system and a federal structure with a division of powers.

The progress achieved on monetary policy is undoubtedly a decisive step forward
for the Community. Monetary union, and the European Central Bank, are back on
the agenda. The last political steps on the way were the German Foreign Minister
Hans-Dietrich Genscher's 'Memorandum on the creation of a European monetary
area and a European Central Bank' of February 1988, the European Council
decision in Hannover in June 1988 to appoint a committee chaired by the then
President of the EC Commission, Jacques Delors, the final report of the Delors
Committee, Spain's entry into the EMS on 19 June 1989 and the decision at the
Madrid summit in June 1989 to embark upon the first stage of the three-stage
Delors Plan on 1 July 1990 and to start work on the necessary amendments to the
Treaties.

The report presented by the Delors Committee on 17 April 1989 is a key element in
the European debate about monetary union. The main item concerns the drafting
of a three-stage plan for EMU, the main institutional aspect being the creation of
a European System of Central Banks (ESCB).

The Treaty on European Union agreed and signed in Maastricht on 7 February
1992 is seen as the most comprehensive reform of the Treaties of Rome. It also
produced a clear timetable for further progress on the road to economic and
monetary union.

The second stage began on 1 January 1994, with the objective of enabling as many EU Member States as possible to qualify for the final stage and of preparing for the establishment of a European Central Bank. The criteria for entry into the final stage are price stability, budgetary discipline, convergence of interest rates and participation in the European Monetary System. By 1996 at the latest, the Heads of State or Government were to decide whether a majority of the Member States satisfy the requirements, before setting a date for completion of EMU. If this majority was not secured, the third stage would begin automatically on 1 January 1999.

The Maastricht summit also paved the way for European foreign and security policy to acquire a new dimension. The Member States committed themselves to developing a common foreign and security policy (CFSP) in all areas. On the basis of unanimous decisions reached by the Council of Ministers subsequent actions can be passed by qualified majority. This is the first time that the European Community has departed from the principle of unanimity on matters of foreign and security policy. As regards security policy, the Western European Union (WEU) is assigned a new role, becoming both a part of the European Union and a part of the Atlantic Alliance at the same time.

In this context it was agreed at the Maastricht summit to introduce citizenship of the Union, to increase cooperation in justice, home affairs and foreign policy, and above all to increase the powers of the European Parliament. Parliament now confirms the Commission, and the terms of office for Parliament and the Commission are concurrent. Parliament has obtained the right to set up Committees of Inquiry and to receive petitions. In terms of Community legislation, Parliament obtained the right of co-decision in matters regarding the single market, consumer protection, the environment and trans-European networks.

The ratification of the Maastricht Treaty by the Member States proved to be a more troublesome and protracted process than had been expected. Referendums were held on the Union Treaty in Denmark, France and Ireland. Whereas France and Ireland voted in favour of the Treaty, the Danish referendum sparked a crisis, as 50.7% of the Danes voted against the decisions reached at Maastricht and threatened to block the major reforms they contained. 1992 – the magical year when the single market was to be completed – turned out to be a roller coaster of a year. Although it proved possible, by means of concessions, to transform the Danish 'No' into a 'Yes', the near mythical incomprehensibility of the Treaty on European Union proceeded to colour the bitter debates raging, above all, in Germany and the United Kingdom. After the British Parliament had finally given its approval and the complaints of unconstitutionality had been rejected in Germany, the last hurdles had been cleared. All the States had ratified the Treaty and deposited their instruments in Rome. In November 1993, almost one year later than planned, the Treaty came into force.

Beyond Maastricht: deeper and wider Notwithstanding its achievements, the Union Treaty cannot conceal the need for reform on matters of European policy. Even if it was not possible to include the aim of a federally organized Union in the new Treaty, in the long term it is inevitable that the Community will develop on strictly federal lines with a clear separation of powers based on the principle of subsidiarity. The list of tasks ahead in the post-Maastricht era are moulded by two aspects concerning the form European integration should take: on the one hand, increasing the capacity for action by deepening the Union and developing existing policies, on the other hand, coming to terms with the expansions that have already taken place and those still to come.

In the shadow of the Maastricht crisis, the fact that the 'magic date' of 1 January 1993 for the completion of the single market was not adhered to passed almost unnoticed. While the implementation of 95% of the planned measures can be seen as an impressive success, the range of unresolved problems – the harmonization of the tax systems and internal security – made it impossible to generate any sense of jubilation about Europe. The report by a group of experts under the chairmanship of former European Commissioner Peter Sutherland had earlier made it clear that political organization and continued close cooperation would be essential for the single market to function successfully. Maastricht and the single market display the common characteristics of the process. They can both be seen as attempts to increase the Community's capacity for action enabling it to tackle what is still a long agenda of tasks relating to European affairs with a more effective set of instruments.

1995

1 January 1995
Austria, Finland and Sweden join the Union following the treaties of accession signed in Corfu on 24–25 June 1995

On 1 January 1995 the Union expanded again with the accession of Finland, Austria and Sweden and now comprises 15 Member States; but the problem of deepening the Union is still present, now more urgent than ever. In view of the evident magnetic attraction offered by the Union, the key problem of having the capacity for action will grow increasingly important, from the Six to the Fifteen of today, then on to the twenty-one, twenty-five or twenty-eight states with a population of about 500 million in the years to come. This raises the crucial question: how can a community of States so politically, economically and culturally heterogenous be organized at all?

Careful study of the history of European unification reveals that differentiation is the key to success: various forms of organization, different memberships, different speeds for implementation from the very beginning. The structures housing political union, the common foreign and security policy, economic and monetary union and the single market will no longer all be identical. Such a complicated, differentiated system can only be organized when it is on a predictable course. Differentiation could be arrived at by grading the degree of integration. Three models suggest themselves: firstly, the rapid integration of a hardcore Europe on the basis of the decisions reached at Maastricht on economic and monetary union; secondly, the establishment of a political union independent of participation in economic and monetary union; thirdly, the establishment of a political union by the members of the WEU, an option which puts a security union at the heart of the political deepening process.
On the basis of Franco-German initiatives, several central aspects could be developed in western Europe with sufficiently high levels of aspiration to counter the development of a Europe *à la carte*. Furthermore, these central aspects would overlap, thus limiting any loss in effectiveness.

The current state of affairs already contains an element of differentiation: the European Monetary System, the period of transition accompanying every enlargement, social policy, the opt-outs, additional agreements such as the Schengen Accord, exceptions in environmental policy, health and safety at work, the single market. And the next enlargement will necessitate institutional reform.

In a European Community of 20 or 30 States it will not be possible for every country to appoint a commissioner, nor would it be viable to continue to apply the same rotation principle for the presidency. It is equally true that the simple continuation of the weighting of votes and of the number of votes required for qualified-majority decisions would lead to the larger States being outvoted by the smaller ones. Therefore the European Union needs to find a way of organizing integration at a high level, but one that is differentiated along various lines. All these reform packages would create a new kind of Europe, continuing the astonishingly successful story of European integration.

The creation of a pan-European Community The end of the ideological conflict between East and West has left Europe on the threshold of unity. The same idea underlies the numerous cooperation agreements with Central

and East European countries, the Treaty on the European Economic Area, accession negotiations, not forgetting the close cooperation in the OSCE, in the Council of Europe or other forums, namely that a network of contractual relationships should secure stability throughout Europe and help to accelerate economic development in the new democracies. Where integration remains incomplete and where the capacity for action for the future remains underdeveloped, tragedies are waiting to happen. The nightmare of the war in former Yugoslavia will continue to haunt European policy.

As the major player in Europe, the European Union has a great responsibility. As the centre of gravity for all hopes of peace, stability, democracy and economic prosperity the Union cannot shirk its responsibilities. It must optimize its decision-making structures and clarify its objectives if it wishes to be taken seriously and be able to play its part on the European and world stages. From the very beginning, at the heart of what is now only the torso of European unification – limited as it is to western Europe – there is a vision of a future pan-Europe: a Europe without borders that separate, a Europe where opinions, capital and services can be exchanged freely and a Europe where conflicts can be resolved peacefully, without resort to violence.

Both internally and externally, in the transfer of powers and in the further development of the institutions, European policy is in need of a new, fundamental *raison d'être*. For a long time, the principles and decisions concerning integration were greeted with broad approval. Nowadays, each tiny step needs justifying to a sceptical public.

Europe needs to provide what is in the shared interests of its States. Above all, it needs to secure the future. This means providing economic prosperity, international competitiveness, peace, safety from the risk of new conflicts and the development of a pan-European Union in which Europeans can pursue their own fulfilment.

Werner Weidenfeld

The views expressed in this article are those of the author.

Guide to Europe

Agricultural policy

Treaty basis: Articles 38 to 47 of the EC Treaty.

Aim: To increase agricultural productivity and thus to ensure a fair standard of living for persons engaged in agriculture, to stabilize markets, to assure the availability of supplies and to ensure that supplies reach consumers at reasonable prices.

Instruments: Common market organizations with strong protection of prices through intervention in the internal market, import levies and (for milk and sugar) production limits, improvement of production conditions by supporting farms and inter-farm measures, improvement of the marketing structure, subsidies to compensate for natural handicaps, special programmes for disadvantaged areas and Mediterranean areas.

Budget 1995: ECU 40 980 million (54.3% of the total EC budget) was allocated to agriculture (including fisheries).

Literature from the European Union: European Commission: How does the European Union manage agriculture and fisheries?
Luxembourg 1996 (Cat. no.: CM-43-96-006-EN-C. Free).
European Commission: GATT and European agriculture.
Luxembourg 1996 (Cat. no.: CH-NF-95-001-EN-C. Free).
European Commission: The common agrigultural policy in transition.
Luxembourg 1996 (Cat. no.: CM-98-96-817-EN-C. Free).
European Commission: EC agricultural policy for the 21st century.
Luxembourg 1994 (Cat. no.: CM-84-94-444-EN-C. ECU 30.00).

According to Article 38 of the EEC Treaty (since 1993 EC Treaty), the common market extends to agriculture and trade in agricultural products. Article 39 specifies the goals of the common agricultural policy (see above), and Article 40 lays down the step-by-step development of a common agricultural policy and gives several options for organizing the agricultural markets, of which only the introduction of common market organizations proved to be practicable. Consequently, agricultural policy and the agricultural market gained a special position in the EC, which continues unchanged in the Treaty on European Union. Because of the high degree of regulation in this area, the majority of Community legislative provisions relate to the agricultural market. High costs and differing national interests have repeatedly made the common agricultural policy a Community flashpoint. The attempt to ensure a fair standard of living for the agricultural community primarily through support for Community prices at above world market prices led to the Community being accused by the outside world of protectionism, and to increasing surpluses. In spite of growing public expenditure, the goal of guaranteeing farmers' income was not achieved.

Market and price policy The key element of the market and price policy is the agricultural market organization, which separates the Community's internal market from the world market. This is done mostly through levies, i.e. taxes which correspond to the difference between the lower world market price and a threshold price that is set so that imported goods cannot be offered at below the target or guide price set for the Community's internal market. For exports, refunds calculated in the same way are paid. All prices applicable within the common agricultural policy are established annually by the → Council. Costs connected with price support are borne by the Guarantee Section of the European Agricultural Guidance and Guarantee Fund.

Percentage of labour force employed in agriculture
Men and women

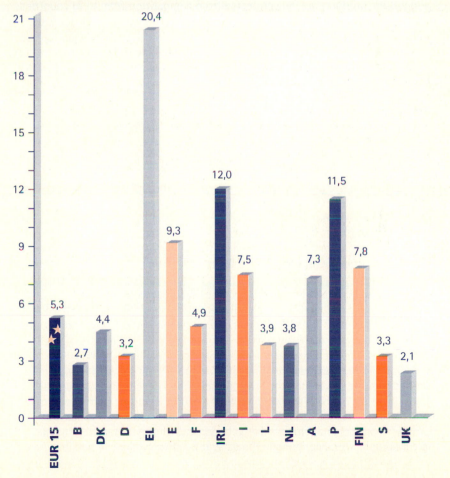

The 21 market organizations can basically be distinguished according to three organizational principles.

1. *Market organizations with price support.* For about 70% of agricultural products, the market organization gives a market and price guarantee, as well as external protection. This covers the most important cereals, sugar, dairy products, meat, certain types of fruit and vegetable, and table wine. Goods that cannot be sold at a given price, the intervention price, are bought up by State intervention agencies. The intervention mechanism has been relaxed in many market organizations in that the agencies only intervene when the market price drops below certain thresholds, and the full intervention price is no longer paid. The market organizations for milk and sugar also still contain quota rules, i.e. the price support is only given for production quantities established for each individual farm.

2. *Market organizations with common external protection.* Around a quarter of agricultural products are only protected from competition from third countries, without a price guarantee for the → single market. This group includes eggs, poultry, certain types of fruit and vegetable (those that do not belong to group 1), ornamental plants and types of wine other than table wine. As a rule, external protection is provided by means of customs duties. If the offer prices drop below certain thresholds, an additional levy is imposed.

3. *Market organizations with direct subsidies.* Until the reform of the common agricultural policy there was a distinction between supplementary and flat-rate subsidies. The former were supposed to secure an adequate income without raising consumer prices. Oilseeds and pulses are imported duty-free. Until the reform, the processors received a subsidy for the amount bought from Community production, and since the reform it is the producers that receive this. For olives, tobacco and durum wheat the producers receive a subsidy in addition to market prices being supported by external protection and intervention measures. Flat-rate subsidies are given for products that are only produced in the Community in small quantities. These include flax and hemp, cotton, silkworms, hops, seed and dry feed.

A fundamental problem arises when there are divergent exchange rate movements. Since the market organization prices are set in European currency units (ECU), they must be reduced in national currencies in the case of revaluation and raised in the case of devaluation. In order to avoid the drawbacks of such sharp changes, the exchange rates used within the agricultural market organization (green parities) are different from the central rates. In revaluing countries they are lower than the central rates and in devaluing countries they are higher. The result of this was that in revaluing countries duties were imposed on imports and refunds were paid on exports. In devaluing countries, duties were imposed on exports and refunds paid on imports. With the introduction of the single market in 1993, duties and refunds at the border became impossible. Any new monetary gaps (differences between agricultural exchange rates and representative rates) that might arise were to be eliminated in accordance with certain arrangements: for floating currencies adjustments in both directions would be possible, and for currencies with fixed margins, only price rises in the countries with weak currencies would be possible. After the decision on 2 August 1993 to widen the margins to 15% within the → European Monetary System, the rule was introduced that monetary gaps between two countries should not add up to more than five percentage points which could be taken up in full by the country with the positive gap.

Agricultural structures policy The 1972 structural directives introduced the first Community programme for agricultural structures. The principal aim was to restrict investment aid to viable farms. This was extended in 1975 by the directive on agriculture in mountain and hill areas and certain less-favoured areas, the aim of which was to maintain farming activity even where local conditions were not favourable. All these measures were taken over in 1985 in the regulation on improving the efficiency of agricultural structures (efficiency regulation). The rate of Community funding, which comes from the EAGGF Guidance Section, is higher in low-income countries than in high-income countries.

As part of the 1988 reform of the Structural Funds, use of the resources from the EAGGF Guidance Section was coordinated with those from the European Regional Development Fund and the European Social Fund for Objective 1 (Promoting the development and structural adjustment of regions whose development is lagging behind) and Objective 5b (Facilitating the development of rural areas). Objective 5a (Adjustment of production and processing structures in agriculture and forestry) largely represents the continuation of the agricultural structures policy under the 'efficiency regulation', is financed exclusively from the EAGGF Guidance Section and is not tied to a specific region. A separate demarcation of areas was made for Objective 5b, which covers extensive areas in France, the United Kingdom and Germany. Of the resources made available for structural development, which were doubled between 1989 and 1993 and came to ECU 60 billion in total, ECU 3.4 billion was allocated to Objective 5a and ECU 2.8 billion to Objective 5b. Before the end of the aid period, the Council adopted a supplementary arrangement for the years 1994 to 1999, with a further doubling of resources for structural policy measures scheduled. The resources available for Objective 5b were increased by 40% and the eligible regions considerably expanded.

Reform of the common agricultural policy Increasing financial burdens due to technical progress and unlimited market guarantees meant that a slight course alteration had to be applied. As a first step, the guaranteed quantities arrangements for milk were introduced in 1984. For the other products, the market organization prices were either no longer increased or only slightly increased and the intervention system was less automatic. On the basis of a decision made at the special Brussels meeting of the → European Council in February 1988, stabilizers were introduced for cereals, oilseeds and protein plants, which triggered an automatic lowering of intervention prices when fixed guarantee amounts were exceeded. All the Member States had to propose a land set-aside programme, but this was only partially successful. The same happened with an early retirement programme which the Member States have been able to propose since 1988, whereby participating farmers of 55 years of age or more can draw their pension if they give up market production for at least five years or sell their land to other, expanding, farms.

In order to prevent agricultural spending from getting out of hand again, a ceiling ('agricultural guideline') was imposed on the growth of compulsory expenditure under the EAGGF Guarantee Section in 1988, limiting it to 74% of the growth rate of the Community's gross national product from a starting point of ECU 27.5 billion.

At the core of a reform adopted in 1992 is the reduction in price support, the impact of which on agricultural incomes should largely be offset by direct payments. Between 1993/94 and 1995/96, the intervention price for cereals was cut, in stages, by 33%. In return the producers receive aid, which rises proportionally with the lowering of prices to ECU 207/ha (EU average), with the exception of small producers, but only if they set aside part of their land that was previously sown with cereals and oilseeds, for which a premium of ECU 262/ha was paid. For oilseeds the producer only received the world market price plus a premium of, on average, ECU 384/ha. For beef, the intervention price was reduced by 15% in three annual instalments. For the first 90 cattle for fattening per farm a premium of ECU 180 per head was paid.

Among the flanking measures, extensification and the use of production processes which particularly protect the environment and natural resources are encouraged. Setting aside areas of arable land for the purpose of protecting the environment can be subsidized for a period of 20 years. The promotion of reafforestation was made more attractive by increasing the Community part-financed subsidies.

Conclusion of the GATT Uruguay Round After seven years of negotiations, the Uruguay Round of the General Agreement on Tariffs and Trade was concluded on 15 December 1993. The results entered into force on 1 July 1995. In the negotiations agriculture proved to be a major stumbling block, above all because of opposing interests between the EU and the USA. The solution came in November 1992 with the Blair House Agreement, which was incorporated into the final act with minor changes. The main points were as follows.

• Market support was reduced by 20% from the 1986-88 bases, taking into account reductions made since 1986. Compensatory payments by the EU within

the framework of reform of the common agricultural policy were not concerned by this reduction.

- All external protection measures were converted into customs duties, to be reduced by 36% on average and by at least 15% per product by 2000.

- Expenditure on export refunds are to be reduced by 36% compared with the 1986-90 bases by 2000, and the quantities exported with refunds by 21%. Alternatively, 1991/92 could be chosen as a base period for the 1995-2000 transitional phase.

- From 1995 there is to be minimum market access of 3% of domestic consumption on the 1986-88 base, which is to be increased to 5% of domestic consumption by 2000. Adequate tariff reductions are to be made at the rate of the minimum market access.

- The EU undertakes to introduce a base area of 5.128 million ha for oilseeds (sown area 1989-91), of which the same percentage as for cereals, and at least 10%, must be set aside.

- If the EU's imports of cereal substitutes rise to over 19.2 million tonnes and imports of feedstuffs to over 40.5 million tonnes (imports for the years 1990-92), negotiations are to be opened between the EU and the USA.

The results of the Uruguay Round will entail extensive restrictions in some markets (sugar, beef, cheese) going beyond the reform of the common agricultural policy.

Enlargement of the Community In the accession negotiations with Austria, Sweden, Finland and Norway, concluded on 1 April 1993, agriculture proved to be a particularly difficult area, because the acceding countries gave agriculture relatively generous support, not least for reasons of regional policy. One of the main problems was how to sustain agriculture in the Arctic and subarctic regions of Scandinavia and the mountain areas of Austria after adjustment to Community levels of support. The acceding countries' desire for transitional arrangements was not met, since accession compensatory amounts and additional trade mechanisms would involve border controls and these would have been incompatible with the principles of the single market. The Community accommodated the regional policy issue by promising extensive compensatory payments. In the Scandinavian countries, areas qualifying for aid under the new Objective 6 were identified simply on the basis of population density (fewer than eight inhabitants per km^2). As support for agricultural adjustment to the conditions of the common agricultural policy the Community offered the new members compensatory payments of ECU 2.97 billion for the period 1995-98. For structural expenditure up to 1999, a budget framework of a total of ECU 8.89 billion was set.

Prospects The EU must adjust certain parts of its agricultural policy to the new conditions under the GATT agreement. In the long term the question will arise of whether the reform of the common agricultural policy has led to definitive stability. Since technical progress will undoubtedly continue in the future, production will keep growing and the GATT decisions will also have a limiting effect where this is not the case today. The Community will then once again face the question of whether it wants to take tougher measures to limit production or allow reductions in prices. The question will also become increasingly pressing with time after the compensatory payments introduced by the reform are accepted. In terms of foreign policy, the common agricultural policy will have to face the task of integrating the countries of Central and Eastern Europe into the European Union (→ Enlargement).

Winfried von Urff

Budgets

Treaty basis: Articles 199-209a of the EC Treaty; Articles J.11(2) and K.8(2) of the Treaty on European Union; Council Decision of 31 October 1994 on the system of the European Communities' own resources.

Aims: To finance the expenditure and activities of the Union and its policies; to lay down financial priorities for political action by the Union.

Instruments: Own resources and other EU financing instruments; general budget of the Union and individual sections of the budget; audits by the Court of Auditors.

Literature from the European Union:

The Community budget: The facts in figures.
Luxembourg 1996 (Cat. no.: C-69-59-62-13-EN-C. ECU 20.00).
European Commission: General budget of the European Union for the
financial year 1996: The figures.
Luxembourg 1996 (Cat.no.: C-69-19-56-97-EN-C. ECU 7.00).
European Court of Auditors: Auditing the finances of the European Union.
Luxembourg 1995 (Cat. no.: MX-89-95-632EN-C. Free).
European Commission: General Report on the Activities of the European Union 1996.
Luxembourg 1997 (Cat. no.: CM-93-95-152-EN-C. ECU 33.00).

The common budget policy of the → European Union forms the basis for its political activities. It defines the Union's financial scope for action and at the same time gives an indication of the resolve that actually exists to pursue integration and achieve the Union's objectives. At the heart of budget policy is the annual procedure of drawing up and finalizing the general budget for the Union and its institutions. This procedure involves laying down the structure of the budget and setting the level of the Union's operating and administrative expenditure (the use of financial resources). The budget procedure is firmly embedded in the Union's financial system.

Financial system of the European Union There have been several stages in the development of the Union's financial system since the founding of the European Coal and Steel Community (ECSC) in 1951 and the EEC and the European Atomic Energy Community (Euratom) in 1957, and since the institutions of the three Communities were merged in 1967.

Early on, the EEC and Euratom were financed by national contributions. This system was gradually changed with the introduction of 'own resources'. In 1970 the Council adopted a Decision 'on the replacement of financial contributions

from Member States by the Communities' own resources', which entered into force on 7 January 1971, after ratification by all the Member States. Under this Decision the old budget contributions were to be phased out by 1 January 1975 and superseded by a system whereby the Community would be financed entirely from its own resources. This timetable was extended by another five years, so that the Community budget became fully self-financing from 1 January 1980.

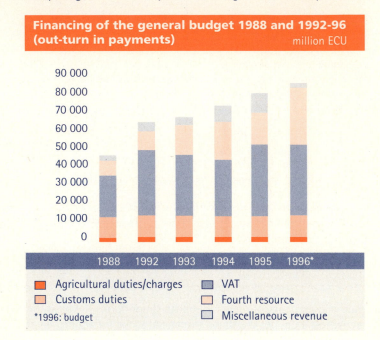

Financing of the general budget 1988 and 1992-96 (out-turn in payments) million ECU

*1996: budget

- Agricultural duties/charges
- Customs duties
- VAT
- Fourth resource
- Miscellaneous revenue

The Union's own revenue The term 'own resources' is not specified any further in Article 201, the main legal base for the 1970 Council Decision. Within this broad framework, three main sources of revenue were established in 1970:

(i)   agricultural levies (levies, premiums and additional or compensatory amounts which are imposed on trade with non-member countries);

(ii) customs duties levied on trade with non-member countries on the basis of the Community's Common Customs Tariff, and other customs duties;

(iii) revenue from VAT collected in the Member States, initially limited to a rate of 1% of a uniform, harmonized tax base applied in all Member States.

By far the largest proportion of the Union's revenue comes from its share of Member States' VAT receipts. This share was increased from 1 to 1.4% in

connection with the enlargement of the Community to 12 Member States on
1 January 1986 and has remained at that level, for the time being, even after the
enlargement to 15 Member States on 1 January 1995. When the VAT ceiling was
raised, the proportion of own resources accounted for by VAT rose to 66%. In 1995
it was around 54%.

Reform of the financial system The Community's finances were placed
in a new, medium-term framework in 1988 (after the Community had been
reformed by the Single European Act in 1986) and again in 1992 (with a view to
implementation of the Treaty on European Union). The medium-term framework
ties in with the completion of the → single market and the implementation of a
targeted structural policy and puts the budget on a secure footing until 1999. On
12 February 1988 the → European Council, meeting in Brussels, agreed on the
'Delors package', a set of coordinated budgetary measures concerning
 → agricultural policy and → regional and structural policy. The main elements of
the reformed own resources system, which was applied retrospectively from
1 January 1988, are as follows:

(i)   the overall ceiling for own resources, including all types of own resources, was
      set at 1.2% of the total annual gross national product (GNP) of the
      Member States at market prices;

(ii) binding intermediate ceilings were fixed for annual expenditure from 1988 to
      1992 so that the overall own resources ceiling would not be reached too soon;

Financing of the 1996 general budget by Member State

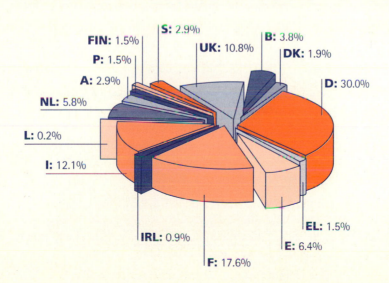

(iii) a fourth source of Community financing was established, alongside the three original resources, to be based on the total GNP of all Member States at market prices, calculated from a uniform base;

(iv) the fourth source of revenue is called in as an additional resource only where the Community's financial requirements cannot be covered by the three original resources. The maximum share of Member States' VAT revenue called in by the Community was kept at 1.4%, but an important change was also introduced here: under the new rules, the VAT assessment base of a Member State taken into account for financing own resources may not exceed 55% of its GNP. The aim of this 'capping' rule is to ensure that the financial burden is shared more evenly between Member States.

At the Edinburgh summit on 12 December 1992, the European Council reached agreement on the 'Delors II package', which, building on the foundations of the 1988 financial reform, sought to guarantee the future financing of the Union up to 1999, taking into account the full implementation of the Union Treaty (including the expansion of structural aid, measures to make European industry more competitive and the financing of the CFSP). Important features of the Delors II Package were:

(i) changes to the structure of the Union's own resources from 1 January 1995 aimed at reducing the role of VAT revenue and increasing the contribution from the GNP-based resource;

(ii) a mandate given to the → European Commission to investigate and report on the possible introduction of a fifth source of revenue by 1999.

The Union's own resources are collected by the Member States and made available to the Commission, which implements the budget (Article 205 EC). The Commission exercises certain inspection and monitoring powers.

In addition to own resources the Union may also borrow to finance investment in the coal and steel industry (ECSC borrowings) and in nuclear energy (Euratom borrowings); in the economic field borrowings may also be used to finance Community assistance and investment in industry, research and technology, energy and infrastructure (EC borrowings), for example through the New Community Instrument (NCI), which was set up in 1979 to promote investment projects in the Member States and to reduce regional disparities in the Community.

Structure of the budget Since 1967 there has been a single general budget for the three Communities, which have now been brought together under one roof as part of the European Union. The general budget is drawn up annually. It must be complete, showing all Union revenue and expenditure, which must be in

balance (Article 199). The same applies to administrative expenditure under the
→ common foreign and security policy (CFSP) and cooperation in the field of
→ justice and home affairs. The financial year runs from 1 January to 31
December.

On the expenditure side, the budget covers the administrative expenditure of the
Union institutions and expenditure on operations by the European Community (in
particular the agricultural, regional, cohesion and social funds) and Euratom
(research and investment). Certain categories of expenditure are dealt with
separately, the main ones being the ECSC operations, the EC's borrowing and
lending operations and the European Development Fund (EDF) for the ACP
countries associated with the Community under the Lomé Convention
(→ development policy), which is financed by Member States' contributions.
A distinction is made in Union expenditure between commitment appropriations
and payment appropriations. Commitment appropriations provide the financial
framework in which commitments for multiannual programmes can be made
during one financial year. Payment appropriations cover the actual expenditure
arising from the commitments in the current financial year or commitments
carried over from previous financial years. Since the switch to a self-financing
system between 1975 and 1980, the Community/Union budget has constantly
grown in volume. Between 1973 (which saw the accession of the United Kingdom,
Ireland and Denmark) and 1981 (when Greece joined), Community expenditure
rose by an average of 23% per year and the upward trend continued at a similar
pace in subsequent years. In the 1986 budget, the first to cover Spain and
Portugal, the growth rate fell for the first time to around 18%. Between 1988 and
1992 the Community budget increased by an average of 4.8% per year.

Structure of the EC/EU budget 1958-94 (UA/EUA/ECU million)[1]

	1958	1960	1970	1980	1990	1994
Totale expenditure	8.6	28.3	5 448.4	16 057.1	46 604.6	70 013.5
of which:						
EAGGF (agriculture)	–	–	5 228.3	11 596.1	27 233.8	40 222.0
Social Fund	–	–	64.0	502.0	3 212.0	5 819.0
Regional Fund	–	–	–	751.8	4 554.1	7 701.9
Industry/R&D[2]	–	–	–	212.8	1 738.7	2 593.0
Administration	8.6	23.4	114.7	938.3	2 298.1	2 428.0
Other	0.0	4.9	41.4	2 056.1	7 567.9	11 249.6

[1] UA (unit of account) until 1970, EUA (European unit of account) – 1980, ECU from 1990
(ECU 1 =).
[2] 1980 and 1990: industry, energy research; 1994: research and technological development,
industry.

Sources: European Commission Annual Economic Report 1993; OJ, L 34, 1994.

In terms of structure, the objectives set in the Union budget are now at least partly similar to the tasks undertaken by national budgets, demanding high levels of investment expenditure (e.g. regional policy and technological research funding). However, in financial terms the annual volume of the Union budget, although on the increase, is still relatively modest – in 1995 expenditure for the enlarged 15-member Union came to ECU 77.2 billion in payment appropriations – and can hardly be compared to the volume of a national budget, which is intended to cover all the expenditure and organizational targets of a modern industrial State and social welfare system. The cost of → agricultural policy and the common agricultural market organizations still accounts for the bulk of expenditure and is the area where most changes occur. Between 1968 and 1975 agricultural expenditure accounted for around 72 to 93% of the budget. After 1976 its share was between 60 and 75%, dropping to around 57% in 1992. Since 1992 the proportion of the budget devoted to agriculture has fallen further, amounting to 52% in 1994.

Breakdown of Union expenditure

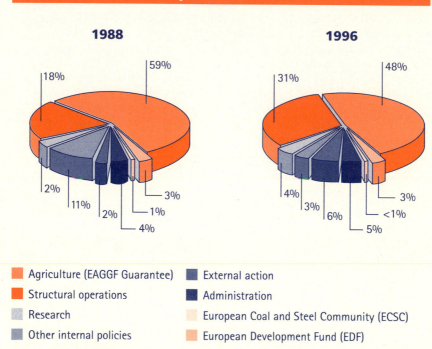

1988

59%
18%
2%
11%
2%
4%
1%
3%

1996

48%
31%
4%
3%
6%
5%
<1%
3%

- ■ Agriculture (EAGGF Guarantee)
- ■ Structural operations
- ■ Research
- ■ Other internal policies
- ■ External action
- ■ Administration
- ■ European Coal and Steel Community (ECSC)
- ■ European Development Fund (EDF)

In addition to agricultural policy and the Union's administrative expenditure (which accounts for around 5% a year), there are four main policy areas financed by the general budget (not including the CFSP and justice and home affairs): structural policy, development cooperation, → research and technology and other

policies (→ culture, → energy, → industry, → transport and the → environment). Aside from agricultural policy, around 36% of Union expenditure goes on other areas, that is, on creative and forward-looking Union activities.

The EU budget procedure The procedure for establishing the general budget comprises various stages and involves the → European Commission, the → European Parliament and the → Council of the European Union. The individual stages of the procedure are laid down in Article 203. Supplementary and amending budgets, which are necessary to accommodate unavoidable or unforeseen developments in expenditure, are established in the same way. When the Community's financial system was changed to introduce its own sources of revenue, the budget procedure was also reformed in two stages under the 1970 and 1975 Treaties. Since 1975, Parliament and the Council together constitute the budgetary authority of the Community (or Union) with complementary and dovetailing decision-making powers.

The budget procedure runs as follows: the Commission lays before the Council and Parliament the preliminary draft budget, which contains the individual proposals from Parliament, the Council, the Commission, → the European Court of Justice and the → European Court of Auditors. On this basis the Council establishes the draft budget, which it then lays before Parliament. During subsequent stages of the procedure Parliament enjoys various powers.

1. In the case of 'compulsory' expenditure, Parliament may address proposals for modifications to the Council, which has the final say. Compulsory expenditure is defined in principle as expenditure which, because of its basis or the sums involved, constitutes a legal obligation arising from the Treaties or from legislation derived from the Treaties ('secondary' legislation) or from commitments under international or private law (the prime example is agricultural expenditure);

2. In setting 'non-compulsory' expenditure (Community Structural Funds and other creative policies, e.g. research and technology), Parliament may amend the Council's spending proposals, within an annual margin calculated by the Commission, and, acting by a qualified majority, have them adopted even in the face of opposition from the Council. Since the distinction between compulsory and non-compulsory expenditure determines whether the Council or Parliament has the final say in setting the level of spending, it has been the subject of a power struggle between the two institutions. Other stages in the procedure are as follows:

(i) the Council adopts an amended draft, taking into account Parliament's amendments and proposed modifications;

(ii)   under the special 'conciliation procedure', the Council and Parliament try to close the gap between their respective positions;

(iii) Parliament examines the draft budget at second reading and establishes the budget in its final form. The budget is then published in the *Official Journal of the European Communities*;

(iv) Parliament can, however, reject the entire budget, if it has 'important reasons' to do so, and ask for the Council to lay a new draft before it (Article 203(8)).

If the budget has not been adopted by the beginning of the financial year, the provisional twelfths laid down in Article 204 come into play, using the previous year's budget as a reference.

Dialogue between the Union institutions is another feature of the budget procedure and the coordination of budget policy. It developed gradually as the Community became financially independent after 1970 and takes a variety of forms, including consultation on legal instruments with financial implications, the budget 'trialogue' and the more recent measures on budgetary discipline, which also laid the basis for medium-term financial planning up to 1999. The aim of the budget 'trialogue' and interinstitutional agreements is to avoid or defuse conflicts between the institutions in establishing the budget and to make the budget procedure run as smoothly as possible.

Implementation of the budget Once the budget has been established, the Commission implements it on its own responsibility (Article 205). This is particularly true for Section III, which contains all important operating expenditure of the Union. The other institutions implement their own sections of the budget themselves. Within each institution a financial controller supervises all payments and receipts. In addition, the independent European Court of Auditors monitors the execution of the budget as a whole and determines whether financial management has been sound. Each year the Commission must lay before the Council and Parliament the accounts of the preceding financial year. On a recommendation by the Council, Parliament gives the Commission a discharge for the implementation of the budget on the basis of the Commission's annual accounts and the Court of Auditors' annual report, together with the replies of the institutions.

Assessment and prospects The financial system is more than just one aspect of the Union's general make up; it is also a means of measuring progress on the road to full integration. The Union's budget and finances are therefore tied closely to its political and institutional development and constitute an important vehicle for carrying integration forward.

It is clear from the present structure and weighting of budget expenditure that it will be very difficult to finance further development of the Union, particularly towards → economic and monetary union and political union, on the basis of the present system of own resources and volume of funding. That is why, in December 1992, the European Council, acting on the basis of the Maastricht Treaty, decided to change not only the Union's institutional structures, but also the outlines of its financial system (in the Delors II Package), in order to adapt it to the demands of closer integration in the years leading up to 1999. Deeper integration will also require greater financial autonomy, that is, new own resources which would have to flow direct to the Union (e.g. tax-raising powers). Moreover, the Union budget would clearly have to be restructured so that agricultural policy no longer predominates and creative policies are given greater scope in the allocation of expenditure. In this respect the Delors II Package negotiated in 1992 is merely an intermediate step which can apply only to the immediately foreseeable programming period from 1993 to 1999.

The next stage in reform is the → Intergovernmental Conference, from which Parliament is expecting an extension of its budgetary powers and a review of the Union's financial system. It is already clear that if the European Union is to be expanded in future to include more than 15 Member States, its financial system must be radically overhauled.

Thomas Läufer

Committee of the Regions

Treaty basis: Articles 4(2) and 198a-198c of the EC treaty.
Responsibilities: To give the Commission and Council opinions either at their request or on its own initiative.
Composition: 222 representatives from the regional and local authorities of the EU: 24 each from Germany, France, United Kingdom and Italy, 21 from Spain, 12 each from Belgium, Greece, the Netherlands, Austria, Portugal and Sweden, 9 each from Denmark, Finland and Ireland, 6 from Luxembourg.
Budget 1995: ECU 27 million.
Literature from the European Union:
Committee of the Regions.
Luxembourg 1995 (Cat. no.: GF-88-95-969-EN-C. Free).
European Commission: Serving the European Union. A citizen's guide to the institutions of the European Union.
Luxembourg 1996 (Cat. no.: FX-89-95-939-EN-C. Free).

The task of the Committee of the Regions, which was set up by the Treaty on European Union, is to represent the interests of the regional and local authorities in the → European Union (EU) and to ensure their participation in the integration process.

The Committee of the Regions is made up of 222 independent representatives of the regional and local authorities and the same number of alternates, who are appointed for four years by the → Council of the Union, acting unanimously, on nominations from the Member States. The Treaty does not contain any rules on the distribution of the seats within the Member States or on the internal organization of the Committee. In almost all the Member States there was keen and, in some cases, controversial debate between the various levels of authorities over the distribution of the seats. Despite all the difficulties in allocation, the Committee of the Regions is, for its first term (1994-98), composed of about half regional and half local authority representatives.

Within the organizational structure of the EU, the Committee of the Regions has a position as advisory body to the Council and the → European Commission. Its role is to focus on regional and local interests and bring them into the → decision-making process, and in particular to monitor the compatibility of EU legislation with regional and local problems and with administrative practice. The Committee of the Regions is therefore concerned with bringing European decisions closer to

the people and to their concerns. In order for it to fulfil its tasks it must be consulted in a number of 'typical' regional policy fields (Articles 126, 128, 129, 129d, 130b, 130d and 130e of the EC treaty) and, furthermore, may be asked to give an opinion on all other questions or decide to do so itself. Committee of the Regions opinions have no delaying effects and are in no way binding on the decision-making bodies. It does not, therefore, have any formal possibility of gaining any influence for its views, and cannot take legal steps against any violation of its right of consultation.

Committee of the Regions

Advisory body of the European Union

222

representatives of economic and social groups

Policy areas in which the Committee must be consulted by the Council and the Commission

Promotion of general and vocational training

•

Culture

•

Health

•

Trans-European networks

•

Structural and regional policy

COMPLEMENTARY OPINIONS WHEN MATTERS ON WHICH THE ECONOMIC AND SOCIAL COMMITTEE IS CONSULTED INVOLVE REGIONAL INTERESTS

Internal organization The opinions of the Committee are discussed in eight specialist committees and then presented in plenary for adoption. With a view to the 1996 Intergovernmental Conference it has set up, in addition to the specialist committees, an *ad hoc* committee for institutional affairs. The demands on the time of regional and local politicians in the Committee of the Regions are therefore unusually high.

Cooperation between the members of the Committee of the Regions is formally carried out within the framework of political groups, of which four have so far been formed (EPP, PES, Liberals and 'Radicals'). However, unlike the situation in the → European Parliament, belonging to a political group is not strongly linked to a corresponding national party political affiliation, but is primarily connected with the membership of that particular group.

The administration of the Committee of the Regions is headed by a Secretary-General (until 1999, Dietrich Pause).

Assessment and prospects The Committee of the Regions undoubtedly started work under very difficult conditions. However, it very quickly managed to become operational, and to give opinions on issues that are sometimes extremely important in a regional policy perspective (for example, Community Structural Funds initiatives, EU citizens' right to vote in local elections, Green Paper on the EU's audio-visual policy). In future, what it needs to do above all is consolidate the internal working structures as quickly as possible and, in terms of content, avoid the risk of getting bogged down and concentrating on those EU policy questions that are of central importance from a regional and local point of view. Under these conditions the Committee of the Regions could develop its own institutional profile, becoming a forum of consensus-oriented and grassroots European politics.

Christian Engel

Common foreign and security policy

Members: All Member States of the European Union
Treaty basis: Treaty on European Union, Articles B and C (objectives, single institutional framework, consistency), Article J (provisions on a common foreign and security policy), Articles L and P.2 (final provisions) and four declarations annexed to the Treaty. Repeal of Titles I and III, Article 30 of the Single European Act of 28 February 1986.
Aims: To safeguard fundamental foreign policy interests, in particular the independence and security of the Union, taking into consideration the possibility of a common defence policy and a common defence, to preserve peace and to consolidate democracy, the rule of law and human rights.
Instruments: Common positions and joint actions, coordinated voting and joint positions in international organizations and conferences, joint representations, joint investigative missions, merger of diplomatic and Community instruments.
Literature from the European Union:
European Commission: The European Union's common foreign and security policy. Luxembourg 1996 (Cat. no.: CC-97-96-443-EN-C. Free).
European Commission: Intergovernmental conference 1996.
Commission opinion. Reinforcing political union and preparing for enlargement. Luxembourg 1996 (Cat. no.: CM-94-96-356-EN-C. Free).

The common foreign and security policy (CFSP) is a single worldwide system of cooperation between the Member States of the → European Union (EU) in international political affairs. The CFSP forms the second pillar of the European Union after the European Community (EC). For the governments involved it is also a vital means of protecting national interests in an era of global interdependence. The purpose of the CFSP is to safeguard the identity of the European Union on the international scene. Its most important declared objectives are to establish a practical, ongoing exchange of information and opinions on international political affairs, to align national positions, notably by developing a common basic approach, and to put these basic positions into practice through joint actions.

Important advances and shortcomings in the 1970s and 1980s
By the early 1970s, if not before, it became apparent that the decision by the Community's founding fathers not to pursue a coordinated foreign policy – even one that was not fully integrated into the Community – was increasingly unrealistic. Firstly, the Community had become a player on the international scene simply by virtue of its external economic policy; secondly, there was a growing realization that as the Community was progressively integrated into the world

economy, it would become dependent on developments outside its own borders, and that Western Europe might be able to cope better with international pressure of this kind if it could agree on a common position. The 1973 Arab-Israeli conflict was one of the first – although not always successful – testing grounds of European political cooperation (EPC). The Organization for Security and Cooperation in Europe (OSCE) is another field where the Member States have traditionally acted together, first as a Community of Six and now, after successive waves of enlargement, as a 15-member Union.

This policy of public pronouncements was often criticized as too reactive and passive, but it did have an impact on its targets, for example in definite cases of human rights abuse. However, the EPC approach on its own was too selective and ineffective in certain crisis situations. The Community realized that to wield any credible influence it would also have to offer – or withdraw – economic and, possibly, military support. It seemed inevitable that EPC diplomacy would have to be combined with the machinery of the Community (for example in the case of the Iraqi invasion of Kuwait and the war in Yugoslavia or in response to the break-up of the former Soviet Union and the democratization process in Central and Eastern Europe), which inevitably had implications for decision-making structures and procedures. The emergence of new challenges in foreign policy, the boost to integration supplied by the single market programme and the debate over EMU in 1990-91 sparked a discussion on the principles of a European foreign and security policy, leading to the adoption of provisions in Article J of the Treaty on European Union, which have been in force since 1 November 1993.

Basic elements of the CFSP and early experiences
It was hoped that by introducing all-embracing powers under the CFSP in the security field, 'including the eventual framing of a common defence policy, which might in time lead to a common defence' (Article J.4 of the Treaty an European Union), the Union's policy could be made more coherent and its capacity to act strengthened. This substantial increase in powers reflects a change in Western Europe's security policy interests, which can no longer be covered solely by the Atlantic Alliance. In institutional terms this task falls to the Western European Union (WEU), an institution devoid of significance for the last decade. As 'an integral part of the development of the (European) Union' WEU acts at the 'request' of the Union, drawing up and implementing decisions and measures which have defence implications (for example the deployment of a police force for the EU administration in the Bosnian city of Mostar). Like other CFSP provisions, Article J.4 was the outcome of a conflict between national interests and consequently open to interpretation in practice. The institutions of WEU and CFSP thus remain independent of each other, at least until the WEU Treaty expires in 1998, a rather dubious arrangement from the point of view of efficiency, particularly since the WEU is extending its operational capacities in fields such as crisis management, where it touches on areas of EU responsibility. To reduce any negative effects,

efforts have been made to establish systematic working relations between WEU and the EU since the Union Treaty entered into force. Initial attempts to flesh out the EU's military dimension, now enshrined in the Union Treaty, have so far proved highly controversial. At first the notion of security was interpreted in a broad sense, leaving untouched the conceptional and operational aspects of a common defence, which are regarded as highly sensitive. Points at issue here include the obligation to come to the assistance of fellow members as well as security guarantees for present and future members, the implications for the Atlantic Alliance and the question of military capabilities with or without NATO support.

The decision to abandon the consensus principle, a major innovation in the CFSP according to the traditional diplomatic view, and to establish a new instrument in the form of joint actions which are expressly binding on Member States, was intended to counter the justifiable criticism that internal decision-making procedures are inefficient and that the Union comes across in the outside world as lacking unity and being too reactive. It is hardly surprising that these provisions were written into the Treaty only after a hard struggle and that the United Kingdom in particular wants to apply them as restrictively as possible. Majority decisions are specifically confined to joint actions, and even here only in the case of implementation, whereby the Council, as the main decision-maker at all stages of the procedure, may determine whether the unanimity or majority rule applies.

Bearing in mind these and other institutional shortcomings (for example in the reorganization of expert committees and the division of tasks between the Political Committee and the Permanent Representatives Committee), the success of the CFSP during its start-up phase has been rather mixed.

Although the Member States did react swiftly – at least for a while – in their first joint actions in October and November 1993, this was often offset by the fact that the decisions they took failed to come up with suitable answers to international problems or created unforeseen difficulties such as the question of who finances joint actions. By way of example, the exercise of sending European observers to elections in Russia was not properly thought out and lacked coordination, as it could cover only a marginal part of the strategy of stabilizing the Russian President and lay outside the far more important framework of the partnership agreement between Russia and the European Union. Elsewhere, the Union's efforts to carry out a joint action to 'polish up' its seriously tarnished image in relation to the war in former Yugoslavia had little impact on the media or on European public opinion. The Union's position was further compromised by the fact that the → Council struggled for months to reach a basic decision on how to meet the costs of the CFSP which are described in Article J.11 as operational expenditure. As the Member States' coffers were empty, charging these costs to the Community budget seemed an attractive proposition. However, this would also mean, at least in the eyes of the main supporters of integration, in particular → the European

Parliament and the → European Commission, that the rules governing the Community budget procedure would apply, which in turn attracted the attention of those favouring an intergovernmental approach to the CFSP. Finally, in 1994, it was agreed that joint actions could be financed either from the Community budget or by national contributions, which would be calculated on the basis of the GNP of the Member States. Union contributions for operational measures have been included in the Commission budget (Section III B 8) since 1995, thus making the Commission and Parliament important players in the CFSP. Purely administrative expenditure, for example for CFSP meetings and interpreting services, is covered by appropriations in the Council budget and therefore not subject to Parliamentary influence under existing interinstitutional rules.

Another of the early joint actions was the stability pact, much praised as a model of preventive diplomacy, which is aimed at channelling potential disputes between the countries of Central and Eastern Europe into talks – through a series of procedural proposals and conferences – which may also include representatives of the European Union. Ideally, disputes would be resolved by agreement before conflict breaks out. The Union also launched a joint action in an attempt to maintain a presence in one of its traditional areas of activity, the Middle East. It laid down a framework for EU aid totalling around ECU 500 million to consolidate the agreement between Israel and the PLO on the autonomy of the former occupied territories of Gaza and Jericho. The first series of joint actions *vis-à-vis* South Africa has been judged by CFSP participants and observers as at least a one-off success. The Union's first aim was to help prepare the first elections in South Africa in 1994 with a European election team of over 450 people, focusing on technical and organizational aspects, advice and training for election helpers and public information through the media. As the democratic process continues, the Union plans to pursue existing Community aid programmes, put an end to remaining sanctions and conclude a wide-ranging cooperation agreement, including what is now a customary security clause on human rights and democracy.

On more than one occasion discussions in this field – and on Union positions in other international matters (for example relations with Ukraine and aid for Rwanda) – were hampered by disputes over the demarcation of powers, which went beyond purely technical and legal aspects, reflecting the tension between supporters of Community orthodoxy, who fear CFSP 'interference' with the first pillar, and those following the traditional foreign policy line under the second pillar, who believe that the CFSP must lay down comprehensive guidelines.

Between 1994 and 1996 guidelines or legal instruments were adopted for more joint actions, dealing for the first time with security policy. However, these actions were concerned primarily with procedural matters, such as the preparations for the Conference on the Nuclear Non-Proliferation Treaty and the introduction of a system for controlling Union exports to non-member countries which could be used for either civilian or military purposes ('dual-use' goods).

The structure of the CFSP Like the old EPC, the CFSP has four tiers of hierarchy. At its head is the European Council, which defines general guidelines (Article J.8(1) of the Treaty on European Union), has ultimate authority in the event of irreconcilable differences of opinion between the bodies beneath it, initiates proposals for reform and expresses common positions *vis-à-vis* the outside world. The second tier of decision-making – and the one which plays the leading role in day-to-day affairs – is occupied by the Council, i.e. an institution of the European Union (Article J.8(2)). The idea behind this merger is to improve consistency and the efficiency of decision-making structures, but at the same time such an approach harbours considerable potential for conflict and for new problems regarding the delimitation of powers, as early experiences have shown.

It is therefore not surprising that the fusion of EPC and EC bodies at political level has had an influence on the bureaucratic machinery. This is particularly true of the activities and self-image of the Political Committee, which consists of the heads of political departments in Member States' foreign ministries. Although the Committee is supposed to continue preparing the substantive work of the Council, either on its own initiative or at the Council's request, and to monitor the implementation of the CFSP, its old EPC role as a pivot between political and administrative authorities has been diminished by the 'intrusion' of a newcomer, the Permanent Representatives Committee (Coreper), an ambassadorial body which is also staffed by high-ranking representatives from the Member States and has been traditionally responsible for preparing and finalizing the Council's work, including CFSP affairs. It seems that the rough division of responsibilities envisaged between the two bodies – the Political Committee examines the content of the CFSP, while Coreper acts more as a technical coordinator or looks after Community-related aspects – has established a *modus vivendi* acceptable to both parties, although rivalry and inefficient decision-making cannot be ruled out. The Political Committee and Coreper are assisted by over two dozen expert groups. The European Correspondents Group has hitherto enjoyed a special status, examining and monitoring the general organization of the EPC/CFSP. In the long run this function could also be taken over by the CFSP Secretariat, which was integrated into the General Secretariat of the Council under the Union Treaty, provided that it has an adequate staff complement. Another important element in this fourth tier of the hierarchy consists of meetings between the ambassadors of Union Member States to non-member countries and international organizations and conferences, which are normally held every month.

The internal management of the CFSP and its representation in the outside world depend very much on the Presidency, which is held by each Member State in turn for six months in accordance with the rota laid down in Article 146 of the EC Treaty, a system with undoubted benefits but still far from being entirely satisfactory.

A further example of how the institutional structures of the CFSP and the

Community have become noticeably closer is that the Commission, long-feared as a potential member of EPC, now has a right of initiative in the CFSP comparable to that of the Member States. This right enables it to become a more active, 'fully associated' partner (Article J.9). In practice this means, for example, that Commission representatives participate in all outside contacts by the Presidency under the Troika system and are included in consultations between embassies of Union Member States in non-member countries concerning the CFSP. Another innovation is that the Commission is required to inform the European Parliament about the development of the CFSP, a task it shares with the Presidency.

In principle – and particularly in the eyes of governments – the European Parliament's role in the CFSP remained unchanged. Article J.7 confirmed the existing – and widely used – right of MEPs to ask questions and the Presidency's obligation to report to Parliament regularly. However, it should not be forgotten that Parliament has considerable opportunity to intervene by virtue of its right to give or withhold approval on all major Union agreements with non-member countries and its budgetary powers, especially where Community funds are needed to implement CFSP decisions, and that it intentionally uses these opportunities in order to boost its standing in the CFSP.

Future prospects As the CFSP provisions have so far been interpreted in a rather restrictive fashion and the Member States tend to stick to customary practices, the Intergovernmental Conference on the revision of the Treaties has little room for manoeuvre. The United Kingdom in particular still seems to insist on applying the intergovernmental method, but there is also a certain reluctance to abandon the unanimity rule on the part of the new Member States and France. The Benelux countries and Germany clearly seem to regard such a step as vital, especially with the prospect of an enlarged Union of 20 or more members. There are considerable differences of opinion between the 15 Member States and within the European Parliament over whether and how the WEU should be brought under the Union structure, for example as a fourth pillar, with the option of a merger with the CFSP under a phased plan to be drawn up at a later date. The Commission and the Governments of the Member States are also warning that the CFSP's analysis and planning capabilities must be improved. It has been proposed that a unit be set up consisting of representatives of the Commission, the Member States, the General Secretariat of the Council and WEU. Whether such a body should only act internally within the CFSP or have an external role, how it would fit in to the CFSP hierarchy and who should lead it are questions which still need to be clarified and promise to be highly controversial.

Elfriede Regelsberger

Competition policy

Treaty bases: Articles 4, 5, 65 and 66 of the ECSC Treaty, 3(g), 5 and 85-94 of the EC Treaty.

Aims: To ensure an economic system that guarantees undistorted competition between equal market participants.

Instruments: Ban on cartels, prohibition of the abuse of dominant positions on the market, merger controls, controls on State subsidies.

Literature from the European Union:

European Commission: XXVth Report on competition policy 1995.
Luxembourg 1996 (Cat. no.: CM-94-96-429-EN-C. ECU 20.00).
European Commission: European Community competition policy - 1995.
Luxembourg 1996 (Cat. no.: CM-94-96-421-EN-C. Free).

The aim of competition policy is to create and maintain a system permitting undistorted competition within an economic region. In liberal economic theory, competition policy aims to ensure markets with perfect competition and endeavours to prevent the emergence of monopolies and oligopolies able to dictate prices to the disadvantage of consumers. Only in exceptional cases are monopolies permitted, to guarantee the reliable provision of goods or services of significant public interest. For example, Europe has had state monopolies in transport, postal services and telecommunications. Through its Treaties, the → European Union has at its disposal a wide range of competition policy instruments for banning cartels in the European → single market, prohibiting the abuse of dominant positions on the market, ensuring equal treatment for public and private enterprise, imposing merger controls and monitoring national subsidies. Because of the globalization of the economy, however, the European Union finds itself increasingly confronted with the problem of reconciling the maintenance of competition within the European single market with the competitiveness of European enterprises on the world market.

Principles The → European Commission sees itself as the guardian of competition both within and outside the European Union. However, its powers of intervention in these two areas differ widely. In three chapters containing Articles 85 to 94, title V of the Treaty establishing the European Community regulates the various subjects and procedures of competition policy. Under these provisions, the Commission intervenes in principle in those areas covered by the Treaty where State aid, agreements between enterprises, mergers or other forms of cooperation jeopardize competition.

Articles 85 and 86 of the EC Treaty prohibit anti-competitive agreements between enterprises that may affect trade between Member States, and the abuse of 'a dominant position within the common market'. On being informed of agreements by firms, following complaints or at its own initiative, the Commission can investigate the matter and, where necessary, impose legally binding penalties on anti-competitive conduct. These two articles are of central importance for European competition policy, as they have a direct impact on the conduct of companies. The total number of cases investigated under Articles 85 and 86 of the EC Treaty has grown considerably over the past 15 years. For example, the number of cases examined in 1980 was 299, but by 1993 the figure had risen to 404. However, Articles 85 and 86 also provide for exceptions. If European oligopolies need to be established in order to be able to hold their own against the intensified international competition, the Commission may consent to such alliances in individual cases. Vertical agreements between companies can also be approved if they result in increased efficiency through access to new markets. However, such agreements may not be of a price-fixing nature or divide up territories. Since 1990, Articles 85 and 86 have been supplemented by the Merger Control Regulation. This provides for preventive control of mergers between firms with a Community-wide impact. It permits proactive intervention in economic concentration processes, that is to say, mergers can be approved or banned beforehand.

Also of great importance for competition policy are State aid and subsidies that may distort competition. Articles 92 to 94 of the EC Treaty regulate the procedure for the monitoring of aids by the Commission, an activity which has had to be considerably stepped up since the end of the 1980s as a result of the escalation in subsidies. However, the Commission does not in principle refuse to approve national aid programmes, provided they are explicitly aimed at correcting structural imbalances in certain sectors of production. For example, it has consented to various programmes for restructuring steel firms, subsidized by the Member States of the European Union, but in return has called for a considerable reduction in capacity to put this sector on a sound footing. The principle in the control of subsidies is that State aid must have a structural impact, be final in character and benefit the entire branch of industry.

In addition to monitoring competition, the European Commission is also striving for an active role in regulating competition. In 1993, for example, it took the initiative to introduce competition in several sectors hitherto dominated by a few firms with a monopoly position. For sectors such as transport, energy and telecommunications, which are important for the competitiveness of European enterprises, the European Commission is pursuing a policy of liberalization to ensure that these sectors are opened up to competition in the interests of the consumer. In April 1993, for example, the Commission issued a communication on services in the telecommunications sector, which proposed a complete liberalization by 1998. The aim is to create the conditions for a universal service by then. This deadline is intended to be sufficient to allow the firms in question, which have hitherto had exclusive rights, to adjust to the new circumstances.

Assessment Europe both seeks and avoids competition. This apparent paradox characterizes the situation in the European Union, which is confronted with a dilemma resulting from the differing levels on which European competition policy operates. Competition policy in the European Union is concerned in the first instance with the behaviour of enterprises and States within the Union and takes insufficient account of economic globalization. In the single market, the European Union has a legal system for effectively penalizing anti-competitive behaviour. However, such measures have no effect on a global scale. Consequently, measures to ensure competition may increase competition within the single market, but weaken the competitiveness of European firms *vis-à-vis* their international competitors. An international system for regulating competition has yet to emerge. The formation of oligopolies or monopolies may result in imperfect markets at world level, preventing free competition. To prevent such processes, use is made of industrial policy and trade policy as State regulation instruments to protect home markets against aggressive international competition. There is a regulatory conflict between competition policy on the one hand and industrial and trade policy on the other. Industrial policy and trade policy both aim to secure optimum market results, while competition policy is concerned with optimum market processes. The outcome of this conflict, and the different standpoints of the Member States of the Union, is a regulatory impasse that prevents Europe from taking consistent action oriented to both the European single market and the world market. In view of international economic trends, however, Europe increasingly needs a competition policy that ensures both competition on the European single market and the competitiveness of European firms on the world market. To this end particular efforts are required at multilateral level, within the international economic organizations such as the OECD, G7, the General Agreement on Tariffs and Trade (GATT) the WTO, the World Bank or the International Monetary Fund, to arrive at legally enforceable rules for international competition to ensure free competition between market participants.

Jürgen Turek

Consumer policy

Treaty base: Articles 3(s) and 129a of the EC Treaty.
Objectives: Protection of consumer rights in the areas of safety and health, compensation for damage, protection of economic interests, representation, information and education.
Instruments: Action programmes and legal instruments.
Budget: 1996: consumer information: ECU 8 million; consumer representation and access to the courts: ECU 6.15 million; quality control and production monitoring: ECU 5.9 million, total: ECU 20.05 million.
Literature from the European Union:
European Commission: European consumer guide to the single market.
Luxembourg 1996 (Cat. no.: C-59-095-776-EN-C. ECU 9.00).
European Commission: The European Union - What's in it for me ?
Luxembourg 1996 (Cat. no.: CM-43-96-001-EN-C. Free).

The → single market of the → European Union (EU) offers a vast range of goods and services. The consumer market is growing but its transparency is on the wane. Consumers often find it difficult to see the wood for the trees in the European market. It is incumbent on the EU, through action programmes and legal instruments, to harmonize trade conditions and requirements throughout the Union so as to provide a dependable basis for all parties to business transactions. With a view to guaranteeing Union citizens a 'high level of consumer protection', the Treaty on European Union, which entered into force in November 1993, introduced Article 3(s) and Article 129a, for the first time enshrining European consumer policy as a Union domain in its own right.

Development of consumer protection The preamble to the Treaty establishing the European Economic Community calls for 'constant improvements of ... living and working conditions' in the interests of consumers in the Member States. Article 2 of the EEC Treaty enshrined 'accelerated raising of the standard of living' as an objective. → Agricultural policy (Article 39) is also designed to ensure that supplies reach consumers at reasonable prices. And, last but not least, the Community's competition rules (Article 86) outlaw all abuses 'to the prejudice of consumers'.

As European integration gathered momentum, the need for a common consumer policy became increasingly obvious. In 1975 the Council of Ministers (→ Council of the European Union) adopted the 'Preliminary programme of the European

Economic Community for a consumer protection and information policy'. It focused on the protection of five basic rights: 1. protection of health and safety; 2. protection of consumers' economic interests; 3. the right to reliable information; 4. consumer redress and, 5. consumer representation at Community and national level.

Further consumer policy programmes were adopted for 1981-86, 1990-93 and 1993-95. Basically, they followed up the criteria and objectives of the first action plan. But despite continuous adaptation, consumer protection in Europe was initially slow to get off the ground. All too often the ambitious plans clashed with powerful economic interests.

Consumer protection got a new impetus with the adoption of the Single European Act in 1987: the new Article 100a (3) of the EC Treaty stipulated that in developing the single market in the domains of health, safety, environmental protection and consumer protection, a 'high level of protection' had to be taken as a base. Thus the Single Act enshrined the concrete legal basis for consumer protection in Europe. In the Union Treaty this provision is supplemented by 'specific action' to protect the health, safety and economic interests of consumers and to provide adequate information to consumers.

Implementation of consumer protection Like the growth of the internal market, implementation of consumer protection is a gradual process. By harmonizing standards the → European Commission sought to secure a standard level of protection at Community level while simultaneously removing barriers to trade. But the constraints on consumer policy rapidly became evident: the business lobby was too powerful and the legal basis for consumer protection was too weak, while the procedure of harmonizing goods on a case-by-case basis was laborious and time-consuming. Discussions on European directives and regulations dragged on for years, with the requirement that Council decisions be adopted unanimously often leading to stalemate.

In its 1985 White Paper on completing the single market the Commission adopted a 'new approach' to consumer policy. Since then the Council has been adopting directives to protect health and safety *en bloc* for whole categories of products. Thus national legal provisions must not be painstakingly standardized in detail for each individual product. Experts at the private European standards organizations CEN and Cenelec are empowered to draft technical standards on basic safety requirements for products. The CE marking is a seal of approval and guarantees a standard minimum level of protection.

Since 1987 the principle of mutual recognition has applied across the board: anything that is legally manufactured and marketed in one Member State may be sold in all other Member States. This was enshrined by the → European Court of

Justice in its landmark *Cassis de Dijon* judgment. However, besides the advantage of widening consumer choice, this principle also has its downside. This is because goods may be placed on the market throughout Europe even if the manufacturing process in individual countries is deemed to be defective. Hence, in the interest of consumer protection there are certain constraints on the free movement of goods: individual Member States may adopt more stringent protective provisions and in exceptional cases may even ban imports of specific products. There must be serious grounds for doing so – for example protection of consumer health or of consumers' economic interests. A total export ban on British beef was imposed in 1996 following the BSE outbreak. At the same time the Union introduced a programme of measures to combat the disease.

How have consumers benefited? A European directive requires consumer information to be provided concerning the composition and shelf-life of all food. Purity criteria and binding lists clarify which additives are permitted and which are not. A draft regulation would in future make the labelling of genetically modified products compulsory where the chemical structure had clearly changed. National provisions apply to the irradiation of food for the purpose of conservation; to date there are no Union-wide rules.

Since July 1994 the cross-border insurance market is a reality: any insurance company approved in one Member State may market its policies in all other Member States. Because of the singularities of the Member States' domestic legal orders, the EU has not attempted to standardize the various provisions in full. For clients this means that the picture is often complicated and confusing. Hence consumer associations have been clamouring for harmonization of the basic legislation governing insurance contracts.

European consumer organizations have given numerous fillips to consumer protection. One major demand was satisfied in 1985 with the adoption of the Directive on liability for defective products. In the event of damage it is no longer the consumer who has to prove the existence of the defect – instead, the manufacturer must prove that his product was not defective. If he cannot do so, he must pay damages. Another example is the Directive on doorstep selling, which gives buyers a one-week cooling-off period before their contract becomes legally binding. Sellers throughout Europe are obliged to inform clients in writing about this right to cancel the contract. The Community has also adopted many other directives in the interests of consumers, such as the directives on toy safety, cosmetic products, textiles, construction products, mail order purchases, misleading advertising and unfair terms in consumer contracts. There are also standardized rules governing package holidays, consumer credit and the rights of air travellers. To fill consumers in on the plethora of decisions, regulations and directives that apply to shopping in Europe, the Union has created European consumer advice centres. These info-centres see it as their mission to protect citizens and advise shoppers on how to avoid the pitfalls that await them. They provide information on where and how to find the best bargains in Europe. The computer network Coline gives the consumer info-centres swift, focused, and state-of-the-art access to the relevant provisions and rules in neighbouring countries.

Assessment The Treaty on European Union gave a fresh impetus to consumer protection policy. But much remains to be done if consumers are to make the most of the internal market. Above all, awareness of the relevance of consumer issues differs greatly from one country to another. To this day the status of consumer protection in each Member State varies both in legal and organizational respects. While Germany and the United Kingdom have a fine-meshed network of local information centres, consumers seeking advice in Greece are less well-served. There is a clear north-south differential in regard to consumer protection. The spectrum of opinion – ranging from apologists of a liberal policy in the service of industry to advocates of strict regulation – is as variegated as the European Union itself.

Ralf Schmitt

Council of the European Union

Treaty basis: Articles 145-148, 150-154 of the EC Treaty.
Responsibilities: Decision-making powers, coordination of national policies, executive powers.
Composition: Each country is represented by one minister.
Voting: Decisions may be taken by simple or qualified majority, or unanimously.
Literature from the European Union:
European Commission: Serving the European Union. A citizen's
guide to the institutions of the European Union.
Luxembourg 1996 (Cat. no.: FX-89-95-939-EN-C. Free).
Forty-second review of the Council's work: The Secretary-General's report.
Part I + Part II.
Luxembourg 1996 (Cat. no.: BX-51-95-002-EN-C. ECU 20.00).
The Council of the European Union.
Luxemburg 1996 (Cat. no.: BX-94-96-146-EN-D. Free).
Noel, Emile: Working together; The institutions of the European Community. Luxembourg
1994 (Cat. no.: CC-76-92-172-EN-C. Free).

The Council of the Union is the organ which represents the Member States. It does, however, perform the role of a legislative chamber and also has executive powers. Although it was originally intended to carry out its role without an administrative staff of its own, a rapid increase, both quantitatively and qualitatively, in the activities of the European Community led to the Council becoming overburdened and to a multiplication of the sectors in which a ministerial council was established – there are now over 20. As early as 1958, the Permanent Representatives Committee (Coreper) began its support work for the Council. Subordinate to the Coreper, working parties of national officials were established and there are now some 200 of these. Together with the Council's General Secretariat, the Permanent Representatives Committee and the working parties make up the considerably expanded administrative structure of the Council.

Until the Treaty on European Union came into force on 1 November 1993, the history of the Council had been profoundly marked by a lack of decision-making capacity, especially during the 1970-85 period. The failure to make use of the option of qualified majority voting in a number of fields, as offered by the EEC Treaty, the enlargement of the EC in 1973 and the inability of the Member States to move forward to other common objectives after the completion of the → single

market, left the Council in a 'decision-making trap'. The establishment of the
→ European Council of Heads of State or Government (1974), which
institutionalized the earlier irregular summit meetings, was an attempt to create a
political authority which could ease the work of the Council of Ministers and the
other Community bodies by setting clear priorities and guidelines. In reality, the
Council became even less capable of taking decisions once the European Council
was created, since it became the practice to leave important decisions to the
Heads of State or Government.

More dynamic decision-making within the Council of Ministers was brought about
by the 1986 Single European Act and, in particular, the objective – shared by all
Member States – of completing the single market. Rather than tackling head-on
the problem of Member States' refusal to apply the principle of majority voting,
the SEA deftly linked the majority principle with the decisions needed to complete
the single market. Since about 1986, decision-making in the Council has in
practice accelerated and decisions taken on a majority basis are quite normal
occurrences.

The Treaty on European Union abolished the distinction, still drawn in the Single
European Act, between the EC Council of Ministers and meetings of Ministers in
the framework of → external relations. It is the Council which is competent for
the → common foreign and security policy (CFSP) and for cooperation in the fields
of → justice and home affairs: in the case of the CFSP, there is even the option in
special circumstances of taking decisions on the basis of a qualified majority. The
cohesion of the three pillars of the → European Union (EU) is now apparent in the
official title 'Council of the European Union'.

Functions and institutional position The main function of the Council
is to represent the interests of the Member States at EU level. The fact that the
Council at the same time possesses general decision-making powers demonstrates
that the interests of the Member States are the major factor determining the
policy of the EU and that these take priority over the Community interest as
embodied by the → European Commission and → European Parliament.

In the beginning, the Council had sole decision-making powers in all EC policy
fields. Executive powers were also predominantly held by the Council. Although
there has been no fundamental change to the position of the Council within the
institutional system, it has in the meantime been required to delegate its
executive powers to the Commission and to share its decision-making powers with
the European Parliament in connection with the → budget and association
policies, and also in the matter of accession treaties. The introduction by the SEA
of the 'cooperation procedure' (Article 189c) by the Single European Act, and of
the 'co-decision procedure' (Article 189 b) by the Treaty on European Union, has
involved a gradual and significant increase in the influence exerted by the

European Parliament on EC/EU legislation. In the field of → economic and monetary union, the Council is responsible, on the recommendation of the Commission, for the coordination and multilateral monitoring of national budget policies.

The continued dominant position of the Council within the institutional system is limited in particular by the fact that, with some minor exceptions, it can act in fields of common EU policy only on the basis of a proposal submitted by the Commission. Every meeting of the Council, or of its subordinate bodies, is attended by representatives of the Commission who are entitled at any time to amend or withdraw the Commission's proposal. Given that the Council must act unanimously to amend a Commission proposal but in many cases can adopt the Commission's text with a qualified majority, it is very rare for the Council to take a decision without the agreement of the Commission. In the case of the common foreign and security policy, by contrast, proposals may be submitted to the Council by either the Commission or by Member States (Article J8(3)), whereas cooperation in the fields of justice and home affairs accords the right to initiate proposals predominantly to the Member States (Article K3 (2)).

Voting system There is no central voting system in the Council; rather, there are individual prescriptions in the EC Treaty which set out how the individual bodies are involved in the → decision-making process and what voting system is to be employed in each case. The Treaties allow for voting by simple majority in the Council when no other system is stipulated. A vote requiring a particular majority ('qualified majority') or even unanimity is, however, the rule. Certain decisions of constitutional importance require not only a unanimous decision in the Council but also ratification by the Member States in accordance with their constitutional provisions (for example, in the case of the EC's own resources as described in Article 201).

Where provision is made for a qualified majority, the votes of the Member States are weighted in accordance with Article 148(2) as follows: Germany, France, United Kingdom and Italy each 10, Spain 8, Belgium, Greece, Netherlands and Portugal each 5, Austria and Sweden each 4, Denmark, Finland and Ireland each 3, Luxembourg 2.

A qualified majority is obtained when at least 62 of the total of 87 votes support the decision; 26 (29%) of the votes then comprising the 'qualified minority'.

The EEC Treaty envisaged a transitional period, after which certain decisions would be taken by qualified majority. When this transition was due to be effected in 1965, France opposed the move and withdrew its representative from Council meetings ('the empty chair policy'). For the next nine months, the Council was unable to take any decisions until, on 18 January 1966, the so-called 'Luxembourg compromise' was reached. Issues involving a 'vital national interest' of a Member State henceforth required that the search for a compromise should continue until the Member State concerned was able to support the joint agreement. In practice, this compromise meant that with very few exceptions majority voting in the Council between 1966 and 1985 was restricted to budgetary matters. The implicit acceptance by the Member States that the Luxembourg compromise should be interpreted as a right to veto any decision a Member State disliked, resulted in a constant attempt to achieve unanimity and meant that a single Member State could delay a Council decision for years or even block it entirely.

The Single European Act did not abolish the Luxembourg compromise but it did result in suspension of its application. During the negotiations for the accession of Finland, Austria and Sweden to the EU, Britain and Spain long opposed the arithmetic adjustment of the number of votes required for a qualified majority or blocking minority to 62 and 26 votes respectively. Both countries wanted to retain the old 23-vote blocking minority in order to maintain the influence of the 'major' countries, and, in the case of Spain, to maintain the 'southern block'. The solution adopted in April 1994 resembles a partial revival of the Luxembourg compromise: while 26 votes do constitute the qualified minority, the casting of between 23 and 25 votes against a decision would require further negotiations to be conducted – though for how long is not made clear. This is an indication of a widespread pattern of 'renationalization' of European policy.

Operation: a consensus-seeking machine Irrespective of the voting procedure to be used in any particular case, the operation of the Council is that of a machine designed to find common ground between the Member States. Within this machinery, decisions are taken at three different levels. The many working parties of national officials have in particular the task of discussing the technical aspects of the proposals drawn up by the Commission. The working parties send the texts they have examined to the Permanent Representatives Committee as a second 'clearing' house. At this, already political, level an attempt is made to smooth out the remaining clashes between the interests of the Member States and to produce a decision which in specific cases may require only a qualified majority for adoption. At each of these levels, the meetings are chaired by the representative of the Member State holding the presidency of the Council. The close intermeshing of the Member States' administrations and the EU is apparent from the fact that these working parties primarily comprise the same national officials as are on the bodies consulted by the Commission during the preparatory phase of its decisions. The permanent representations to the EU are the most important junction between the Member States and the Union; they are in constant close contact with the Commission and the permanent representations of the other Member States.

Council meetings are major events: the Ministers are accompanied by specialist advisers and over a hundred people may be involved. Accordingly, the various ministerial councils meet increasingly often in so-called 'informal' sessions attended by the Ministers alone. In order to tackle particularly serious problems, so-called 'Jumbo-Council meetings' – attended by two or more ministers from each Member State – are sometimes held. As a result of the openness debate set in train by Maastricht, the first public meetings of the Council took place in 1993.

Despite increasing recourse to the option of qualified majority voting, the practical work at all levels of the Council continues to be dominated by the search for consensus. Member States in a majority on one issue know that they will find themselves in a minority position on others and thus dependent on the understanding of their partners. Moreover, discussions in the Council generally feature highly changeable coalitions of Member States. Overhasty isolation of some Member States could later mean that no qualified majority can be obtained. In practice, therefore, majority decisions are taken only where one or more Member States are unwilling or unable to accept a compromise.

One of the important aspects of the operational capability of the Council is the chairmanship, or 'presidency', which rotates among the Member States every six months. With the assistance of the Council's General Secretariat, the 'memory' of the institution, it is the task of the presidency to prepare the work of the Council, to lead discussion and to pilot the Member States towards compromises. In this latter role, the presidency often works closely with the Commission, since a compromise can often only be reached with its help.

Prospects The question with regard to the future of the Council is whether it will develop further in the direction of a European Upper House or Senate. It is, however, only realistic to expect that the Council will adhere to its past practice of only gradually sharing its responsibilities with other EU bodies, in particular the European Parliament. More strongly than in classical federations, the European Union will continue in the future to be marked by the double legitimacy of the Member States in the Council and the elected representatives of the people in the European Parliament. It should be noted that the Council has comprehensive responsibilities under the existing Community treaties and in the non-Community fields of the common foreign and security policy and cooperation in matters of justice and home affairs. It is accordingly responsible for coherence in the activities carried out under the various pillars of the Union.

Christian Engel

Culture

Treaty basis: Article 128 of the EC Treaty; Article 92(3)(d) of the EC Treaty.
Aims: Improvement of the knowledge and the dissemination of culture and history; conservation of cultural heritage; non-commercial cultural exchanges; encouragement of artistic and literary creativity; development of a European culture industry.
Instruments: Cultural activities and programmes, employment and social policy.
Budget: 1995: ECU 15.2 million, about 0.02% of the EU budget.
Literature from the European Union:
European Commission: Grants and loans from the European Union.
Luxembourg 1995 (Cat. no.: CC-90-95-106-EN-C. ECU 35.00).

European Union policy on culture Until the Treaty on European Union came into effect there was no explicit treaty basis for cultural affairs and cultural policy within the framework of the European Community. Some Member States had constitutional or political reservations about general cultural policy being 'subsumed' under Community policy. The cultural activities of the Community were therefore based on individual decisions made by the → Council of the European Union. Since the advent of the Treaty on European Union, Article 128 of the EC Treaty provides a treaty basis for the inclusion of culture as a sphere of activity, requiring, on the one hand, that the Council reaches its decisions unanimously and, on the other, that the → Committee of the Regions be consulted.

In the Union all the institutions have an input into cultural affairs and cultural policy. The → European Council provides the decisive stimulus for developments in cultural matters. General aspects of cultural policy are dealt with at Council meetings of Culture and Education Ministers. The → European Commission is responsible for preparing and implementing Council decisions. Nowadays cultural affairs and cultural policy fall within the remit of Directorate-General X, which is responsible for information, communication, culture and audio-visual media. By using its budgetary powers the → European Parliament can exercise an influence on the degree of financial provision for cultural programmes. It also participates in the decision-making process under Article 189b of the EC Treaty.

As a rule, the Union can make use of the same legal instruments in the sphere of cultural affairs as are available in the other areas of Community policy. However, harmonization of national legislation and administrative regulations is expressly excluded. The Council mostly limits itself to arriving at decisions and conclusions to which the Member States commit themselves politically rather than legally. Nevertheless, these provide the Commission with important instruments with which to implement programmes.

In the areas of → economic and → social policy, EU cultural programmes aim both to improve the economic and social position of people in the cultural sector and to develop a 'cultural industry' in Europe, an aim which also ties in with the completion of the → single market. The most important issues here concern national subsidies and taxation of cultural productions and cultural goods, questions of copyright and the protection of performing rights, social provision for those involved in the cultural sector, the promotion of the audio-visual industry (→ media policy) and vocational and advanced training in the cultural sector.

Article 128 sets out the general aims of cultural policy as encouragement, support and, where necessary, supplementing the actions of Member States in the following areas: improvement of the knowledge and dissemination of the culture and history of the European peoples; conservation and safeguarding of cultural heritage of European significance; non-commercial exchanges; artistic and literary creation, including in the audio-visual sector; cooperation with non-Member States and international organizations, in particular the Council of Europe.

While the themes of EU cultural programmes frequently coincide with the work of the Council of Europe, the methods of implementing them differ, especially with regard to developing and financing practical activities. There are many examples of this, such as the concerts by the 'European' youth, baroque and jazz orchestras; poetry festivals and cultural events mostly organized by unemployed artists under the Kaleidoscope 2000 programme; further vocational training for young people involved in the cultural sector; the conservation of cultural heritage under the Raphael programme; the development of and training in the use of conservation technologies; the encouragement of literary translation through the Ariane programme, and participation in the activities centred on European cities of culture.

Conclusion Apart from cultural activities with a direct economic importance which are areas for 'tough politics', above all in the Union, cultural policy is aimed more than anything at encouraging as wide a range of private cultural activities as possible. Having been provided for by the Heads of State in the Maastricht Treaty, the non-commercial cultural policy is still waiting for the Commission to give it real substance by implementing programmes and activities, and the Member States are making sure that the subsidiarity principle is being followed to the letter. In the sphere of European culture, the wide range of activities will, however, remain a matter for private initiative and will develop in their own way.

Bernd Janssen

Decision-making procedures

Treaty basis: Articles 137, 138b, 141 and 142 (EP); Articles 145 and 148, 150-152, and 189a (Council); Articles 155, 189a (Commission); Articles 189-191 of the EC treaty. For special decision-making procedures for the common foreign and security policy and cooperation in the fields of justice and home affairs see Articles J and K of the Treaty on European Union.

Bodies concerned: European Commission, European Parliament and Council of the European Union. These bodies are assisted by the Economic and Social Committee and the Committee of the Regions acting in an advisory capacity (Article 4(2)).

Decisions: EC instruments under Article 189 of the EC treaty. Decisions adopted under the budget procedure (Article 203 of the EC treaty) and the common foreign and security policy and cooperation in the fields of justice and home affairs (Articles J and K of the treaty on European Union) are of a special type.

Literature from the European Union:

European Commission: 'The EU's future shape - the 1996 Intergovernmental Conference': A new database on the 1996 Intergovernmental Conference.
Luxembourg 1996 (Cat. no.: CC-97-96-136-EN-C. Free).
European Commission: Intergovernmental Conference 1996. Commission report for the Reflection group.
Luxembourg 1995 (Cat. no.: CC-89-95-357-EN-C. Free).
European Commission: Serving the European Union. A citizen's guide to the institutions of the European Union.
Luxembourg 1996 (Cat. no.: FX-89-95-939-EN-C. Free).

Decisions of the European Community and the European Union are reached in accordance with a variety of procedures governed by legal acts; together these make up the decision-making process of the → European Union (EU). At the centre of the decision-making procedure is Community legislation, which is in theory divided into three stages, initiative, consultation and decision-making (which form the basic structure of legislation); however, Community legislation follows a number of different procedures, the details of which vary according to the subject matter (Community policy). Under the basic model for general legislation the → European Commission, → European Parliament (EP) and the → Council of the European Union work closely together. The Commission, with its right of initiative, is responsible for the preparatory work. The EP consults public opinion on the proposal, taking into account the positions of the political forces represented within it, and produces opinions in the form of resolutions. Both the Council and Parliament may themselves call on the Commission to make proposals and influence its right to propose legislation by means of corresponding initiatives of their own. Although, at the moment, the final power of decision still lies with the Council, as the Union's principal legislator, Parliament has secured a partial role as a joint legislator under the Treaty on European Union (co-decision procedure under Article 189b).

For the purposes of the legislative procedure, the Community bodies are locked into a fixed and binding system of competences. This system is based on the principle of 'specific conferment powers': whether the bodies may act at all, what measures they may adopt if they do, what legal form these measures must take and what procedural rules must be observed are all matters deriving solely from the actual terms of the Treaties and especially the EC Treaty as updated by the Treaty on European Union. Decisions in the fields of → common foreign and security policy and cooperation in the fields of justice and home affairs (→ justice and home affairs) are adopted by special procedures (Articles J and K).

Legislative procedures The distribution of powers between the three acting institutions as laid down in the EC Treaty means that in effect all basic legal instruments are to be adopted by the Council, since its structure makes it the political link to the Member States on whose consent the creation and development of the EC/EU has been dependent since its foundation.

Legislation takes the form primarily of regulations and directives ('secondary Community legislation') under Article 189. Regulations have general application; they are binding in their entirety and directly applicable in all Member States. Directives, on the other hand, are binding on the Member States to which they are addressed only as to the result to be achieved; the form and method for implementing them is left to the Member States, who have a given time in which to do so. Under Article 191, Community instruments only take effect after they have been published in the *Official Journal of the European Community* (in the case of regulations) or notified to those to whom they are addressed (in the case of directives).

Consultation procedure Under the general consultation procedure the Commission normally drafts proposals for legislation by virtue of its right of initiative (Articles 155 and 190); the Council refers them to Parliament for an opinion (Articles 137 and 190) before taking a final decision (Article 145). Articles 152 and 138b allow the Council and Parliament to request the Commission to submit certain proposals. A distinction needs to be made between matters on which consultation of the European Parliament is compulsory under the Treaties and those on which such consultation is optional. This distinction is also important because of the legal consequences if the Council fails to consult Parliament or does not comply with the procedures laid down in the Treaty. Proper consultation of Parliament in those cases in which it is compulsory under the Treaty is a formal requirement. Following a ruling by the → European Court of Justice in 1980 failure by the Council to fulfil this requirement renders the Council act in question null and void.

The significant feature of the consultation procedure is that only one reading takes place in Parliament. The following sequence of events has developed in practice: the Council formally transmits the Commission proposal to Parliament for an opinion; the President of Parliament refers the proposal to the committee responsible and, where appropriate, to any committees which must also be consulted for their opinion. The committee's conclusions are presented to the full House in the form of a report and the proposal is either approved without amendment or amendments are suggested. Parliament's opinion is sent to the Council and the Commission so that the latter can, if necessary, revise its original proposal in line with Parliament's suggestions. The Commission and the Council examine Parliament's proposals for amendments and adopt a position on them, mostly on an informal basis. They inform Parliament whether or not they accept its suggested amendments. Finally, the Council adopts the Community act by the appropriate majority and weighting of votes (Article 148(2)) and thus concludes the procedure.

What is a qualified majority? The 15 Member States' governments have a total of 87 votes in the Council, distributed according to the size of the countries. A minimum of 62 of the 87 votes constitute a qualified majority (Article 148) where the EC Treaty specifically provides for a decision by qualified majority. Where a simple majority is sufficient for a Council decision to be adopted, on the other hand, at least eight of the 15 Members must vote in favour.

The votes are currently weighted as follows:

Belgium	5	France	10	Austria	4
Denmark	3	Ireland	3	Portugal	5
Germany	10	Italy	10	Finland	3
Greece	5	Luxembourg	2	Sweden	4
Spain	8	Netherlands	5	United Kingdom	10

EP-Council cooperation procedure From 1958 until 1987, the sequence of events outlined above constituted the Community's customary legislative procedure. From 1 July 1987, a special 'cooperation procedure' between the Council and Parliament and with the participation of the Commission was introduced for Community acts concerned primarily with the establishment and operation of the → single market (see Article 100a of the EC treaty) with the dual aim of protecting decision-making by qualified majority in the Council and ensuring greater involvement of Parliament in decisions on the single market. The new procedure required extensive changes to the Treaty rules. The amendments introduced the following stages to the procedure for adopting decisions relating to the single market, which since 1987 have required two readings in Parliament and the Council: as before, the Commission makes a proposal and Parliament adopts a position on it; the Council examines the proposal at first reading and drafts a 'common position' which is transmitted to Parliament along with an explanation. Parliament must approve the Council draft within three months, reject it or propose amendments. An absolute majority of its members is required in the latter two cases. If Parliament proposes amendments, the next stage of the procedure must be initiated by the Commission (within a period of one month). It has two options: firstly, it can incorporate Parliament's amendments, in which case the Council need only muster a qualified majority for the final adoption of the proposal as amended by Parliament. If the Council wishes to depart from the amended text, however, it requires a unanimous vote. If this is not forthcoming, the Council must accept Parliament's proposals or be liable to legal action for failure to act (a decision must be taken within three months). Secondly, the Commission may reject Parliament's amendments, in which case the rule applied (not confined to this procedure) is that the Council can accept the Commission proposal by qualified majority and only depart from it by unanimous vote. Parliament proposals rejected by the Commission may be accepted by the Council, but again only by unanimous vote. The Council may adopt a proposal rejected by Parliament only by unanimity.

Within the cooperation procedure, the involvement of Parliament in the legislative process depends on the Council actually taking majority decisions, as provided for in the Treaty. It is therefore essential that Member States refrain from resorting to the so-called 'Luxembourg compromise' of 29 January 1966, which made it possible in practice for Member States, by claiming vital national interests, to impose a veto preventing majority decisions being taken in the Council of Ministers, which led in effect to a situation in which all decisions required unanimity.

Co-decision procedure Article 189b of the EC Treaty introduced a new way of involving Parliament in the Community's legislative procedure in the form of a Parliamentary right of co-decision in certain Community acts; among other things the co-decision procedure provides for the possibility of a third reading in Parliament. The new procedure has been in use since 1 November 1993. Co-decision builds on the 'cooperation procedure', but goes beyond it in two important respects: firstly, in the event of differences of opinion between the Council and Parliament a conciliation procedure is activated, with the convening of a special Conciliation Committee, and, secondly, Parliament has the right to reject the proposed act if, despite the conciliation procedure, agreement cannot be reached. This requires an absolute majority of its members. No act can therefore be passed against the will of Parliament. The importance of the co-decision procedure is underlined by the areas to which it applies – it is compulsory for legislation on culture, education, health, consumer protection, trans-European networks, research and technology and environmental protection.

Co-decision procedure
(Article 189b of the EC Treaty)

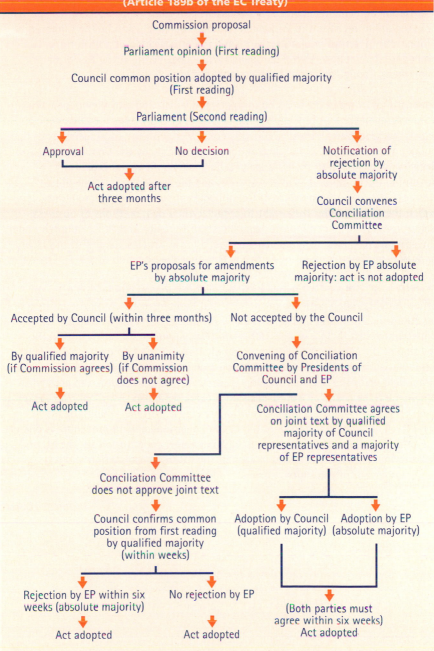

Commission proposal

↓

Parliament opinion (First reading)

↓

Council common position adopted by qualified majority
(First reading)

↓

Parliament (Second reading)

Approval   No decision   Notification of
rejection by
absolute majority

Act adopted after
three months

Council convenes
Conciliation
Committee

EP's proposals for amendments
by absolute majority   Rejection by EP absolute
majority: act is not adopted

Accepted by Council (within three months)   Not accepted by the Council

By qualified majority   By unanimity   Convening of Conciliation
(if Commission agrees)   (if Commission   Committee by Presidents of
does not agree)   Council and EP

Act adopted   Act adopted   Conciliation Committee agrees
on joint text by qualified
majority of Council
representatives and a majority
of EP representatives

Conciliation Committee
does not approve joint text

Council confirms common
position from first reading
by qualified majority
(within weeks)   Adoption by Council   Adoption by EP
(qualified majority)   (absolute majority)

Rejection by EP within six
weeks (absolute majority)   No rejection by EP

Act adopted   Act adopted   (Both parties must
agree within six weeks)
Act adopted

Assent procedure This procedure is used above all for 'constitutional' acts which shape the identity and structure of the EC/EU. In addition to accession and association agreements covered by the assent procedure since 1987, other matters now requiring the assent of Parliament include the conclusion by the Community of important international agreements and the establishing of a uniform procedure for elections to the European Parliament. Without the assent of Parliament, Council decisions have no legal force.

Special procedures In addition to general legislation and the cooperation, co-decision and assent procedures, the EC Treaty also provides for other special legislative procedures. These are mainly concerned with the establishment of the budget and the conclusion of international agreements by the Community, the decision on elections to the European Parliament, the financial provisions governing the Community's own resources and the procedure for amending treaties. The rules of procedure of Union bodies are also special Community acts, which they adopt under their right to organize their own methods of business. Decisions relating to common foreign and security policy and those adopted under the special procedural arrangements provided for in Articles J and K of the Treaty on European Union are not legislative acts within the meaning of the EC Treaty.

Further reforms On the one hand procedures are too cumbersome, on the other there has been criticism of the fact that Parliament has too little influence on European legislation and as a result the Council's acts lack legitimacy. The hopes which rest mainly on the 1996 → Intergovernmental Conference on the revision of the Maastricht Treaty accordingly rank the 'parliamentarization' and democratization of Community legislation alongside streamlining and simplification of the decision-making process. In this connection, the possibility of widening the scope of the co-decision procedure, in use since 1993, has also been created on the basis of an 'evolutionary clause' (Article 189b(8) of the EC Treaty). A fundamental reform of the Union's decision-making procedure is one of the priorities and central tasks of establishing a new constitution for the EU and will become even more pressing in view of the future consolidation and → enlargement of the Union.

Thomas Läufer

Development

Treaty basis: Articles 131 to 136 (Association of the overseas countries and territories), Article 238 (Lomé Conventions), Article 113 (Commercial policy) and Article 43 of the EC Treaty (Food aid). Extensive Community powers introduced by the Treaty on European Union in the field of development cooperation (Articles 130u-y of the EC Treaty).
Instruments: Association agreements with groups of States and trade and cooperation agreements, generalized system of preferences, financial assistance, food aid and emergency aid, coordination and harmonization of national development policies.
Budget: For 1995: ECU 2.651 billion, or about 3.4% of the Community budget; approximately ECU 2.5 billion a year for cooperation under Lomé.
Literature from the European Union:
European Commission: EU-ACP cooperation in 1995.
Luxembourg. Special issue: July 1996 (Cat. no.: CF-AA-96-004-2A-C. Free).
European Commission: Trade relations between the European Union and the developing countries.
Luxembourg 1995 (Cat. no.: CC-AM-95-071-EN-C. Free).
European Commission: 20 questions and answers. Development.
Luxembourg 1996 (Cat. no.: CC-AM-96-084-EN-C. Free).

Since the mid-1970s the → European Union has been increasingly involved in development policy. In the absence of clearly defined powers, it gradually developed its own range of development policy instruments and a financial framework which corresponded fully with the scope for action of its Member States. But only since the entry into force of the Maastricht Treaty on European Union in November 1993 has the EU had clearly defined responsibilities to complement the activities of the Member States. There are no plans – for the time being at least – to transfer more extensive powers on development policy to the EU. The declared aim, however, is greater coordination of the activities of the Union and the Member States.

Although the EU had no development policy powers of its own until the early 1990s, it developed a wide range of activities in the field of north-south cooperation; primarily for agricultural policy reasons it has been a party to international food agreements since 1969 and since 1971 it has granted developing countries unilateral trade benefits under its generalized system of preferences. On the basis of a number of Council Decisions adopted in accordance with Article 235 of the EC Treaty, the European Union has also provided financial and emergency aid since the mid-1970s and it works very closely with (private) international aid organizations.

The Treaty on European Union considerably strengthens the legal basis for the Community's development policy. Articles 130u-y add to the EU Treaty a new title, 'Development cooperation', which lays down three goals: fostering economic and social development, integration of developing countries into the world economy and the campaign against poverty. It expressly states that Community development cooperation is to be complementary to national policies.

Aid to the Third World
Public aid from the principal donor countries (million dollars, 1992)

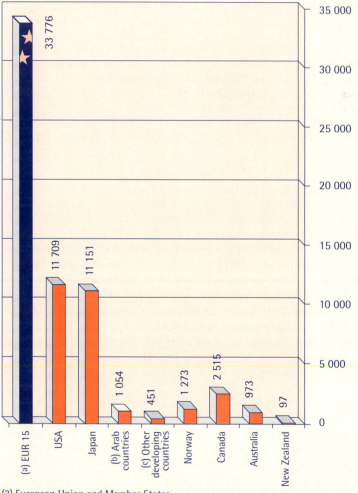

(a) European Union and Member States
(b) Including Saudi Arabia and United Arab Emirates
(c) Including China, India, South Korea, Taiwan, Venezuela

Aims and instruments The early 1980s saw a reorientation of Community development policy. In the 'Pisani Memorandum' of October 1982 the → European Commission, at the instigation of the first → European Parliament to be directly elected (in 1979), set new objectives which have since been revised on a number of occasions. In addition to a number of general considerations – most importantly peace throughout the world – this document gives priority to six practical aims: support for developing countries' own efforts; promotion of self-sufficiency in food with emphasis on agricultural development; development of human resources and respect for the cultural dimension; development of independent capabilities in scientific and applied research; systematic use of all available natural resources; restoration and maintenance of the ecological balance. This system of priorities is now increasingly used in the allocation of resources. In May 1992, the Commission presented a communication on development cooperation policy in the run-up to the year 2000, in which it explains the consequences of the Maastricht Treaty. Special importance is nowadays also placed in cooperation on respect for human rights and good governance.

The instruments of Community development policy include trade, association and cooperation agreements with selected groups of States and individual States as well as a wealth of instruments directed at the world as a whole. These include the generalized system of preferences, which grants simplified access to EU markets for the countries involved, and food aid, emergency aid and financial aid for Asia and Latin America.

The Lomé Conventions Cooperation under the Lomé Conventions lies at the heart of Community development policy. The first Lomé Convention was concluded in 1975 between the nine Member States of the time and 46 ACP countries. It was the successor to the Yaoundé Convention. In December 1989 the representatives of the European countries, which then numbered 12, and 69 developing countries signed the fourth Convention (Namibia followed in 1990). Lomé IV runs for 10 years (from March 1990 until February 2000), with provision for renegotiation of the financial assistance in 1995. In material terms, the heading on commercial policy allows 99% of all ACP products to enter the EU market free of duty. Sensitive products, covered by the rules governing the Community's agricultural markets, are still largely excluded from free access to the Community market. Conversely, ACP States may levy duties on EU imports provided they are not discriminatory in relation to other industrial nations. One of the most important instruments of the EU-ACP agreement is the System of stabilization of export earnings (Stabex) developed as part of Lomé cooperation. This has now become recognized worldwide as a tried and tested model, albeit of limited scope. Stabex applies to over 40 agricultural raw materials and guarantees compensation from Brussels in the event of a fall in income from sales, subject to maximum rates and provided the appropriate conditions are met. A similar system has also existed for the poorest countries of Asia and Latin America since 1987.

Other headings of the fourth Lomé Convention are concerned with the question of indebtedness, environmental protection and human rights. Financial resources for the period 1990-95 were increased from ECU 9 billion under Lomé III to ECU 12.6 billion. Following protracted negotiations and hard bargaining on the part of some Member States, the 1995 Cannes European Council agreed to allocate ECU 13.3 billion to the EDF for the period 1996-2000.

So far the results of Lomé have been far from satisfactory: the ACP share of EU trade has been declining for years. By the early 1990s it had fallen to between 4 and 5% compared with over 7% before 1975, and to make matters worse raw materials prices have declined and the indebtedness of the Lomé partners has increased. According to a special report by the → European Court of Auditors in July 1995, the annual Stabex tranches were insufficient in every one of the first three years of Lomé IV. Between 1990 and 1992 only 40.7% of eligible applications could be financed. The food situation continues to give cause for concern. Even though the results are not entirely satisfactory – and also because they have no realistic alternative – the ACP States are still very interested in continuing cooperation under the Lomé Convention.

Conclusions EU development policy in the mid-1990s has the following features: firstly, the Community, as a transnational coalition, gives priority to supporting regional integration projects, such as cross-border infrastructure projects.

Since 1990, the Union has been making more resources available for humanitarian aid including certain aspects of Community food aid, aid for refugees, rehabilitation projects following crises and crisis prevention measures. Between 1990 and 1994 the funds provided rose steadily from ECU 114 million to ECU 764 million. The European Community Humanitarian Office (ECHO) was set up to handle the technical side. With the exception of minor concessions under the Lomé Convention, the Union has not so far made any significant contribution to solving the debt problem which, it says, it is not its responsibility.

Otto Schmuck

Economic and monetary union

Treaty basis: Articles 102a–109m of the EC Treaty.
Aims: Price stability, irrevocably fixed exchange rates between EU currencies by 1999, introduction of a common currency, the euro.
Instruments: Development of a common monetary policy, close coordination of economic policies, establishment of a European System of Central Banks (ESCB).
Literature from the European Union:
European Commission: Economic and monetary union. (Part I: The path to economic and monetary union. Part II: The scenario for the changeover to the single currency).
Luxembourg 1996 (Cat. no.: CW-96-96-166-EN-C. Free).
Borchardt, Klaus Dieter: European integration: The origins and growth of the European Union.
Luxembourg 1995 (Cat. no.: CC-84-94-355-EN-C. Free).
Fontaine, Pascal: Europe in ten points.
Luxembourg 1995 (Cat. no.: CC-86-94-755-EN-C. Free).
European Commission: When will the 'euro' be in our pockets?
Luxembourg 1996 (Cat. no.: CM-43-96-004-EN-C. Free).

The completion of economic and monetary union (EMU) is one of the most ambitious and controversial aims of the European Union. The signing of the Treaty on European Union and its ratification on 1 November 1993 represent a binding commitment to the creation of EMU. Internally, a Community currency will strengthen the → single market, while externally it will add to the economic weight of the Union. Under the terms of the Maastricht Treaty, the exchange rates for the currencies of the countries participating in EMU will be irrevocably fixed from 1 January 1999. Their national currencies then become merely an expression of a common currency, which, under the terms of the Treaty, will be swiftly introduced.

The need for close monetary cooperation is conditioned, above all, by strong external economic influences. The closer the interlacing of economic systems, the more disruptive exchange rate fluctuations are for their economic relations. Consequently, the European Union is counting on EMU first and foremost to improve its competitiveness.

The Community has already made several attempts to step up economic cooperation. In the 1970s, the Werner Plan for an economic and monetary union foundered on a lack of willingness to deepen integration and the differing economic outlooks of the Member States. After this, pragmatic schemes were tried in a bid to limit the risk of exchange rate fluctuations by means first of the currency snake (1972), then of the → European Monetary System (1979). The objective of EMU, which had in the meantime been put on the back burner, only reappeared on the agenda when the deepening of integration, the foreseeable completion of the → single market and convergence of views on economic matters in the mid-1980s created the necessary basis.

The Delors Report and the Maastricht Treaty

The provisions in the Treaty on European Union are to a large extent based on the ideas expressed in the Delors Report. This report, presented by a group of experts including the Governors of the national central banks in April 1989, saw the transition to EMU as a three-stage process. The essential objectives of the first stage, which began on 1 July 1990, were to increase monetary coordination, to bring all Member States into the EMS, to complete the → single market and to carry out preparatory work on the Treaty amendments that would later be necessary. The most important aspect of the second stage is the setting up of a European System of Central Banks with what will initially still be limited powers. The third phase provides for the transition to fixed rates of exchange and a single currency.

As early as 1989 the Madrid European Council decided to embark on the first stage, agreeing to convene an Intergovernmental Conference at the end of 1990. In April 1990 the → European Council reached agreement on the convening of a second Intergovernmental Conference on the institutional form of political union, not least with a view to tying Germany, then in the run-up to unification, closer into the Community. As far as monetary policy was concerned, the Member States agreed that the date for the start of the second stage of EMU should be 1 January 1994. Before the Intergovernmental Conference was even convened, the Statute of the European Central Bank was adopted stating that maintaining price stability was a primary objective.

The road to economic and monetary union

The Maastricht Treaty is a historical continuation of European policy in that it gives priority to economic rather than political integration. As far as monetary policy is concerned, it presents a clear timetable for the stage-by-stage Delors Plan, scheduling political aims. The negotiations concerning the provisions regarding the transitional phase and the forms of the second and third stages proved particularly difficult. While it was necessary to avoid blurring the question of national and European competence in matters of monetary policy in the transitional period, it was equally necessary to link both stages closely.

Consequently, although decision-making power concerning matters of monetary policy remained with the Member States during the second stage, under Article 109e of the EC Treaty the process leading to the independence of their central

banks has started. In terms of the institutions, the preparations for EMU resulted in the → European Monetary Institute being set up on 1 January 1994 as a precursor to the European Central Bank. Its function is to support the efforts of the Member States to create the conditions for entry into the third stage. It is also developing instruments and procedures for the implementation of a single monetary policy.

A credible stability policy and a high degree of convergence on the part of the economies involved are essential if a common currency is to be stable. While all EU States are participating in the second stage, for entry to the third stage all the 'convergence' criteria would have to be met (Article 109j):

(i)   A high degree of price stability. This is considered achieved when a country's inflation rate exceeds the average inflation in the three best-performing Member States by no more than 1.5%.

(ii) The sustainability of the government financial position. This condition is fulfilled when annual government borrowing is no more than 3% of the GDP and total public borrowing does not exceed 60% of GDP. Here, however, room has been left for manoeuvre. If the total public borrowing of a State has declined substantially and is rapidly approaching the 60% reference value, the Council may decide that this criterion has been met.

(iii) Exchange rate stability. Currencies are required to remain within the narrow EMS band for at least two years without devaluing against the currency of any other Member State. Since the EMS bands were widened in 1993 the continued relevance of this criterion has been a matter for debate.

(iv) The durability of convergence. This condition is measured by nominal long-term interest rate levels, which may not be more than two percentage points higher than the average of, at most, the three countries with the lowest rates of inflation.

Although the convergence criteria are politically motivated, they can be seen as sophisticated indicators of suitability for entry into EMU. However, they also underline the still clear differences in convergence between the EU Member States. From this perspective, the Maastricht Treaty involves a compromise between the desire for sufficiently long periods of transition and a scheduled, swift and irreversible transition to EMU.

As a first step, acting by qualified majority and on the basis of reports from the EMI and the Commission, the → Council decides whether the convergence criteria have been met. By the end of 1996, the Council, composed of the Heads of State or Government, was to decide whether a majority of Member States had satisfied

the necessary conditions. It would then set the date for the start of the third stage. In the (foreseeable) case of the majority of Member States not qualifying, suitability for entry into EMU will be examined, in a second step, before 1 July 1998. The States qualifying will commence monetary union on 1 January 1999. The supervisory procedure will be repeated at least every two years. All Member States qualifying for the third stage must then join, apart from the United Kingdom and Denmark, which have been released from the obligation to participate under special provisions.

In addition to the Statute of the European Central Bank, Articles 105 to 109d of the EC Treaty establish monetary policy provisions relating to the European System of Central Banks. These provisions draw heavily on the model provided by the German central bank (*Bundesbank*) and emphasize that price stability is the primary objective. Under Article 107 the independence of the ECB is guaranteed so as to enable it to achieve this objective. It is not permitted to finance public deficits in any way. To arrive at convergence the Treaty provides for close cooperation on matters of → economic policy by the Member States under Council surveillance.

Implementation and prospects The Treaty on European Union deliberately left some details regarding EMU unclarified, with the question of implementation in particular requiring further provision before the start of the third stage. A Green Paper presented by the Commission in May 1995 outlined several scenarios for the introduction of a common currency. The EMI has also presented its views on the subject. It appears that, from the beginning of 1999, the common currency will first be used by the Central Banks and commercial banks with sufficiently long transition periods helping to overcome any implementation problems. From 1 January 2002 banknotes and coins in the European currency should be available and six months later the national currencies of the States participating should cease to be legal tender. At the Madrid summit in December 1995 the Heads of State or Government reaffirmed their desire to start EMU in 1999 and agreed on the 'euro' as the name for the new currency. Moreover, by the end of 1996 the range of monetary instruments at the disposal of the Central Bank is to be specified. To prevent EMU from having a lasting divisive effect on the → single market, an 'EMS II' is to be set up to link the currencies of those countries taking part (the 'ins') with the currencies of those not participating (the 'outs'). All in all, the technical preparations for EMU are on schedule.

Since its ratification, the Maastricht Treaty has come in for some criticism. In connection with monetary union, apart from rejection as a matter of principle, public debate has focused on the fact that political union and EMU are not achieved at the same time. Without greater political integration, so the argument goes, there is no basis for monetary union. It also seems questionable whether, in the context of a Community monetary policy, mere coordination of economic policy is sufficient to guarantee the commitment to price stability being adhered to. The conclusiveness of the convergence criteria has also been questioned, doubts being coupled with strong suspicions that the criteria would be weakened before entry into the third stage. It is true that the Treaty contains a fundamental flaw in that it views the convergence criteria as simple entry requirements. Although it does provide for penalties to be imposed if economic policies diverge, the penalties must be approved by qualified majority. Therefore it is not inconceivable that the evident current trend towards stability could be relaxed after the start of the third stage.

The 'Stability Pact for Europe' proposed by Germany in 1995 attempted to deal with this problem. Basically, the proposal contains a procedure enforcing stricter budgetary discipline after EMU has begun. In contrast to the EC Treaty, the Stability Pact provides for automatic sanctions involving heavy fines as a deterrent to economic indiscipline. In September 1996, the Council agreed in principle to introduce such an instrument in order to safeguard monetary union.

The political will to start EMU on time has been reaffirmed time and again. Nevertheless, some Member States are still having problems gaining acceptance for it, and there is also a great deal of sensitivity regarding actual implementation. Although the economic usefulness of monetary union increases with the number of Members participating, in spite of all the efforts made at consolidation, only Luxembourg managed to meet the convergence criteria in 1995. The politicians unanimously reject the possibility of a postponement, arguing that there is too great a danger that the momentum towards integration, with all its disciplining effects, will be lost. Furthermore, they do not wish to see any loose interpretation of the convergence criteria. This would hardly be possible at the same time. Agreement on a stability pact may be an important factor in the resolution of this problem.

Olaf Hillenbrand

Economic and Social Committee

Treaty basis: Article 4(2) and Articles 193-198 of the EC Treaty.
Composition: 222 members from the 15 EU Member States broken down as follows: 24 each from France, Germany, Italy and the United Kingdom, 21 from Spain, 12 each from Austria, Belgium, Greece, the Netherlands, Portugal and Sweden, 9 each from Denmark, Finland and Ireland, and 6 from Luxembourg (Article 194); the Committee elects a President and a Bureau from among its members.
Function: Institutional vehicle for representing (in an advisory capacity) the interests of economic and social groupings in EU Member States.
Instruments: Opinions submitted to the Council and Commission.
Budget: 1995: ECU 26.3 million, plus ECU 57.8 million for its organizational infrastructure, which it shares with the Committee of the Regions.
Literature from the European Union:
Economic and Social Committee: Annual report 1995: Economic and Social Committee. Luxembourg 1996 (Cat. no.: EX-94-96-235-EN-C. ECU 25.00).
European Commission: Serving the European Union. A citizen's guide to the institutions of the European Union.
Luxembourg 1996 (Cat. no.: FX-89-95-939-EN-C. Free).

The Economic and Social Committee (ESC) was set up under the 1957 Rome Treaties to represent the interests of the various economic and social groupings, thus providing them mainly with an opportunity to participate in the completion of the → single market and thus to play a part in the integration process within the → European Union (EU). They were therefore provided with an institutional vehicle for informing the → European Commission and the → Council of the European Union about their views (in the form of an opinion) on any issues of Community interest.

Rights and tasks The Committee may, when deemed appropriate, be consulted as part of the → decision-making procedures by the Council and Commission. In some cases the latter two bodies are obliged to consult the ESC prior to taking certain decisions, *inter alia* in connection with measures required to bring about freedom of movement for workers (Article 49 of the EC Treaty), freedom of establishment (Article 54), cooperation on matters in the social field (Articles 118 and 121), education (Articles 126 and 127), health and consumer protection (Articles 129, 129a), environmental issues (Article 130s) and regional development (Article 130). The Commission and Council may set the ESC a time limit of no less than four weeks for it to submit its opinion. Any opinion issued after expiry of the time limit does not have to be taken into account.

Furthermore, since the Treaty on European Union came into force the ESC is able
to issue an opinion at its own initiative in cases it deems appropriate (Article 198).
The full Committee meets 10 times a year as a rule, and on the basis of the
opinions drawn up by its specialized sections adopts (by simple majority) an
average of some 180 opinions annually, of which about 10% are at its own
initiative. These opinions are forwarded to the Council and Commission and
published in the *Official Journal of the European Communities.*

Economic and Social Committee

Advisory body of the European Union

222

representatives of economic
and social groups

**Policy areas in which the Committee must be consulted by the
Council and the Commission**

Common agricultural policy
•
Transport policy
•
Single market regulations
•
Social policy
•
Training
•
Consumer policy
•
Environment policy
•
Structural and regional policy
•
Industry policy
•
Research, etc.

Structure The ESC's members are divided into three groups – workers,
employers and various interests, including the professions, agriculture,
cooperatives, chambers of commerce and consumer associations. They are
proposed by the individual governments and, after consultation with the
Commission, are appointed for four years by unanimous decision of the Council
and may be reappointed. The ESC's members elect a 30-member Bureau (10 from
each group) from among themselves for a two-year term, and the Bureau has a

President and two Vice-Presidents elected alternately from each of the three groups. The President is responsible for the smooth running of the ESC and, together with the Bureau, is also responsible for relations with third countries. However, his main task is to direct and coordinate the work of the Committee's individual working bodies and provide them with policy guidelines. These bodies include nine specialized sections covering all the areas in which the ESC is active: economic, financial and monetary questions; external relations, trade and development policy; social, family, educational and cultural affairs; protection of the environment, public health and consumer affairs; agriculture and fisheries; regional development and town and country planning; industry, commerce, crafts and services; transport and communications; energy, nuclear questions and research.

Assessment Given its advisory nature, the only real instrument the ESC has – the opinion – often has no more than limited success in securing consideration for the interests of the various economic and social groups. For this reason, these groups are increasingly concentrating on influencing the Commission directly as this approach promises to be more successful in achieving their aims. This is also the reason why the Committee is trying to upgrade from its hitherto ancillary role within the EU's institutional machinery to an institution of equal standing with the ability to influence the legislative process directly.

For several years now the Committee has also been involved in tasks which go beyond its obligations under the Treaties. For example, it is involved – with the support of the other European institutions – in measures to improve relations between Europe's citizens and its institutions in an attempt to demonstrate that it is more than just a lobby for the various interest groups.

Nicole Schley

Economic policy

Treaty basis: Articles 2, 3, 3a, 4a, 102a-104c, 105-109, 109a-109d, 109e-109m of the EC Treaty.

Aims: Consistent and balanced growth, improved living standards, promotion of convergence and cohesion, high employment, stable prices, healthy public finances and monetary conditions and sustainable balance of payments.

Instruments: Monetary Committee with advisory status, Economic Policy Committee, European Monetary Institute, 'multilateral surveillance'; third stage: Economic and Financial Committee, European System of Central Banks.

Literature from the European Union:

European Economy (quarterly).
Luxembourg (Cat. no.: CM-AR-96-000-EN-C. ECU 105.00).
European Commission: Economic and monetary union.
Luxembourg 1996 (Cat. no.: CW-96-96-166-EN-C. Free).
European Commission: When will the 'euro' be in our pockets ?
Luxembourg 1996 (Cat. no.: CM-43-96-004-EN-C. Free).
European Commission: Annual economic report for 1996.
Luxembourg 1996 (Cat. no.: CM-AR-96-001-EN-C. ECU 30.00).

The decisions taken in Maastricht by the Heads of State or Government on → economic and monetary union (EMU) in the context of the Treaty on European Union (TEU), which entered into force on 1 November 1993, have significant consequences for economic policy in a Community enlarged by the accession on 1 January 1995 of Austria, Sweden and Finland.

Objectives, competence and powers under pre-Maastricht law

The rules of the 1957 EEC Treaty (EC Treaty since 1993) on steering the economy in accordance with general economic objectives reflected a compromise between economic and integration policy requirements and national resistance to the surrender of sovereignty over economic policy. The economic policy objectives themselves were not in dispute. Article 2 ('tasks of the Community') refers to a continuous and balanced expansion, an increase in stability, an accelerated raising of the standard of living and the promotion of closer relations between the Member States. In the section of the Treaty on 'economic policy', Article 104 lays down the objectives of a high level of employment, a stable level of prices and the equilibrium of the balance of payments.

The EEC Treaty left economic and monetary policy largely within the sphere of

competence of the national governments. At the same time, however, they were obliged to regard their conjunctural and exchange rate policies as a 'matter of common concern' (Articles 103, 107) and to coordinate their economic and monetary policy in accordance with Article 105, that is to say, bring it into line with the common objective. The Community dealt with the problem of coordination by creating an institutional environment through the establishment of committees, for example, the Monetary Committee and the Committees on Economic Policy, Medium-Term Economic Policy and Budgetary Policy.

Unsatisfactory coordination Faced with growing differences in the Member States' views on stability, which could not be dealt with in the context of the committees, there were uncoordinated economic policy reactions. This process of disintegration in economic and monetary policy was contrary to the requirements of the EEC Treaty, which declared the gradual convergence of the economic policies of the Member States and the establishment of a single market to be the instruments for achieving its objectives.

The EMS as a new approach to cooperation A new attempt at closer cooperation in economic and monetary policy only became possible once ideas on a policy of stability began to converge and the view that only one policy on price stability could help to solve the problem of unemployment began to gain ground. This convergence of objectives finally made it possible to establish the → European Monetary System (EMS) as a system of fixed (and at the same time adjustable) exchange rates with clearly defined rules on intervention.

The German mark took over the function of a lead currency, thus becoming an anchor for the system. A trend towards economic convergence began in the EMS, radiating out from the Bonn-Frankfurt-Paris axis to the other countries participating in the EMS. Some EMS members initially countered the restriction of their economic freedom of movement by retaining restrictions on the movement of capital. The liberalization of capital movements within the Community from 1 July 1990 emphasized the loss of autonomy in economic policy. The logic of the → single market principle would dictate that in the medium term the erosion of national competence in economic and monetary policy should be offset by the development of the Community into EMU with a European System of Central Banks (ESCB).

Economic policy in practice: 1980s to early 1990s At the beginning of the 1980s there was still no agreement between the Member States on the therapeutic approach to overcoming the recession and combating unemployment. With real growth in gross domestic product (GDP) at 2.5%, the rate of unemployment in 1985 was almost 11%, the net borrowing requirements of the Member States amounted to 5.2% of GDP and even the rate of inflation (despite an appreciable fall since the early 1980s) lay at 6%. This was the background to the approval in 1985 by the → Council of the European Union of the cooperative growth strategy for increased employment; cooperative, because it was to be based on close cooperation between government, employers and employees, but also between countries. This strategy provided for a connection between slowing the rise in wages, boosting demand and improving conditions in the goods, capital and labour markets. Improving the allocation of the goods and services markets and, as a result, the conditions for growth was, moreover, part of the 1993 single market programme, which the → European Commission set out in its June 1985 White Paper.

The cooperation strategy was intended to increase the average rate of GDP growth in the EC from 2.5% in the mid-1980s to 3.5% and reduce the rate of unemployment to 8% by 1990. Only at the end of the 1980s was the necessary rate of growth achieved, and the rate of unemployment fell from its peak of 10.8 (1985) to 8.1% (1990). Growth in the Community in the early 1990s could not, however, be maintained in order to continue reducing unemployment (GDP growth, 1994: 1.5%) and the unemployment rate rose to 11% (1994). The rate of inflation fell and, in 1994, with a slight decline in convergence and a temporary increase after 1988, lay at 3.3%. The three new Member States, Austria, Sweden and Finland, had inflation rates below this average.

The total budget deficit of the Member States was reduced in the second half of the 1980s from 5.2% of GDP (1985) to 2.6% (1989), although the trend since 1990 has been clearly upwards (1994: 5.6%). In many Member States, considerable efforts at consolidation are required.

Economic policy in the 1990s The Maastricht decisions on EMU are of far-reaching significance to economic and monetary policy. In a three-stage process, the first phase of which began on 1 July 1990, EMU is to be established by 1 January 1999 at the latest, following completion of the second stage which began on 1 January 1994. It is interesting to note, in the light of the bitter controversies over organization which raged until very recently, the explicit emphasis on the competition-led market economy as the economic system for the Union and the Member States (Articles 3a, 102 and 105 of the EC Treaty). It remains to be seen, however, how this will be reflected in economic practice in the coming years.

The Member States have to conduct their economic policy as a 'matter of common concern' and coordinate it in the Council in accordance with an extended list of principles and objectives (Article 103). The Treaty lays down the guiding principles for economic and monetary policy as stable prices, sound public finances and monetary conditions and a sustainable balance of payments (Article 3a(3)). The Council draws up guidelines for the economic policies of the Member States and of the Union which, after discussion in the European Council, are approved by it as recommendations and addressed to the Member States. To promote and ensure economic convergence, the existing system of 'multilateral surveillance' is extended. Where economic policy is not in accordance with the guidelines, the Council can communicate the necessary recommendations to the Member States and, in certain circumstances, publish them as a means of applying pressure.

The emphasis for coordination and monitoring is on budgetary policy. In contrast to monetary policy (in the third stage) it is not collectivised. The budgetary policy of Member States is, however, subject to a progressively stricter harmonization process. Enshrining important common principles for stability in the Treaty is intended to ensure that stability does not rely solely on monetary policy. Particular principles applying since the beginning of 1994 are as follows: prohibition of credit facilities for public authorities (Articles 104 and 104a); responsibility of each Member State for its own national debt (Article 104b); avoidance by Member States of excessive government deficits (Article 104c). On the basis of established criteria, according to which the total deficit of a Member State's public budgets should in principle not exceed 3% of GDP and total debt should not exceed 60%, the Commission monitors the development of the budgetary situation in the Member States and, on the basis of further criteria, examines whether an 'excessive deficit' exists. Should this be the case, the Council sets in motion a process to reduce the deficit which, in the final stage, also includes the possibility of fines. The Monetary Committee, which is involved in coordination and monitoring, will be dissolved at the beginning of the final stage (when there are no more national monetary policies) and replaced by an Economic and Financial Committee.

On monetary policy, the Treaty provides for the establishment in the final phase of a European System of Central Banks (ESCB) and the fixing of exchange rates with a view to introducing a single currency in the Community by 1999. The ESCB, consisting of the European Central Bank (ECB) and the national central banks, is responsible for determining and implementing monetary policy in the Community. In the transitional phase, monetary policy will remain within national competence. The → European Monetary Institute (EMI), established in Frankfurt early in 1994, therefore has no monetary control functions, but is intended to coordinate monetary policy in a similar way to the (now dissolved) Committee of Central Bank Governors. The ESCB, the statute of which is set out in detail in a protocol to the Treaty, has as its primary objective the maintenance of price stability. Without prejudice to this objective, the ESCB, which is independent in the performance of its tasks, will support the general economic policies of the Community.

The convergence criteria are not without their own problems. Efforts are only directed towards relative price stability. In the event of deficits, the 'national budget' is taken into consideration; deficits could therefore be 'hidden' in shadow budgets. The EU must prove that it is capable of developing and reinforcing a 'stability culture' as a prerequisite for ensuring lasting employment and growth.

The December 1993 White Paper on growth, competitiveness and employment, published immediately after the entry into force of the Union Treaty, was the Commission's reaction to the Union's most pressing problem, the continually increasing unemployment in the Member States of the European Union. The White Paper's subtitle, 'The challenges and ways forward into the 21st century', underlines its forward-looking claim to be a strategy document on reducing unemployment. Its ambitious target is the creation of 15 million jobs by the end of the century. The White Paper makes provision for a wide range of tools for creating the necessary conditions for growth, including: improving macroeconomic conditions, investing in modern infrastructure to open new markets, creating the necessary human capital, intensifying internal and external competition, accelerating the pace of innovation through the targeted promotion of research and development, regaining price advantages by reducing costs and providing more flexible use of labour. The White Paper also examines the relationship between resources, environment and growth. Although overall it offers no finished strategy and is orthodox in many of its statements, it is nevertheless an important basis for discussion and a guide to the decisions to be made at various levels in the European Union in order to determine the success of EMU.

Henry Krägenau

Education and youth

Treaty basis: Articles 3(p), 126 and 127, also one-off operations under Article 235 of the EC treaty.
Aims: EC contribution to the development of a high standard of education; development of a European dimension to education; encouragement of mobility in students and teachers; academic recognition of diplomas and periods of study; cooperation between educational establishments; youth exchanges; the development of distance learning; the promotion and improvement of initial and continuing vocational training and retraining; the promotion and intensification of cooperation between educational establishments in the Member States.
Instruments: Decisions taken (under the Articles 189b or 189c of the EC treaty procedures for the adoption of action programmes, Council directives, European Parliament or Council resolutions, European Commission communications, Green and White Papers.
Budget: 1996: ECU 418 million (approximately 0.9% of the total budget); other budgetary resources if necessary (e.g. from the European Social Fund).
Further reading: European Commission White Paper on teaching and learning – Towards the learning society, COM(95)0590 final.
Literature from the European Union:
European Commission: Education and training. Tackling unemployment. Luxembourg 1996 (Cat. no.: CM-93-95-500-EN-C. Free).

The Treaty on European Union established a new framework for the EC programmes and actions which had existed in the field of education since the founding of the ECSC, and also for general education and youth policy. The new Article 127 gave a concrete form to the instruction directed to the Council to adopt a set of basic principles regarding the implementation of a common vocational training policy with regard to its aims and objectives, as was introduced in Article 128 of the EEC treaty with the Single European Act. At the same time, in order to limit the scope of the policy to vocational training, there is a new Article 126, covering the legal basis for Community activities in relation to general, school, university, non-vocational extracurricular education and for EC youth policy. In terms of its non-vocational educational activities, the Community aims to promote high-quality education, to develop a European dimension to education, particularly by the dissemination and learning of the languages of the Member States, to increase the mobility of students and teachers by means of the appropriate exchange programmes and mutual recognition of diplomas and other qualifications, to promote cooperation between educational establishments, youth exchanges and distance learning. In the field of vocational training, Community efforts generally centre around adapting to industrial change and lay particular stress on improving career prospects by the promotion of initial and continuing vocational training and retraining, by increasing the mobility of trainees and instructors, and by encouraging cooperation between educational establishments and companies. The scope of the measures based on Articles 126 and 127 is limited by the fact that Member States retain exclusive responsibility for the content of material taught and the form of their education systems. This limitation on Community education policy greatly restricts the institutions' scope for action, as neither Article 126 nor Article 127 gives the Community the power to harmonize education policy in the Member States.

When the Community adopts measures relating to education and youth policy, the Council must decide by qualified majority. The procedural basis for general education and youth policy is Article 189b and for vocational training it is Article 189c.

Implementation of education and youth policy Community activity in the sphere of education and youth led to a major revision of existing Community programmes in 1994 and 1995. With a budget of ECU 850 million up to 1999, the Socrates action programme assimilates the previous higher education programmes Erasmus, Lingua, Eurydice, NARIC and ARION and supplements them with a new schools programme, Comenius, and actions in support of distance learning and the European dimension in adult education. With a budget of ECU 126 million up to 1999, the Youth for Europe III exchange programme is a continuation of previous programmes. Lastly, in the field of vocational training the Leonardo da Vinci programme, adopted on the basis of Article 127 with a budget of ECU 620 million up to 1999, brings together the existing Comett, FORCE, PETRA, Eurotecnet and IRIS Community action programmes. All three programmes represent a significant element in the strategy of the Community institutions to link the aim of equal and comprehensive access to general education and vocational training with the desire not only to develop a high-quality standard of education which can compete with the best in the world but also to prevent social exclusion by dovetailing the Community's occupational and educational activities. In this context, on the basis of the conclusions of the Cannes → European Council in June 1995, the → Council adopted a resolution on the response of education to the problem of racism and xenophobia. In response to the European Year of Life-long Learning declared by the → European Parliament and the Council in 1996, the → European Commission published a White Paper entitled 'Teaching and learning – Towards the learning society', setting out its main ideas on methods of combating youth unemployment and on continuing integration into the world of work and further training of young people and adults, and making proposals for how to implement them. The European Commission's strategy on education increasingly revolves around encouraging the people and education establishments of the Union to learn languages and acquire new skills, to extend their individual knowledge and obtain qualifications. It is therefore also involved in creating new validation and accreditation procedures for knowledge acquired. The action plan presented by Commissioners Cresson, Bangemann and Flynn entitled 'Learning in the information society' (→ information society) sets out the main points of the programme to promote the electronic networking of primary and secondary schools with the aim of making increasing use of multimedia teaching methods and learning materials.

Evaluation and prospects All in all, the verdict of the new EC programme and action strategy on education and youth must be positive. However, the fear expressed in some quarters that the European Commission is exerting a direct and what is perceived to be too strong an influence on the content and organization of education is not to be taken lightly. In terms of self-evaluation and analysis of the recently started education programmes, the Commission Green Paper examining education and vocational training reveals different and, in some cases, serious obstacles to the implementation of measures promoting transnational mobility of teachers and students, such as problems regarding the legal status of trainees, tax difficulties in connection with research grants, the condition that training grants are dependent on the training being undertaken in the country offering the grant and the continuing lack of recognition of qualifications acquired abroad. Owing to the separation of powers regarding education policy and the differing interests of the Member States, these problems will not be overcome overnight.

Andreas Maurer

Energy

Treaty basis: Specific provisions for coal in the ECSC Treaty; specific provisions for nuclear energy in the Euratom Treaty; general EC Treaty provisions on the elimination of trade barriers (Articles 12-37) and on competition rules (Articles 85-94), and Article 3(t).
Aims: To guarantee safe, cheap, healthy and environmentally acceptable energy supplies; to develop new energy systems; to complete the single market in energy.
Instruments: Intervention instruments, particularly in the coal and nuclear power industries; nuclear technology programmes and fusion research; programmes and structural subsidies for demonstration projects; regulations on market integration for forms of energy carried on a grid; determination of environmental standards for energy production and consumption.
Literature from the European Union:
European Commission: Energy in Europe: Compendium of legislation and other instruments relating to energy.
Luxembourg 1995 (Cat. no.: CS-83-94-571-EN-C. ECU 24.00).
European Commission: For a European Union energy policy: Green Paper. Luxembourg 1995 (Cat. no.: CM-85-94-721-EN-C. ECU 11.00).
European Commission: European energy to 2020: A scenario approach.
Luxembourg 1996 (Cat. no.: CM-BR-95-002-EN-C. ECU 25.00).

Oil is the most important source of energy for the European economies and has been since the middle of the 1960s. The Community's dependence on oil reached its peak in 1973, when oil accounted for 67% of energy consumption. By the end of the 1980s, the figure had levelled off at 45%. More than four fifths of the oil consumed in the Union has to be imported from outside. The proportion will rise in the near future, when the oil reserves in the North Sea run out. In 1994, two thirds of oil imports came from the OPEC countries. Import dependence for natural gas is over a third. Since the 1980s, Russia has been the leading supplier. Coal, though relatively abundant in the EU, is expensive to extract and cannot compete with cheap imported coal. The EU is self sufficient only in nuclear and hydro-electric power, which accounted for 16% of energy needs in 1994.

The main energy policy issue is how, under these circumstances, to guarantee reliable and cheap supplies in sufficient quantities. In particular, the Union's dependence on oil imports from the unstable Gulf region makes its energy systems very vulnerable. One of the priority objectives of the EU's energy policy is therefore to reduce this vulnerability and develop alternative supplies. The perennial problems with supplies apart, recent years have seen the emergence of new concerns requiring, with increasing urgency, a re-ordering of priorities as far as use of energy is concerned. As well as the quite specific problems associated with nuclear power (risk of fall out, social acceptability and waste disposal), there are various environmental concerns about the use of fossil fuels (coal, oil and gas). With the risk of climate change caused by an excess of carbon dioxide in the atmosphere (the greenhouse effect), the environmental damage done by these energy sources is reaching dangerous levels. Since every country in Europe is facing the same problems, the EU is becoming increasingly prominent as the appropriate forum to address these concerns.

Primary energy   EUR 15 1995(%)

Production   Consumption

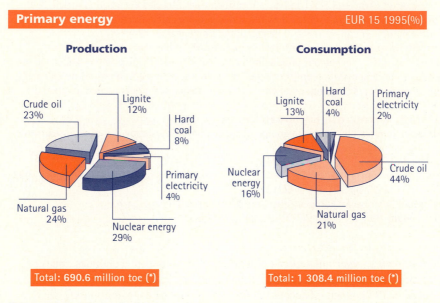

Production:
- Crude oil 23%
- Lignite 12%
- Hard coal 8%
- Primary electricity 4%
- Nuclear energy 29%
- Natural gas 24%

Total: 690.6 million toe (*)

Consumption:
- Lignite 13%
- Hard coal 4%
- Primary electricity 2%
- Crude oil 44%
- Natural gas 21%
- Nuclear energy 16%

Total: 1 308.4 million toe (*)

(*) Tonne of oil equivalent (toe) is a standard unit for measuring quantities of energy. It corresponds to the energy content of one tonne of crude oil with a net calorific value of 41 868 kJ/kg.

Development of the European energy policy No provision was made for a common energy policy as such when the European Communities were first established. The European Coal and Steel Community (ECSC) created the institutional framework for coal in 1951 and the European Atomic Energy Community (EAEC or Euratom) did the same for nuclear power in 1957. The other energy sources fell within the scope of the European Economic Community (EEC), also established in 1957, though there was no direct reference to energy policy in the Treaty. However, it became clear after a few years that the ECSC and Euratom would not live up to initial expectations, while the EEC's approach to energy and to integration proved successful.

Cheap and plentiful energy imports from outside Europe played an important role in Europe's economic growth in the 1960s. But with the 1973 oil crisis, when the price of crude oil quadrupled and the oil-exporting countries in the Middle East threatened to cut off supplies, the risks of depending on outside sources for energy became all too apparent to Europe. In the wake of the crisis, European governments first tried either to break their dependence on oil through national energy programmes (the most notable being the massive expansion of the French nuclear programme) or, together with other industrialized nations, to devise strategies to counter the influence of the OPEC oil cartel. All the western industrialized nations joined the International Energy Agency (IEA), established in 1974 under the auspices of the OECD. The Agency agreed to build up a joint reserve, to be used if oil supplies were interrupted. The EC played only a subsidiary role in this. In November 1983, the Council (Energy) granted the Community the power to formulate its own energy policy for the first time. The European Commission responded by bringing together a number of projects, some new, some old, in a single programme, presented in its report 'the Internal Energy Market' (May 1988). Through a far-reaching liberalization of the European energy market, the Commission hopes to promote growth in the gas and electricity industries, increase the flexibility of the European energy system and remove any obstacles that hinder integration at national level. At the same time, it wants to ensure that environmental concerns are given greater consideration when energy policy is formulated. The Treaty on European Union reaffirmed these objectives but did not contain a new basis for European energy policy.

Instruments, decision-making procedures and individual programmes
The Treaties give the EU a whole range of instruments which they can use to intervene in the energy industries in the Member States: competition rules and trade standards, price limits and quotas, technical standards, limit values, supervisory powers, information systems, subsidies and investment credits. Its power to intervene directly is greatest in relation to the coal and nuclear industries. Of course, the autonomy of the EU is tempered in all of the areas referred to above by the involvement of the Member States.

The EU's → decision-making procedures for energy policy are as diverse as the energy industry itself. In general, the → European Commission has a strong hand in areas governed by the ECSC and Euratom Treaties (i.e. coal and nuclear power): as a supranational supervisory body and the Community's representative on the international scene, it acts directly and autonomously. In areas governed by the EEC Treaty (oil, gas and electricity), the Commission can do nothing more than lay down regulatory frameworks, for which it requires the agreement of the → Council. Irrespective of the Union's formal powers, the extreme politicization of many energy-related issues means that lengthy discussions are often needed at every level of the institutional structure of the EU before an agreement can be reached. Ever since the early 1970s, the → European Council has often stated its views on energy issues. The 1980s saw the start of the → European Parliament's increasing interest in energy-related matters, primarily in connection with the environment and consumer protection.

Traditionally, the EU's efforts to develop new energy sources have focused on nuclear power (fission and fusion). However, energy conservation, the promotion of sensible and environmentally friendly technology and the development of renewable sources (solar, wind and geothermal power) have become increasingly important. The Fourth Framework Programme for Research and Development (1994-98) has earmarked ECU 2.256 billion for these activities, and in December 1994 the European Council adopted a special programme for funding trans-European energy networks. One of the aims was to extend the network of gas and electricity links between the Member States and their main suppliers.

However, all the various measures, programmes and instruments are not enough to conceal the fact that, in the EU budget, energy is about as marginal as the EU's energy policy is when compared with that of the Member States.

Prospects The long-term prospects for European energy policy are quite positive. The objective of ensuring reliable, inexpensive and environmentally acceptable energy supplies for the Member States of the EU, has been largely achieved in the past few decades. There is no guarantee that this success will continue, though. Once the internal market has been completed, certain of the more controversial policies will have to be reformulated and explained. The future of nuclear power and the importance of environmental protection are prime examples. Plans to introduce a European energy tax on greenhouse gas emissions failed as the result of the Member States' conflicting interests. In the future, the EU will face new challenges and possibly new conflicts as it develops closer relations with Central and Eastern Europe, tries to secure oil supplies from the Middle East in the long term and strives to agree on a common approach with its industrialized competitors and the developing countries. This will require action going beyond the EU's existing energy policy. With the conclusion of the European Energy Charter Treaty in December 1994, the 45 signatories defined objectives and established a code of conduct for East-West energy cooperation. However, this has yet to be put into practice.

Erwin Häckel

Enlargement

Treaty basis: Preamble, Articles O and F(1) of the Treaty on European Union, Article 3(a)(1) of the EC Treaty.
Applications for membership: from 10 Central and East European States: Hungary (31.3.1994), Poland (5.4.1994), Romania (22.6.1995), Slovakia (27.6.1995), Latvia (27.10.1995), Estonia (28.11.1995), Lithuania (8.12.1995), Bulgaria (14.12.1995), Czech Republic (17.1.1996), Slovenia (10.6.1996); and four other States: Turkey (14.4.1987), Cyprus (3.7.1990), Malta (16.7.1990), Switzerland (20.5.1992).
Literature from the European Union:
European Commission: International trade and foreign direct investment in 1996. Luxembourg 1996 (Cat. no.: CA-99-96-657-EN-C. ECU 20.00).
European Commission: The impact of the development of the CEEC countries on the EU territory.
Luxembourg 1996 (Cat. no.: CX-85-94-519-EN-C, ECU 23.00)

The Madrid → European Council in December 1995 stated that → enlargement was both a political necessity and a historic opportunity for Europe. The → Council currently has before it applications from 14 countries, including 10 associated Central and East European States. While the → European Commission delivered a provisional negative opinion on Turkey's application as long ago as 20 December 1989, the Council received favourable opinions on the applications from Cyprus and Malta on 30 June 1993. The Swiss application is also still pending, having been suspended following the 'no' vote in the referendum on joining the European Economic Area (December 1992). The Commission is currently preparing provisional opinions on the applications from the countries with Europe agreements, which are central to the present enlargement policy. As mentioned again by the European Council in Florence in July 1996, the first stage of negotiations with the Central and East European countries is scheduled to start at the same time as negotiations with Cyprus, six months after the conclusion of the → Intergovernmental Conference (IGC). The task of the Conference is to start preparing the → European Union for the institutional effects of enlargement to a Union of between 20 and 25 Member States, by reforming the → decision-making procedures and institutional structure according to the yardsticks of efficiency, firmness of action and legitimacy.
The countries of Central and Eastern Europe see EU membership as a means of reinforcing their security and the process of modernization in order to create a stable basis on which to push ahead with the transition to democracy and a

market economy. The political benefits for the Union of the long-term establishment of Western political and economic principles in its immediate neighbours are more important than economic reasons in wanting to extend the → single market. With the end of the Cold War, the EU finds itself with a decisive role to play in helping to create the structures for a society based on security, prosperity, social equality and democracy throughout Europe. The security policy implications of an enlargement to the east must be borne in mind because of Russia. However, enlargement to the east challenges the consensus on integration policy and at the same time severely tests the capacity for reform of the 15 member Community. The challenge cannot be met by falling back on the model used for the previous four rounds of accessions nor can the EU use delaying tactics to evade the issue by making an optimum level of integration an absolute precondition for enlargement to the east. The Union has therefore announced a parallel procedure. Its aim is to coordinate, in terms both of time and ideas, the main points of 'Agenda 2000' (conclusion of the 1996/97 Intergovernmental Conference, reform of the Union's system of own resources, reform of the cohesion, structural and common agricultural policies, transition to the third phase of → economic and monetary union, future of the WEU) with the so-called pre-accession strategy and the negotiations on the accession of the new democracies. Of course, enlargement to the east will exacerbate latent conflicts about distribution between Cohesion Fund countries and net contributors in the EU and will force strategic decisions which narrow down the pragmatic policy of keeping options open on final integration. It is also fanning the debate about allowing different types of European integration and introducing greater flexibility and about a shift in the Union's political and economic centre of gravity.

The Central and East European States are currently proceeding along four interconnected routes towards the goal of EU membership: (1) implementing the provisions set out in the bilateral Europe agreements and making use of the possibilities available for cooperation and dialogue; (2) implementing the national alignment programmes based on the Introduction to the White Paper on the preparation of the associated countries of Central and Eastern Europe for integration into the internal market of the Union; (3) participating in the structured relations with the institutions of the Union, which could be applied to policies and activities in all pillars of the EU. The 10 associated Central and East European countries take part in these multilateral talks, as do Malta and Cyprus occasionally; (4) practical management of accession which began with application for membership and is now the centre of public attention.

Legal bases and general accession procedures The concept of an open structure has been fundamental to the European Communities since their inception. Thus, even the ECSC Treaty provided that any European State may apply to become a member. Articles 237 of the EEC Treaty and 205 of the EAEC Treaty expressed the same idea. With the entry into force of the Treaty on

European Union, Article 237 of the EEC Treaty was replaced with the almost identical Article O of the Treaty on European Union, the central point of which is that 'Any European State may apply to become a Member of the Union'. Meeting the geographical requirement that it must be a European State is not sufficient, however. The new Article F of the EU Treaty stipulates that any acceding State must have a system of government founded on the principles of democracy. As early as 1978 the European Council asserted this principle in its declaration on democracy. In addition, Article 3a(1) of the EC Treaty stipulates that the Member States and the Community shall include the adoption of an → economic policy which is conducted in accordance with the principle of an open market economy with free competition. However, States which meet all the conditions have no legal entitlement to join. The decision on membership is an act of political discretion which devolves in particular on the Council and the Member States. Moreover, Article N of the Treaty on European Union gives the Member States an unlimited right to propose amendments to the Treaty, which could include conditions of membership. The general accession procedure for new members as it has evolved in practice over the years is much more complex than Article O would suggest.

First of all, a European State wishing to join the Union addresses its application to the → Council. This unilateral declaration of intent can be withdrawn by the applicant State at any time before the accession document has been ratified – as happened with Norway in 1994. In its provisional opinion for the Council, the Commission discusses the general opportunities and problems of the application for membership. The Council then decides by simple majority on the opening of negotiations within the meaning of Article O. The negotiations are conducted by the Presidency of the Council on behalf of the Member States and with the assistance of the Commission. Only in the final stages does the procedure described in Article O apply. First, the Council obtains the Commission's final, but non-binding, opinion on the accession. By unanimous vote the Council decides whether to grant the request for membership. It is the Member States, however, which decide in accordance with Article O, in an accession treaty (including the comprehensive acts of accession) with the applicant State, on the practical arrangements for accession: the 'How'. The conditions of membership relate to the transitional arrangements, which allow the applicant State to depart from the EC Treaty for a limited period of time only. The adjustments to be made are for the main part amendments to the EC Treaty required as a result of the accession, for example with regard to the provisions on the Community bodies. During the negotiations, the European Parliament is kept informed of progress of the talks. It has to agree to the accession of new Member States by an absolute majority of its Members. Only then does the Council take a decision once the accession Treaty has been negotiated. The Treaty of Accession is a treaty under international law and requires ratification by all the contracting States in accordance with their respective constitutional requirements. Once the ratification instruments have been deposited the accession procedure is at an end. As soon as the Treaty of Accession enters into force, the acceding State becomes a contracting party under international law to all the Treaties establishing the European Communities. It acquires the rights and obligations of a Member State of the Union. In spite of enlargement, the Community retains its identity as a legal person. From the time of accession the entire body of primary and secondary legislation (*acquis communautaire*) has the force of law in the new Member State.

Conditions, procedures and options for enlargement to the east With a view to enlargement to include the associated Central and East European countries, the June 1993 Copenhagen European Council laid down the criteria for accession which had to be taken into account by the Commission in drafting its provisional opinion. The Copenhagen criteria reflect the economic and political pre-conditions for membership without actually setting out a detailed check list or an objective yardstick. They state that the following five criteria must be met: stability of democracy and its institutions (the rule of law, multi-party system, respect for human rights, protection of minorities, pluralism, etc.); a functioning market economy, which will be able to cope with competitive pressure in the → single market; the ability to assume the rights and obligations arising from Community law; adherence to the aims of political union and → economic and monetary union. The fifth criterion is concerned with the Union's capacity to absorb new members without losing the momentum of European integration. The last of these criteria undoubtedly reflects the general interest within the Union of maintaining all that the Community has already achieved and preserving realistic prospects of further progress on integration. The Union's agreement in principle to enlargement to the east is therefore hedged around with a range of conditions.

At its meeting in Madrid, the European Council referred to the need to create the conditions for the progressive and smooth integration of the associated countries, in particular by developing the market economy, adapting the administrative stuctures of those countries and creating stable economic and monetary conditions. The strategy to prepare the associated countries for accession, adopted in December 1994, focuses on measures to assist the process of catching up and adjustment, for example under the PHARE programme and in the 'White Paper' process.

In each individual case, the Commission assesses the candidate's ability to harmonize its legislation in order to assume and to implement the *acquis communautaire* in all the Union's sectors of activity. It concludes its opinion with a recommendation on opening negotiations. What counts is less a 'snapshot' than an assessment of the progress to be expected from the applicant state before accession, both in the light of an evolving Union *acquis* and in relation to the political and economic situation. The opinions will be published at the earliest in the second half of 1997 after the end of the → Intergovernmental Conference.

EUROPEAN UNION • The power centre of Europe

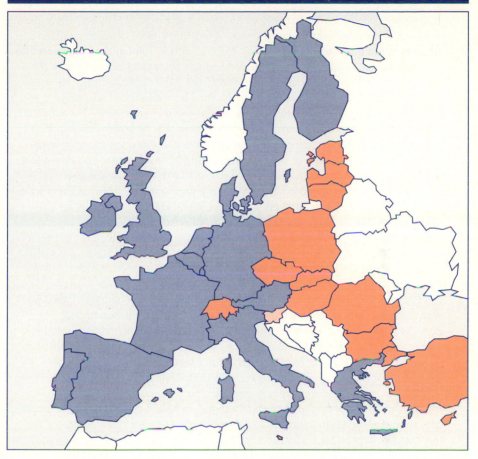

European Union

Applicants for membership
Bulgaria, Cyprus, Czech Republic, Estonia, Hungary, Latvia, Lithuania, Malta*,
Poland, Romania, Slovak Republic, Switzerland*, Turkey.

States which have concluded Europe agreements
Slovenia and the countries which have applied for membership**

* Application in abeyance at present.
** Except: Cyprus, Malta, Switzerland and Turkey (Malta has had an association agreement with
the European Union since 1971 and Cyprus since 1973; since 31 December 1995 there has been
a customs union between the European Union and Turkey).

Accession negotiations are expected to begin some time in 1998.

In drafting its opinion, the Commission will be basing itself mainly on information provided by the applicant States, the most important source being the written answers to the questionnaire sent in by the end of July 1996 and supplemented by a steady flow of follow-up questions. Fleshed out by exploratory talks with the Commission, they provide a detailed profile of the individual countries. As instructed by the Madrid European Council, the Commission will also prepare a number of reports and other documents in relation to enlargement. These include, firstly, detailed impact studies to assess the effects of enlargement on Community policy, especially the → common agricultural policy, and the structural policies (→ regional policy). Some of the key data relate to the importance of agriculture for the labour market and the economy in the 10 Central and East European countries (7.8% of GDP and 26.7% of the workforce, compared with 2.5 and 5.7% respectively in the EU), an increase in demand calculated at ECU 12 billion assuming no change in the common agricultural policy and exorbitant expenditure if the structural and cohesion policies are applied in their present form to the new members, since the average per capita GDP of the 10 applicant States is currently only 30% of the Community average.

The Commission is also drafting a composite document on enlargement, dealing with horizontal questions, such as the nature and duration of transitional arrangements and the future development of the pre-accession strategy in the context of an overall strategic concept. As soon as the IGC comes to an end, the Commission will also have to table a communication on the future financial framework of the Union taking into account the prospects for enlargement. The concerns of the net recipients and the size of the national budget deficits make the revision of the arrangements which run out in 1999 one of the most difficult operations for the EU in adjusting to enlargement. The pace of enlargement to the east will depend on a package of measures covering the availability of political and financial compensation and the balance of power within the Community.

Approximately six months after the end of the Intergovernmental Conference, the Council will adopt the necessary decisions on the start of accession negotiations in the light of the package of communications from the Commission and the results of the IGC. These will include decisions in which Central and East European countries should be involved in the first stage of the negotiations. There are two basic options: firstly, the opening of talks *en masse*, with all 10 Central and East European countries starting negotiations at once but finishing at different times, and, secondly, the politically sensitive but easier to manage 'group' option, whereby negotiations would begin and be concluded with just a few of the 10 Central and East European countries. The countries not involved in the first round would enter into accession talks with the EU in one or more subsequent enlargement rounds. This option, which most clearly reflects the varying degrees

of readiness of the applicants to join the Union and the limited capacity for absorption of the EU, must not overlook the dangers of a setback for the process of reform and stabilization and the resulting political and economic cost to the Union. Both options and their possible variants revolve around the need to treat individual applicant states differently but without discrimination. They must respect the principle of equal treatment in accordance with reasonable uniform criteria. Given the possible duration of the negotiations, the time needed for ratification and dovetailing with 'Agenda 2000', the next enlargement cannot be expected before the middle of the first decade of the new century.

Barbara Lippert

Environment

Treaty basis: Articles 2, 3 (k) and 130r - 130t of the EC Treaty.

Aims: To protect and improve the quality of the environment; to protect the health of the population; the careful and rational use of natural resources; the promotion of measures at international level to overcome regional and broader-scale environmental problems.

Instruments: Legal acts, primarily directives on quality standards for the environment (pollution levels), process standards (emission standards, design standards and operating standards) plus product standards (maximum tolerable pollution levels or emission levels for a product); action programmes on environmental protection; support programmes.

Budget: Approximately ECU 144 million (1995).

Literature from the European Union:

European Commission: How is the European Union protecting our environment?
Luxembourg 1996 (Cat. no.: CM-43-96-007-EN-C. Free).
European Commission: Environmental protection: A shared responsibility.
Luxembourg 1996 (Cat. no.: CC-97-96-063-EN-C. Free).
European Parliament: Nature.
Luxembourg 1996 (Cat. no.: AX-90-95-558-EN-C. Free).
European Community environment legislation. 7 volumes.
Luxembourg 1996 (Cat. no.: CR-26-96-000-EN-C. ECU 74.00).
* Volume 1 - General policy. Luxembourg 1996 (Cat. no.: CR-26-96-001-EN-C. ECU 13.00).
* Volume 2 - Air. Luxembourg 1996 (Cat. no.: CR-26-96-002-EN-C. ECU 15.00).
* Volume 3 - Chemicals,industrial risks and biotechnology. Luxembourg 1996 (Cat. no.: CR-26-96-003-EN-C. ECU 17.00).
* Volume 4 - Nature. Luxembourg 1996 (Cat. no.: CR-26-96-004-EN-C. ECU 13.00).
* Volume 5 - Noise. Luxembourg 1996 (Cat. no.: CR-26-96-005-EN-C. ECU 7.00).
* Volume 6 - Waste. Luxembourg 1996 (Cat. no.: CR-26-96-006-EN-C. ECU 11.00).
* Volume 7 - Water. Luxembourg 1996 (Cat. no.: CR-26-96-007-EN-C. ECU 11.00).
European Commission: Taking European environment policy into the 21st century: A summary of the European Commission's Progress Report and Action Plan on the Fifth Programme of Policy and Action in relation to the environment and sustainable development.
Luxembourg 1996 (Cat. no.: CR-94-96-889-EN-C. Free).
European Union: Financial instruments for the environment.
Luxembourg 1995 (Cat. no.: CR-87-95-418-EN-C. Free).
European Environment Agency: Europe's environment: The Dobris assessment: An overview.
Luxembourg 1995 (Cat. no.: GH-91-95-504-EN-C. Free).
European Environment Agency: European Environment Agency - Putting information to work.
Luxembourg 1995 (Cat. no.: GH-91-95-495-EN-C. Free).

The Treaty on European Union adopted by the European Community established environmental policy as one of the Community's tasks (Article 3), linking the aim of sustainable growth to the need to respect the environment (Article 2). With this step the common environmental policy developed in the 1970s was given a new legal status. As early as 1987 the Single European Act established that responsibility for environmental policy was to be transferred to the EC and that the need to protect the environment was to be taken into account in Community action of all types. This across-the-board principle, which appears nowhere else in the EC Treaty, assigns a special status to the protection of the environment. However, the transition from theory to practice is a long process and is marked, in particular in times of recession, by clashes between economic interests and environmental demands. This was particularly evident when common car exhaust limits were prescribed, initially in 1970 and then subsequently amended on a number of occasions, most recently in 1994. It is still not universally recognized that with an appropriate outline policy economic growth is compatible with a form of development which does not harm the environment, that environmental protection need not restrict competitiveness, and that it may even enhance it.

The trend in EC environmental policy – from aftercare to prevention
Responsibility for environmental policy was not a Community matter under the 1957 treaties. Member States responded to rising levels of environmental pollution by adopting national measures. However, the international-scale problem of environmental pollution cannot be effectively tackled by national-level policy on its own. Moreover, because the environmental measures and environmentally oriented product standards adopted by the Member States were increasingly seen as inhibiting trade and therefore inconsistent with the Community objective of free trade, there were calls for political action on the environment. Shortly after the first UN Conference on the Human Environment in June 1972 an EC summit in Paris called on the European Commission to produce an action programme for environmental policy. The legal basis for this new task was Article 2, which listed 'a harmonious development of economic activities' and 'a continuous and balanced expansion' in the Member States among the tasks of the Community. These objectives were only achievable if consideration was given to protecting the environment. Reference was also made to the preamble to the Treaty, which affirms the aim of a 'constant improvement of living and working conditions'. The legal bases for taking action on the environment are given as Article 235 of the EC Treaty, which assigns to the EC responsibility for taking action in situations otherwise not provided for, and Article 100, which requires the approximation of provisions laid down by law which directly affect the establishment or functioning of the common market. Legal measures on bases such as these could not be adopted by the Council of Ministers other than by a unanimous decision.

It was thus recognized as early as the beginning of the 1970s that a common policy on the environment was both a fundamental and a legitimate need. EC environmental law came into being in the form of regulatory provisions and restrictions, with over 200 directives and regulations covering, primarily, protection of the aquatic environment, air pollution control, chemicals, protection of flora and fauna, noise pollution and waste disposal. European environmental law concentrates on environmental legislation geared to economic requirements. New environmental laws are added all the time. The impact of EC environmental law is determined by the extent to which the Member States play their part, that is to say, by ensuring that directives are transposed into national law. The many cases of infringement proceedings, for example in connection with the protection of the aquatic environment, are an indication that there is room for improvement here. In addition to environmental law the Community also produced action programmes setting out priority guidelines and objectives for environment policy. It was as early as 1983 that the third action programme shifted the emphasis to the basic principles of prevention and safeguarding. The fourth action programme (1987-92) marked the transition towards a policy geared more to prevention. The Community has also set up research programmes geared to environmental protection, for example STEP (Science and technology for environmental protection) and EPOCH (European programme on climatology and natural hazards).

It was only with the adoption of the Single European Act in 1987 that the EC was given clear powers in relation to environmental policy (Articles 130r-130t). The effect of this was also to formally establish guidelines which had long been followed: the principles of prevention and avoidance, the 'polluter pays' principle and the 'at source' principle (priority given to rectifying environmental hazards at source). An environmental subsidiarity principle was added, on the basis of which the EC only takes action if the stated objectives can be better achieved at Community level than at national level. The most important instrument for ensuring that environmental needs are taken into account when EC measures are being established and implemented, as is required by the SEA, is the environmental impact assessment (EIA). The EIA directive came into force in July 1988 after 22 draft versions. The assessment stipulates a standard administrative procedure when economic projects are being planned so that their impact on human beings, flora and fauna and the environment can be gauged. The SEA, too, specified that on environmental issues decisions had to be unanimous and the European Parliament was, in principle, only to be consulted. Only in the event of subsequent decisions could the Council of Ministers vote by qualified majority (→ decision-making procedures). Environmental protection measures subsequently became possible on the basis of the new Article 100a provided that they were of relevance to the completion of the → single market. Under these circumstances the procedure was one of cooperation with the Parliament and this offered scope for majority voting with resultant faster adoption of the decisions. It was not until the Treaty on European Union was adopted that majority voting

became fundamentally possible and a greater involvement of the EP secured (procedures on the basis of Article 189b EC). There are, however, important areas which are exempted, for example regulations relating to environmental taxes and measures in the energy sector, which continue to require unanimity.

A common environmental policy for the 1990s The programme preparing the single market had the effect of raising the profile of environmental policy and lending it a sense of urgency: a study completed for the Commission in 1989 urgently warned of the risk of increases in environmental pollution in the single market, attributable mainly to higher volumes of road traffic. By imposing stringent environmental limits the Commission is seeking to secure a high degree of protection in the single market. In addition, the Member States are free to adopt their own measures to protect the environment (Articles 100a(4) and 130t). Existing national-level protection measures which go beyond a common system of regulation may be retained. They must not be out of proportion, however, and if they turn out to be a hidden obstacle to trade they infringe Community law. It is primarily in the Nordic countries and Germany that relatively high environmental standards apply.

In addition to developing further its environment legislation the Community has adopted a large number of other measures. The strategy for the fifth action programme, 'For sustainable development', adopted in 1993, is aimed at achieving, with the participation of all the parties involved, further progress towards protection of the environment by prevention, in particular with regard to transport and energy. The common environmental tax on energy/CO_2, which has been under discussion since 1990, failed to be adopted again in 1994, however, and it therefore remains a matter for national initiatives.

A number of Member States have already introduced a tax of this type; in 1995 the Commission presented a proposal for a framework directive with common parameters to be applied in the event of voluntary introduction of the tax. The common policy to reduce greenhouse gases is restricted to a system for observing CO_2 emissions to supplement the Altener programme (the promotion of renewable energy sources) and the SAVE programme (the raising of energy efficiency). The Member States are to conduct national programmes to reduce emissions but so far these are neither complete nor comparable. The EC objective of stabilizing CO_2 emissions at 1990 levels by 2000 is unlikely to be achieved this way.

The protection of the climate is also at the centre of environmental policy at international level. In December 1990 – in response to increasing pressure from within, e.g. from environmental organizations, as well as from the USA – the EC Environment Ministers agreed to cut production and consumption of CFCs by 50% by early 1992 and to ban them completely by mid-1997. Prior to this move there had been protracted international negotiations which had started at the end of the 1970s and where the Community (represented by the Commission) – as the world's largest producer and exporter of CFCs – had proved very intransigent, primarily due to French and British resistance. In the wake of new and alarming reports the EC Environment Ministers agreed at the end of 1992 that CFC production would cease as early as January 1995.

Aftercare is still a feature of the common environmental policy. In 1993 the Commission produced a Green Paper to promote a debate on the problem of remedying environmental damage. EC environmental policy also includes financial incentives for investments to improve the environment, the finance in question being made available through the LIFE financial instrument for the environment, with an allocation of ECU 450 million for 1996-99, or the Structural Funds/Cohesion Fund (→ Regional policy). At the end of 1989 the Regional Fund was used to set up the Envireg programme – a Community initiative contributing to the protection of the environment and promoting economic development in the economically weakest coastal areas of the EU. The → European Investment Bank also offers loans for the construction of waste disposal plants and sewage treatment plants, for example. Duly tested products can now be awarded the EU ecolabel, which was introduced in summer 1993, and since 1995 firms can receive an 'environment-friendly' label after an inspection of their environment-friendly operations.

The European Environment Agency, which began its work in October 1993, was designed to operate primarily as an information and documentation centre; during the three years which followed its decision of May 1990 to set up the Agency along with a network of environment observatories, the Council proved unable to agree on a location. By law now, every EU citizen is entitled to receive comprehensive information on environmental protection and environmental pollution and to have unhindered access to the appropriate official bodies.

To fulfil its obligation to ensure environment-friendly operations in all areas of the economy, the EU must also discharge its responsibilities for environmental policy in respect of its → external relations, in particular those with Eastern Europe and the developing countries. Action to follow up its agreement to play an active role in implementing the United Nations environmental action plan adopted in Rio is, however, still awaited. Overcoming environmental problems by international cooperation was included in the catalogue of environmental policy objectives at Maastricht (Article 130(1) of the EC Treaty). The EC is itself party to various environmental protection agreements. Its own agreements with third countries or groups of countries already include a clause on the protection of the environment. In the context of heightened cooperation with the countries of eastern Europe special bilateral cooperation agreements were concluded in connection with the environment. The European Union is involved in a decisive way in the 1993 environmental action programme for the countries of Central and Eastern Europe and the third pan-European Conference of Ministers for the Environment took place in October 1995. The European Environmental Agency is also involved in cooperation with the countries of Central and Eastern Europe.

Assessment and prospects In addition to its activities at national and bilateral levels the EU has become an increasingly important actor for environmental policy in Europe. So far the EU has adopted environmental policies in all fields. An attempt to determine where European environment policy currently stands would, however, produce contradictory results. The rising level of activity does indicate growing environmental awareness and the firmer and more effective European environment policy becomes, the more pronounced the reservations expressed by the industrial sectors concerned will be. The question, however, remains whether the desired move to a sustainable economic development is succeeding. The Commission is working on appropriate strategies, an example being its White Paper on growth, competitiveness and employment, which appeared in 1993. The achievement of an ecological realignment of the economy, of technology and of society calls for the introduction of environmental taxes and charges coupled with ecology-geared reform of taxation systems. The failure of the common environmental tax on energy leaves little else offering scope for progress. It is still also unclear where the increasingly politically motivated subsidiarity principle will lead as regards the environment – the Commission has already withdrawn some legal measures it was planning. Another possibility is the threat of EC environmental standards being watered down.

The touchstone for the European Union will be the effective merging of the environmental dimension into other areas of policy. To ensure that environmental requirements are taken into account in all areas of Community activity, the Commission appointed an official charged with this task in every directorate-general and in 1994 it also set up the general consultation procedure on the environment. The common environment policy will also not be spared future conflicts of interest between the economy and ecology. Even a number of the infrastructure projects promoted and deemed necessary by the EU run counter to environmental interests. In the middle of the 1990s what the common environmental policy needs above all are new impulses and so it is to be hoped, it will be the new Member States, for example Austria, with its concern about an ecological transport policy, which will bring their influence to bear.

Anita Wolf-Niedermaier

The euro

Treaty basis: Articles 102a to 109m of the EC Treaty, on EMU.
Aims: Introduction of the Euro as a stable currency in the European Union.
Literature from the European Union:
European Commission: When will the 'euro' be in our pockets?
Luxembourg 1996 (Cat. no.: CM-43-96-004-EN-C. Free).

Under the Treaty on European Union the third stage of economic and monetary union is to begin on 1 January 1999. Subsequently, a common currency, the euro, is to be gradually introduced in those Member States which have qualified for EMU.

Originally, the EC Treaty called the new currency the ecu (European currency unit). The ecu has served as the unit of account between the Member States since the introduction of the → European Monetary System. It is a basket currency made up of the weighted values of the currencies of the EU States. This is why, in recent years, the value of the ecu has declined against the stable currencies of some countries. The new currency will not be a basket currency and will tend to take the value of the most stable currencies. It is also intended to be a symbol of European identity. For these reasons the Heads of State or Government agreed, in December 1995, that it should be called the euro. One advantage of this name is that it is short. It can also be written in the same way in all European languages. The euro is further divided into 100 cents.

The replacement of European currencies by the euro is an ambitious task. To limit the technical difficulties involved in the transition to a minimum – for example, the conversion of vending machines – the first step of EMU is to irrevocably fix the exchange rates for the currencies of the countries participating, so that each national currency is simply the expression of the common currency. Under the terms of the Treaty, after the beginning of EMU, monetary policy will be determined by the European Central Bank, which will be politically independent and will have the prime objective of maintaining currency stability.

According to current plans, after the decision is taken in 1998 about which countries qualify for membership, production of euro banknotes and coins will commence. A unanimous decision by the Council of the Economics and Finance Ministers will irrevocably fix the exchange rates of the participating Member

States' currencies, with effect from 1 January 1999. At this point, only public borrowing will be partly converted into euros. It will, however, already be possible to use the euro for payments by cheque or money transfer. On 1 January 2002, European notes and coins will be issued. For a period of at most six months it will be possible to use the euro and the national currencies alongside each other, but from 1 July 2002 the euro will be the only legal tender in the countries participating in EMU.

Contrary to some fears, the euro is a currency conversion and not a currency reform. All money amounts will be converted, but their actual value will remain unaltered. The conditions applying to all existing contracts –such as leases or bank loans – will be the same as before. The difference is that the European Central Bank, due to be established in 1998, will assume responsibility for the stability of the common currency. The European Central Bank is modelled on the successful *Deutsche Bundesbank* in terms of structure and orientation. However, unlike national central banks, the ECB can adapt its monetary policy to the situation in the currency area as a whole. The monetary instruments at the disposal of the ECB are being prepared by its forerunner institution, the European Monetary Institute. The details of these instruments have yet to be set out, but there is common ground between the Governors of the national central banks, who make up the EMI Council, on the basic ideas. After the ECB has been set up, the ECB Council will take decisions regarding monetary policy, monetary instruments and the design of the banknotes.

All in all, there are still a whole series of technical details to be clarified before EMU actually begins, for example, the exact procedure for fixing the exchange rates on the day the currencies are converted or the introduction of a binding legal framework for conversion to the euro so as to guarantee all economic actors the highest possible degree of certainty for their planning. To convince Europeans of the usefulness of a common currency it is necessary both to provide them with comprehensive information and to take the political decisions pending in a manner that is as comprehensible as possible. That the people accept their new currency is, however, only one prerequisite for the success of monetary union. The euro must also live up to all the promises made on its behalf in the long run.

Olaf Hillenbrand

Steps leading to the euro

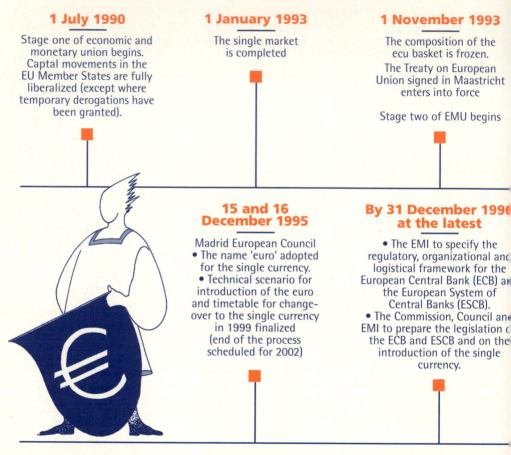

1 July 1990

Stage one of economic and monetary union begins. Captal movements in the EU Member States are fully liberalized (except where temporary derogations have been granted).

1 January 1993

The single market is completed

1 November 1993

The composition of the ecu basket is frozen.

The Treaty on European Union signed in Maastricht enters into force

Stage two of EMU begins

15 and 16 December 1995

Madrid European Council
• The name 'euro' adopted for the single currency.
• Technical scenario for introduction of the euro and timetable for change-over to the single currency in 1999 finalized (end of the process scheduled for 2002)

By 31 December 1996 at the latest

• The EMI to specify the regulatory, organizational and logistical framework for the European Central Bank (ECB) and the European System of Central Banks (ESCB).
• The Commission, Council and EMI to prepare the legislation on the ECB and ESCB and on the introduction of the single currency.

1 January 1999

Stage three of EMU begins.
• Council to fix irrevocably the conversion rates of the currencies of participating countries both among themselves and against the euro.
• The euro is to become a currency in its own right and the official ecu basket will cease to exist.
• Council regulation establishing the legal framework for introduction of the euro is to enter into force.

From 1 January 1999

• ESCB to frame and implement single monetary policy in euros and conduct foreign exchange operations in euros.
• Member States to issue new public debt securities in euros.

1 January 1994

- The European Monetary Institute (EMI) is set up in Frankfurt.
- Procedures for coordinating economic policies at European level are strengthened.
- Member States strive to combat 'excessive deficits' and to achieve economic convergence.

31 May 1995

The Commission adopts Green Paper on the single currency (reference scenario for the transition to the single currency).

As early as possible in 1998

The Heads of State or Government to decide which Member States will be the first to take part in the single currency, on the basis of the convergence criteria and in the light of economic data for 1997.

As soon as possible after that decision

- Member States to appoint Executive Board of the ECB.
- ECB and Council to set the date for introduction of euro notes and coins.
- ESCB to start issuing banknotes in euros.
- Council and Member States to start minting euro coins.

Before 1 January 1999

Final preparation of the ECB and ESCB:
- Council to adopt legislation on the key for capital subscription, collection of statistical information, minimum reserves, consultation of the ECB, and fines and penalties which can be imposed on undertakings.
- ECB and ESCB to get ready for becoming operational: setting up the ECB, adopting the regulatory framework, testing the monetary policy framework, etc.

From 1 January 1999 to 1 January 2002 at the latest

- ESCB to exchange at par value currencies with irrevocably fixed conversion rates.
- ESCB and public authorities in Member States to monitor changeover developments in the banking and finance sectors and assist the whole of the economy to prepare for the changeover.

1 January 2002 at the latest

- ESCB gradually to put euro notes into circulation and withdraw national banknotes
- Member States gradually to put Euro coins into circulation and withdraw national coins.

... The process comes to an end ...

1 July 2002 at the latest

The changeover to the euro is complete in all the participating Member States.

European Commission

Treaty basis: Articles 155 to 163 of the EC Treaty; in the context of the CFSP, Articles J.5(3), J.6, J.7, J.8(3) and J.9 of the Treaty on European Union; in the context of justice and home affairs cooperation, Articles K.3(2), K.4(2), K.6 and K.9 of the Treaty on European Union.

Aims: To ensure the smooth functioning and development of the common market; representation of Community interests both internally and externally.

Instruments: Right of initiative in the Community legislative process; participatory powers regarding the creation, execution and supervision of Community law; international representations.

Budget: Administrative appropriations of ECU 2.7 billion, operational resources of ECU 77.8 billion (1996).

Literature from the European Union:
European Commission: Serving in the European Union.
A citizen's guide to the institutions of the European Union.
Luxembourg 1996 (Cat. no.: FX-89-95-939-EN-C. Free).
European Commission: The European Commission 1995-2000.
Luxembourg 1995 (Cat. no.: CC-86-94-973-EN-C. Free).
Pascal Fontaine: Europe in Ten Points.
Luxembourg 1995 (Cat. no.: CC-90-95-623-EN-C. Free).
Klaus-Dieter Borchardt: European Integration. The origins and growth of the European Union.
Luxembourg 1995 (Cat. no.: CC-84-94-355-EN-C. Free).

'The Commission of the European Communities' - to use the correct legal title, although by way of simplification the term 'European Commission' was introduced in November 1993 – is made up of the 20 Commissioners and the complex Brussels-based administrative machinery that is under their control. The administration consists of 26 Directorates-General and other horizontally-integrated services (the Secretariat-General, the Legal Service, the Official Publications Office, the Statistical Office, the Translation Service, the Interpreting and Conference Service, etc.), employing some 15 500 people in permanent or temporary posts, of whom some 11% are in the language service.

Historical development and function The forerunner of the Commission was the High Authority of the European Coal and Steel Community (ECSC), which was expressly granted a supranational character in the ECSC Treaty. Its first President, Jean Monnet (1952-55), set up a lean, flexible administrative organization to solve factual problems. Following the signing of the Treaty of Rome the 'Commission of the European Economic Community' was established in 1958. Its first President was Walter Hallstein (1958-67). Whereas the Council of Ministers (→ the Council of the European Union) was intended to represent the interests of the Member States, the Commission was thought of as the guardian of the Community's interests. To this end it was instructed to carry out clearly defined duties, described in general terms in Article 155 of the EEC Treaty, which can be summed up in three roles. Firstly, the Commission is the initiator in the decision-making process, meaning that the Council can only take decisions on proposals made by the Commission. The Commission has a legislative function, whereby it takes binding decisions and concludes international agreements on the basis of the powers granted to it. The Commission also has an administrative and monitoring role, acting as the executor of EU laws and monitoring the proper application of Community laws by the Member States.

The Merger Treaty, which came into force on 1 July 1967, joined together the High Authority, the EEC Commission and the European Atomic Energy Community (Euratom) Commission to form the 'Commission of the European Communities'.

The appointment, in 1985, of Jacques Delors as President of the Commission, and the passing, in 1986, of the Single European Act with the aim of establishing a → single market by the end of 1992 heralded a period of dynamic activity on the part of the Commission. The large number of instruments detailed in the White Paper on completing the internal market, together with the incorporation of new political spheres into the Community (→ research and technological development, → regional policy, → environment policy) made the Commission an important address for pressure groups, companies, regions and local authorities. The collapse of the Berlin Wall and the end of the Cold War gave the Commission new room for manoeuvre as regards the → external relations of the Community. These developments, as well as Jacques Delors' dynamic leadership between 1985 and 1995, strengthened the role of the Commission in two respects. Firstly, the Commission's role as a broker between national governments has been enhanced, especially as more Council decisions have been taken on a majority basis. Secondly, the Commission's international profile has grown in the wake of the development of trade and economic relations.

The replacement of Jacques Delors, on 1 January 1995 by the Luxembourger Jacques Santer signalled the start of a new era which is characterized by moderation and consolidation.

The Commission in the decision-making process The Commission is one of the main protagonists in the preparation, formulation, implementation and monitoring of binding decisions taken by the European Union. On matters falling within the scope of the first pillar of the European Union it is involved in all four of these processes. As far as the preparation of decisions is concerned, in most areas (the exceptions being association with non-member countries and enlargement) the Council can only enact legislation on the basis of a Commission proposal. Proposals are drawn up in specialized committees and working parties (between 700 and 1 000 in all) which are made up of independent experts, representatives from pressure groups and officials from Member States as well as officials from the Commission. Once a proposal has been formally presented to the Council, the Commission can amend or withdraw it at any time during the decision-making process. Recommendations, opinions and other formal communications by the Commission (e.g. White or Green Papers on specific policy areas) are an informal presentation of positions and not formal legislative proposals for the Council. They can, however, often provide the impetus for subsequent legislation. On matters of external relations the Commission can be mandated by the Council, within a clearly laid-down framework, to conduct negotiations with non-member countries or international organizations (e.g. countries in Central and Eastern Europe or GATT).

The Commission participates in the formulation of decisions; it is represented in the Council's working parties (approximately 250) by senior officials and by the Deputy Secretary-General in Coreper. The Commission officials can influence the representatives of national governments but have no right to vote. Council meetings are attended by the Commissioner concerned, but he can do very little to influence the negotiations between ministers. The Commission does have its own powers concerning decision-making which it can exercise independently of the Council. These relate primarily to its own organization, matters of budgetary law and laws on competition (e.g. decisions concerning State aids or company mergers).

Article 205 of the EC Treaty makes the Commission responsible for the implementation of the EU budget (→ budgets). Within the framework of the powers assigned to it by the Council regarding the implementation of Council decisions it can issue directives and regulations and take decisions on its own – especially on matters concerning the single market and agricultural policy – which are just as binding on the Member States as the Council's decisions. In 1994 the Commission issued a total of 7 034 legal instruments of this kind. As the implementation of acts is extremely important, the Member States are involved in the Commission's implementation work by means of a highly complex system of committee procedures, involving some 380 committees of various types, known as advisory committees, management committees and regulatory committees. With representatives of the Commission chairing the committees, officials from the Member States discuss and decide on the Commission's implementation measures. The degree of influence the national officials can exert on the executive powers of the Commission depends on the type of committee involved. In an advisory committee they are simply consulted, whereas in a management committee they

can even reject the Commission's measures. Regulatory committees provide the greatest scope for exercising national influence. According to a variant in the decision-making procedure, which is generally known as the safety-net procedure, should a committee vote against a measure the Council can be called together and can decide by simple majority that no implementation measure is to be taken. Although the committee procedure clearly has supervisory characteristics it has turned out in practice to function well as an advisory body and an intermediary between national governments and the Commission administration, so that only in exceptional circumstances does the Council have to step in.

The Commission monitors the implementation of decisions within the framework laid down in Article 169 of the EC Treaty, which allows the Commission to bring proceedings before the → Court of Justice (ECJ) should a Member State fail to fulfil an obligation under the Treaty, or to observe current EC/EU legal provisions. As a consequence the Commission is known as 'the Guardian of the Treaties'. In 1995, the Commission initiated around 1 000 such procedures; 72 cases were brought before the Court; 39 rulings were given in 1995, 36 in the Commission's favour. Since the → Treaty on European Union came into force, if a Member State fails to take the necessary measures to comply with the Court's judgment, under Article 171 the Commission can request the imposition of a penalty payment. The Commission can also take other EU institutions to the Court of Justice.

In the Treaty on European Union the Commission is mentioned in a decision-making context in the areas of both → common foreign and security policy (CFSP, the second pillar of the Union) and cooperation in → justice and home affairs (the third pillar of the Union). Its actual participation rights, however, are far more limited than on matters coming under the first pillar, as these areas basically require action at intergovernmental level. Within the framework of the CFSP, the Commission may submit proposals to the Council under Article J.8(3) of the Treaty on European Union. Article J.9 goes on to state that the 'Commission shall be fully associated with the work carried out in the common foreign policy and security policy field'. The same applies to the Commission in the field of justice and home affairs (see Article K.4). Article K.3 gives the Commission the right to submit proposals on specific aspects of the third pillar to the Council but it does not have a monopoly on the submission of proposals.

Administrative structure and internal procedures Broadly speaking, the Commission can be seen as consisting of three levels. The first level comprises the 20 Members of the Commission (including the President of the Commission whose role is that of primus inter pares), who are nominated by the Member States and approved by the → European Parliament for a period of five years. They must be completely independent in the performance of their duties and can be required to resign if the Parliament passes a motion of censure (Article 144). The second level consists of the staff of the Members' Offices. These work directly for the Commissioners and are made up of a small number of close political advisers. There are also the 26 Directorates-General and other departments which are structured hierarchically on a departmental basis in much the same way as national ministries. They are organized in directorates and units. In addition, the Commission maintains its own representatives in all Member States as well as 126 delegations in non-member countries and to international organizations. Commission staff are subject to the staff regulations of the European Communities and are paid from the Union budget. There are also experts employed on a temporary basis and national civil servants who are seconded to the Commission for a limited period.

Acting in response to initiatives not only from the Commission, but also from the Council or the European Council, the officials in the relevant administrative units prepare proposals. The Directorate-General which holds overall responsibility for the proposal works together with other Directorates-General concerned, either through interdepartmental working parties or *ad hoc* meetings. Rivalries may arise with regard to certain political fields or the 'strong' Directorates-General (External Relations, Agriculture, and Internal Market) may try to impose their wishes on the 'weak' ones. In every case the Legal Service must be consulted, and its approval increases the chances of getting a proposal through the administration. The Chefs de cabinet (Heads of Members' Offices) hold weekly meetings at which they determine on which items there is agreement among the departments. These items are known as 'A' items. There are also 'B' items, which require further discussion and decisions on the part of the Members of the Commission. In this way the Members' Offices can exercise a great deal of influence over the preparation and adoption of proposals. In the past this power of position was exploited above all by President Delors' Office to attain important goals. At Commission meetings, chaired by the President of the Commission, decisions are taken on the basis of a simple majority vote. However, as a rule, a consensus is found before a vote is taken. In order to lighten the load on the Members of the Commission two procedures have been introduced known as the delegation of powers procedure and the written procedure. The delegation procedure empowers a Commissioner to decide alone on a technical matter (especially in the field of agricultural policy) although the Commission maintains its collective responsibility. The written procedure allows the Secretary-General to notify in writing the departments and Members' Offices of matters on which there is general agreement, thereby fulfilling an important coordinating function. If no objections are expressed nor amendments made within a given time the draft is deemed to have been accepted.

Think-Tank or European government? There is a widely held view that the Commission is a technocracy run by 'Eurocrats'. What is not so widely known is that decisions are arrived at after very close cooperation with representatives of associations, the regions and national governments. This dovetailing of different

organizations and their ability to bring into play expert knowledge and quickly to produce proposals for solutions to problems lend the Commission the air of a dynamic think-tank. One thing is clear: the Commission's profile has grown, particularly during the Delors Presidency, and it has moved into fields, such as the reduction of unemployment and foreign policy, which tend to be seen as the classic preserves of government. The increase in the importance of the European Parliament in appointing the Commission has increased the amount of feedback given to the Members of Parliament and the people as a whole, without, however, overcoming its fundamental lack of democratic legitimacy. At the Intergovernmental Conference which began in 1996 there is discussion about reducing the number of Commissioners and reforming the Commission structures, but this is not likely to take the direction of forming a European government. In future the Commission's role will depend on the degree to which it can make an effective contribution to meeting the concrete economic, political and social challenges the Union faces.

Dietrich Rometsch

European Council

Established: 10 December 1974.
Treaty basis: Article D (common provisions) of the Treaty on European Union.
Frequency of meetings: At least twice but usually three times a year.
Composition: The Heads of State or Government of the Member States, plus the President of the European Commission, supported by the Ministers for Foreign Affairs and a Member of the European Commission.
Voting procedure: Consensus.

No other 'institution' has influenced the process of integration in Western Europe in the 1970s, 1980s and early 1990s quite as much as the European Council, which brings together the Heads of State or Government of the Member States. Of particular importance have been the European Council's decisions on the Single European Act (SEA), the Treaty on European Union and other 'constitutional' issues affecting the EC/EU, such as the various enlargements and the incorporation of the five new German *Länder* into the EC.

From a strictly legal point of the view the European Council is not an institution of the EC: following a government agreement reached at the 1974 Paris Summit, the European Council was first mentioned in Article 2 of the SEA, a legally binding text but not part of the EEC Treaty. In the Maastricht Treaty it figures in the 'common provisions' (Article D) as a body above the European Community and, consequently, not subject to the constitutional checks and balances to which the Community is subject.

Tasks and responsibilities Article D of the Treaty on European Union states that 'the European Council shall provide the Union with the necessary impetus for its development and shall define the general political guidelines thereof'. According to Article 103(2) of the EC Treaty, the European Council also has the task of discussing conclusions 'on the broad guidelines of the economic policies of the Member States and of the Community', whilst Article J.8(1) of the Treaty on European Union requires the European Council to 'define the principles of and general guidelines for the → common foreign and security policy'.

Actual role The range of the European Council's actual activities is much wider and more varied than outlined above.

In the first place, it acts as a 'constitutional architect'. In the 1970s it was very reluctant to assume this role, i.e. that of giving a general political impetus to the construction of Europe and deliberating on questions relevant to → European Union. It was not until the 1980s that the European Council took major initiatives such as convening the intergovernmental conferences on the Single European Act, → economic and monetary union (Strasbourg, 1989) and political union (Dublin, 1990), ending with the conclusion of the Treaty on European Union in Maastricht in 1991.

In this way the Heads of State or Government considerably expanded the range of their joint activities. On repeated occasions they defined Western European problems as joint tasks for the EC and for new forms of cooperation and specified the ways and means for tackling these problems, beginning with the 1969 Summit in The Hague, which established the framework for European Political Cooperation, and finally approving the essential points in the Single European Act and the Maastricht Treaty on European Union, which explicitly brought new areas of policy within the scope of the Treaties or other 'pillars' of the Union.

Another function of the European Council is to lay down general guidelines on matters of economic and social policy and to issue statements on foreign policy, which are regarded as particularly important. In recent years there has been a substantial increase in the European Council's involvement in foreign affairs. It has issued declarations on every international crisis in the 1970s, 1980s and early 1990s (e.g. South Africa, the Middle East and the break-up of the Soviet Union).

Of central importance to the development of the EC has been a function of which the European Council itself makes little or no mention, namely its adoption of key decisions on behalf of the European Community (such is the de facto situation, at least). Particularly in the case of financial or institutional disputes the European Council has become the Community's central decision-making body, even if it has at no time adopted any legally binding decisions on behalf of the EC/EU. The policies approved by the Heads of Government have been given shape by EC/EU legislation adopted in accordance with the normal procedures laid down in the Treaty.

Decision-making procedures The decision-making procedures of the European Council present a number of constant features. One is the 'package deal'. Only the Heads of State or Government have the power to offset against each other the various demands and concessions made by Member States in different policy areas. Just as the Single European Act reconciled the interests of some Member States in the completion of the → single market with those of others demanding economic and social improvements, so has the European Council been successful, on several occasions, in paving the way for the further development of the Community by means of 'horse trading' between the Member States. On each occasion the process takes considerable time and trouble but the progress of the Community depends largely on such negotiations at the summit, as has again been demonstrated by the agreement on the essential sections of the Maastricht Treaty on European Union. On that occasion the Heads of State or Government had to step outside their original role and grapple with specific formulations. Their attempts to limit themselves to issuing general political guidelines proved ineffective. It is only when the technical details have to be settled that political controversy rears its head and tough decisions have to be taken.

The Heads of State or Government of the larger Member States have more influence over the discussions in the European Council than in the → Council of the European Union. Depending on the subject under discussion, however, the President of the → European Commission or individual Heads of State or Government from the smaller Member States may also play an important role. The style of negotiation is more direct and personal than in the Council of the EU. To a greater extent than in the Council the current President of the European Council takes responsibility for the preparation and shaping of decisions.

Impact on other EU institutions When the European Council was set up there was justifiable concern that such a body would in the long term alter the original institutional balance within the Community. Many expected the Heads of State or Government to undermine the European Commission's exclusive right of initiative, reduce the Council to a subordinate status and by-pass the few powers available to the → European Parliament (EP). In practice, however, the impact of the European Council has been variable. In those areas with which the Heads of State or Government have concerned themselves directly, they have taken the actual decisions (after due preparation by the Commission and the Council) and have thus frequently reduced the rules laid down in the Treaty to formal 'ratification procedures'. In many other areas, however, the European Council has had little or no impact on the normal process of institutional cooperation. The Commission and its President have in fact gained in status as a result of the European Council, since they are represented at these summits and can use the conclusions of the European Council as a 'mandate' from a higher authority for many of their EU activities. Decisions taken by the European Council have also extended the Commission's powers into such intergovernmental spheres as the common foreign and security policy and cooperation in justice and home affairs.

The effects on the European Parliament have been less favourable, however. Although the President of the EP has for some time been allowed to outline Parliament's views at the beginning of each meeting of the European Council, Parliament's actual powers *vis-à-vis* the Council often remain 'formal', the stance of the latter body having been predetermined by the European Council so that little room is left for negotiation under EC procedures.
More problematic from the constitutional point of view is the European Council's

position outside the system of 'checks and balances' explicitly provided for in the Maastricht Treaty. The activities of the European Council are not subject to any review by the Court of Justice of the European Community ($\rightarrow$ European Court of Justice; Article L of the Treaty on European Union).

Contribution to integration The European Council has made a lasting contribution to integration. By their direct intervention the Heads of State or Government have taken (and continue to take) direct responsibility for the stability, efficiency and development of the EC and the European Union. It is not just the by-product of some political whim entertained by a few Heads of Government; it indicates the underlying trend in Western Europe towards the joint use of government instruments and the consequent merging of institutions.

Wolfgang Wessels

European Court of Auditors

Treaty basis: Articles 4, 188a–188c and 206 of the EC Treaty.

Tasks: To audit the accounts of the EU and its institutions and to ensure the legality and regularity of the underlying transactions; to ascertain whether the financial management of the EU has been sound.

Instruments: After the close of each financial year the Court of Auditors draws up an annual report which the European Parliament examines before it grants discharge to the Commission. The Court may also submit special reports on specific questions.

Composition: Fifteen Members (one from each Member State), appointed for a term of six years by the Council acting unanimously after consulting the European Parliament. The President of the Court is elected for a term of three years. The Court sits in Luxembourg.

Voting procedures: The Court of Auditors is a collegiate body and usually takes decisions by a majority vote of its Members. Particular areas of responsibility are allocated to individual Members.

Literature from the European Union:

European Court of Auditors: Auditing the finances of the European Union.
Luxembourg 1996 (Cat. no.: MX-98-96-857-EN-C. Free).
European Commission: Serving in the European Union.
A citizen's guide to the institutions of the European Union.
Luxembourg 1996 (Cat. no.: FX-89-95-939-EN-C. Free).

The Court of Auditors has grown with the → European Union itself. The Treaty on European Union of 7 February 1992 elevated the Court to the rank of institution. It was originally set up by the Treaty amending certain financial provisions, which was signed by the governments of the Member States on 22 July 1975 and came into force on 1 June 1997. The aim was to expand and improve the checks on the Community budget, alongside the strengthening of the European Community's financial rules and the transfer of own resources to the EC, which has since been targeted even more closely on the completion of the EU as a result of the decisions taken by the → European Council in December 1992 (→ budgets). The establishment of the Court of Auditors went hand in hand with the redistribution of budgetary powers and the introduction (from 1975 onwards) of a new budgetary procedure which gave the → European Parliament in particular greater powers over the drafting and adoption of the Community budget. The Treaty of 22 July 1975 also conferred on Parliament the exclusive right to give a discharge to the → European Commission in respect of its implementation of the budget. In this context Parliament must work with the Court of Auditors, which submits an annual report after the close of each budgetary year.

The Court of Auditors examines all revenue and expenditure of the Community and the European Union. It has the task of examining the whole range of EC/EU finances. This began with the scrutiny of the 1984, 1985 and 1986 budgets and now encompasses the entire EU budget and those of the three Communities which it comprises. In principle, its competence extends also to the subsidiary bodies set up by the institutions themselves. The Court of Auditors' most important task is to submit its annual reports on the EC budgetary accounts, the financial activities of the ECSC and (on occasion) those of subsidiary EU bodies. These reports, however, constitute only a retrospective audit of budgetary management. To ensure that the implementation of the budget is transparent and open, the main instrument used is an arrangement whereby the Court of Auditors may at any time give its opinion on specific matters and subject current accounting procedures to ongoing scrutiny, the results being presented in the form of special reports. The Court may do so either on its own initiative or at the instigation of other European institutions.

Since 1977 the Court has developed into an autonomous inspectorate and control body whose authority and competence are generally recognized. In institutional terms, however, the Court is in a difficult position. This is because there is a degree of natural tension between the European Parliament, which is the other body responsible for budgetary control and for which the Court does most of its work, and the Commission, to which Parliament gives a discharge in respect of its management of the budget on the basis of the Court's annual reports. The Court of Auditors has been particularly active in its investigations of the common → agricultural policy, which it has accused of failing to maintain market balance and failing to lay down effective rules for recording and assessing stocks of surplus products. For some time, Parliament has been calling for the establishment of an independent Community control body with powers to take immediate action to combat fraud, a matter in which the European public has shown a keen interest.

Thomas Läufer

European Court of Justice

Treaty basis: Articles 165 to 188 of the EC Treaty; Article L of the Treaty on European Union.

Aims: The Court of Justice ensures that the law is upheld in the interpretation and application of the EC and EU Treaties.

Composition: Judges and Advocates-General (Articles 165 and 166), appointed for a term of six years by common accord of the Governments of the Member States. The judges elect the President of the Court of Justice from among their number for a term of three years. Every three years there is a partial replacement of the judges and Advocates-General (Article 167). The Court sits in Luxembourg.

Voting procedures: In the case of actions brought by Member States or European institutions the Court of Justice sits in plenary session if so requested. Otherwise it forms Chambers, each consisting of three, five or seven judges (Article 165). Its deliberations are not public. The decisions of the Court reflect the majority opinion of the Judges. Cases are heard in the official languages of the EU. The working language is French.

Literature from the European Union:

The Court of Justice of the European Communities.
Luxembourg 1996 (Cat. no.: DY-88-95-597-EN-C. Free).
Report of Proceedings 1992-94: Synopsis of the work of the Court
of Justice and the Court of First Instance of the European Communities.
Luxembourg 1995 (Cat. no.: DX-87-94-022-EN-C. Free).
Noel, Emile: Working together: The institutions of the European Community.
Luxembourg 1994 (Cat. no.: CC-76-92-172-EN-C. Free).
European Commission: Serving the European Union: A citizen's
guide to the institutions of the European Union.
Luxembourg 1996 (Cat. no.: FX-89-95-939-EN-C. Free).

The European Court of Justice (ECJ) is one of the five main institutions of the Community (Article 4(1) of the EC Treaty). It was originally set up by the Convention on certain institutions common to the European Communities of 25 March 1957, as the single Court of Justice for the EC. The Advocates-General examine the cases before the Court at the same time as the judges, give their independent views in the course of the hearing and, most importantly, submit their opinion with specific recommendations for the Court's decision. The Advocates-General are members of the Court as an institution but they do not take part in its deliberations or voting. The Court's pre-eminent role in the Community system and as the authority on the interpretation and application of Community law derives mainly from the fact that it takes decisions by majority vote and relies solely on its own understanding of the law and justice. In this sense it is a truly supranational institution and is not influenced by the interests of the Member States.

Tasks and responsibilities As the EU's only control body of a legal nature the ECJ has been given a number of tasks which go beyond its customary judicial function. The Court of Justice may also act as:

(i) a constitutional court: clarification of the rights and obligations of the European institutions *vis-à-vis* each other and clarification of the legal relationship between the Member States and the EU;

(ii) a legislative watchdog: verification of the compatibility of secondary legislation (acts adopted by the → Council of the EU and the → European Commission) with the Treaty and general legal principles;

(iii) an administrative court: ruling on actions brought by natural or legal persons against EU measures and on complaints lodged by European officials as regards their terms of employment;

(iv) a civil court: establishment of non-contractual liability and examination of claims for damages, particularly where the liability of public authorities is involved;

(v) an arbitration court: subject to agreement between the parties, the ECJ may be competent to arbitrate in certain specific cases.

The Council, the Commission or a Member State may also obtain the Court of Justice's opinion on the compatibility with the EC Treaty of any agreement planned between the EU and third countries or international organizations (Article 228(6)). In this respect the ECJ has at least partial responsibility for monitoring the validity of international laws. These tasks and responsibilities did not change with the ratification of the Treaty on European Union by the national parliaments. Article L of that Treaty explicitly limits the competence of the ECJ to certain Community acts (in particular, treaty amendments and accession treaties).

Actions and proceedings The following types of action may be brought before the Court of Justice:

(i) applications by EU institutions, Member States or – in certain cases – individuals (Article 173 of the EC Treaty) for the annulment of binding acts adopted by Community institutions;

(ii) actions brought by the Commission or a Member State against another Member State for non-compliance with obligations arising from the European treaties and the secondary legislation adopted by European institutions (Articles 169 and 170) or from treaties concluded by the EU (e.g. Article 228);

(iii) actions brought by EU institutions or Member States against the Council or Commission for failure to act as required by Community law (Article 175);

(iv) disputes between the EU and its staff (Article 179).

In addition to its judgments relating to the provisions of the Treaty or the validity of EU legislation, the Court of Justice is increasingly called upon to give preliminary rulings (Article 177 of the EC Treaty), that is to decide on the interpretation and application of Community law in cases before courts in Member States and referred to the ECJ by those courts. Such preliminary rulings are binding on the national courts and form an important link between the ECJ and the courts of the Member States. They ensure that Community law is applied uniformly throughout the EU and constitute a body of consistent European case law.

Court of First Instance A Council Decision of 24 October 1988 provided that a Court of First Instance (CFI) should be attached to the Court of Justice. The CFI has jurisdiction to hear and determine at first instance (e.g. in disputes between the Community and its staff and in competition cases), subject to a right of appeal to the ECJ. The basis for setting up the CFI was provided by the Single European Act (Article 168a). The CFI has 15 members who may both judge cases or perform the task of the Advocate-General. Their term of office is six years. The CFI commenced work on 31 October 1989, thus easing the burden on the ECJ. In 1993/94, the CFI became competent to hear all actions brought by natural or legal persons against measures taken by European institutions. This should enable the European courts to handle the increasing volume of actions brought by individuals and should make for a more equal division of labour between the ECJ and the Court of First Instance.

Case law From the outset the ECJ has played a central role in moulding the EC into a Community based on law. It has repeatedly provided the impetus towards the further development of the Community rules and even closer European integration. This is particularly reflected in its review of the legality of acts adopted by the Council (Article 189) and in its interpretation of Community law, whereby the Court consolidates its case law and makes its political mark. The judgments handed down by the ECJ have closed many gaps in Community law, which has been consistently viewed as a legal system in its own right, quite independent of the Member States, and which, in case of doubt, should be interpreted for the benefit of the Community, its integration targets and its individual citizens.

The ECJ has particularly applied itself to the task of protecting the basic and human rights of Community citizens *vis-à-vis* the sovereign power of the EC. In 1977 the → European Parliament, the Council and the Commission signed a Joint Declaration on the Protection of Human Rights in the Community. On many previous occasions, however, the ECJ had already ruled on questions of fundamental human rights. Most of the Court's judgments are in the economic field, dealing in particular with competition law and the implementation of the EU's common policies. Infringement proceedings under Articles 169 and 170 are especially common, although in recent years they have not increased in number. In 1993 the Commission initiated 1206 such proceedings; 44 cases came before the ECJ, which handed down 35 judgments to the effect that obligations under Community law had not been met.

Effect of judgments The ECJ's judgments are, in the first place, binding on the parties to proceedings. They are published in the European Court Reports; the operative part of each judgment also appears in the *Official Journal of the European Communities*. Should any EC/EU legislation be declared invalid by the Court, the latter's decision is binding on all concerned but only those judgments which require payments to be made and which can be implemented by the Member States are in fact enforceable. Until the entry into force of the Treaty on European Union the power of the ECJ extended only as far as the Member States' willingness to submit to its decisions. Since 1993, however, the ECJ has been able to impose penalty payments on individual Member States which have failed to comply with a Court judgment (Article 171).

Thomas Läufer

European Investment Bank

Founded: 1 January1958.
Headquarters: Luxembourg.
Membership: All EU Member States.
Treaty basis: Articles 198d and 198e of the EC Treaty.
Bodies: Board of Governors of the 15 Finance Ministers (lays down general directives on credit policy); Board of Directors (ensures that the Bank is managed in accordance with the provisions of the Treaty, grants loans and gives guarantees), Management Committee, Audit Committee.

Literature from the European Union:
European Commission: Serving the European Union.
A citizen's guide to the institutions of the European Union.
Luxembourg1996 (Cat. no.: FX-89-95-939-EN-C. Free).
EIB: European investment bank: The European Union's financing institution 1958-1996.
Luxembourg 1996 (Cat. no.: IX-94-96-405-EN-C. Free).
EIB:Annual report 1995: European Investment Bank.
Luxembourg 1996 (Cat. no.: IX-94-96-388-EN-C. Free).
European Commission, European Investment Bank: Infrastructure for
the 21st century. Trans-European networks for transport and energy.
Luxembourg 1996 (Cat. no.: IX-01-96-002-EN-C. Free).

The European Investment Bank (EIB) is both a bank and an independent institution within the → European Union. It grants credits and gives guarantees for the financing of investment projects which contribute to the balanced development of the Community. As a bank it observes the usual economic and banking principles governing the granting of credit and collaborates closely with other financial institutions. In doing so it operates on a non-profit basis; the interest rates on the loans cover the cost of its own borrowing plus a margin of 0.15%. By means of loans and guarantees its task is to finance projects (generally up to 50% of the cost of the project) which are in accord with the economic aims of the Community. When selecting projects the bank aims to choose those which will make use of the investments to develop something solid and of lasting value. Credits can be granted to public and private borrowers for investment in the infrastructure, energy, industry, services and agriculture sectors. To enable it to finance these projects the EIB mostly borrows on the capital markets of Member States and on the international capital markets. The capital of the EIB, subscribed by the Member States, has since 1 January 1995 amounted to ECU 62 billion. According to its statute, the aggregate outstanding amount of loans and credits may not exceed 250% of the capital.

In 1994, the EIB granted loans to a total value of ECU 19.2 billion, of which ECU 17.7 billion was destined for the financing of Community capital projects. In 1994 the lion's share of this sum (72%) was earmarked for the EIB's most important task – the development of economically weaker regions, enabling the bank to support the aims of the Structural Funds (→ regional policy) and other Community financing instruments. In addition to regional measures for the improvement of the infrastructure, the catalogue of projects receiving assistance includes the development of transport and communication infrastructures, protection of the environment and the quality of life, structural measures to improve urban areas, measures to guarantee the Community's energy supply and improvement of the international competitiveness of industry and integration at European level, in particular by means of support for small and medium-sized companies.

In its activities outside the Community the Investment Bank makes a considerable contribution to → development policy. To date financial protocols have been concluded with 12 Mediterranean countries. In cooperation with the World Bank and other institutions, an environmental programme for the Mediterranean has been developed and supported. In all, the EIB has carried out finance projects in about 130 countries which share common economic interests with the EU.

In 1990, for the first time, the EIB was empowered by the Board of Governors to grant credits in Poland, Hungary and the former GDR for project financing in sectors of the economy designated as development priorities. Since then this facility has been extended to 10 countries in Central and Eastern Europe. Up to 1997, loans of ECU 3 billion may be made. In 1994, the provision of finance outside the Community again increased, to ECU 2.246 billion. The EIB has subscribed 3% of the capital of the London-based European Bank for Reconstruction and Development, founded in 1990 as the EIB's counterpart in eastern Europe.

The European Investment Bank has continued to grow in significance, to the point where it is one of the major international players on the banking scene. Its activities prevent the EU States from drifting apart economically. One of its strengths is its flexibility enabling it to adapt to the aims of the Community. As a consequence of the growth initiative agreed by the → European Council in 1992 and the White Paper on growth, competitiveness and employment, the 860 or so staff of the EIB are facing new tasks. In addition to an ECU 7 billion temporary credit facility and the European Investment Fund, which was set up in 1994 to finance trans-European network projects, the EIB has supported small and medium-sized companies with job-creating investments by means of interest-subsidized loans totalling over ECU 1 billion.

Olaf Hillenbrand

European Monetary Institute

Established: 1 January 1994.
Members: Full-time President, plus Governors of Member States' issuing banks (EMI Council).
Treaty basis: Article 109f, as amended on 7 February 1992 by the Treaty on European Union; Protocol on the Statute of the European Monetary Institute, annexed to the Treaty on European Union.
Structure: President, Secretariat, four Directorates.

With the entry into force of the second stage of → economic and monetary union, the European Monetary Institute was officially established at the beginning of January 1994, though it actually started operating on 1 November 1993. It is based in Frankfurt. A Belgian, Alexandre Lamfalussy, was appointed the first full-time President by the EU Member States.

The EMI took over the functions of the Committee of EC Central Banks. It is the predecessor to the European System of Central Banks (ESCB) and the European Central Bank, which will be established at the next (third) stage of EMU in or after 1997.

The EMI's main job is to prepare for that stage. That means chiefly developing the requisite instruments and procedures for the common monetary policy by the end of 1996, but the EMI is also to strengthen cooperation between the central banks in the EU, strengthen the coordination of national monetary policies and bring these policies into convergence on a price stability objective. The → European Monetary System (EMS) is to be supervised by the EMI, which is to assist with the introduction of the → euro. The Institute is required to promote the efficiency of cross-border financial transactions and supervise the technical preparation of future banknotes.

The central decision-making body is the EMI Council, which consists of the Governors of the national central banks; each Member has one vote. It may neither seek nor take instructions from any Community institution or national Government. It generally takes decisions by simple majority; opinions and recommendations require a two-thirds majority and decisions to publish them require unanimity. The EMI has power to prepare, advise and coordinate but no veritable monetary policy powers – intervention in the foreign exchange markets and with it the power to exercise genuine authority are excluded. The EMI is a transitional institution.

Eckard Gaddum

European Monetary System

Established: 13 March 1979 with retrospective effect as of 1 January 1979.
Members: As regards the composition of the European currency unit, all EU Member States; Greece not involved in exchange rate mechanism; membership suspended by UK.
Treaty basis: Council Regulations of 18 December 1978 relating to the European Monetary System and changing the value of the unit of account used by the European Monetary Cooperation Fund (EMCF); Council Decision of 21 December 1978 setting up machinery for medium-term financial assistance; agreement between the national Central Banks of 13 March 1979 on the *modus operandi* of the EMS; decision of the national Central Banks of 13 March 1979 on short-term financial assistance; decision of the EMCF Management Board of 13 March 1979.
Organs: Council of Finance Ministers; Monetary Committee (two representatives of each Member State and of the Commission); EMCF (Governor of Central Banks, the Commission having only observer status).
Literature from the European Union:
European Commission: Economic and monetary union.
Luxembourg 1996 (Cat. no.: CW-96-96-166-EN-C. Free).
European Commission: When will the 'euro' be in our pockets ?
Luxembourg 1996 (Cat. no.: CM-43-96-004-EN-C. Free).

The European Monetary System (EMS) was established in 1979. Its principal architects were the French President Valérie Giscard d'Estaing and the German Chancellor Helmut Schmidt.

Background Monetary cooperation played only a minor role in the original treaties. All the EEC had was a few basic rules, though later, in 1964, a Monetary Committee was set up, to be followed by the Committee of Governors.

On the initiative of the → European Commission and the subsequent Declaration by the Heads of State or Government (The Hague, 1969), the Werner Plan emerged at the close of the 1960s (approved on 8 October 1970). It envisaged a three-stage plan over 10 years to achieve → economic and monetary union. It failed as a result of deteriorating economic fundamentals (collapse of the Bretton Woods fixed exchange rates system, oil crises, recession). But above all there was a fundamental conceptual clash between the proponents of two opposing theories: one was that convergence should precede and culminate in the single currency (chiefly Germany and the Netherlands), and the other was that the single currency should be brought in as a means of generating convergence (chiefly France, Belgium and the Commission).

The currency snake set up in 1972 between central banks likewise failed as a result of the incompatibility of these two concepts. Weak-currency countries always tended to abandon their close cooperation just when they would have done well to adjust their policies under pressure from the relatively stable German mark.

Establishment of the EMS Even so, in 1979 the EMS was set up. Under Giscard d'Estaing France opted for a more thoroughly stability-oriented economic and monetary policy (→ economic policy). With the plan for EMS Germany offered its western neighbour the face-saving possibility of returning to monetary cooperation. The EMS made no fundamental inroads on the Member States' monetary sovereignty. The founding instrument had little to say on prospects for future integration. The original objective of moving on to a definitive EC system after two years was unchanged. The EMS did not slot neatly into the Community system but had a combination of Community and national legal bases. Only when the Single European Act came into force in 1987 was there a reference to the EMS in a Community Treaty, as it was given if only a passing mention in Article 102 of the EEC Treaty.

Structure and operation The EMS has three components – the ecu (European currency unit), an exchange rate and intervention system and various credit facilities.

(a) The ecu (successor to the earlier EUA – European Unit of Account) is an artificial means of payment based on the EU currencies – an artificial currency in effect. It is calculated as the weighted average of all the participating currencies, reflecting their respective economic strengths. The German mark, with 30.4%, is by far the largest of the 15 items in the basket; the French franc accounts for 19.3% and the pound sterling for 12.6%. The ecu's primary function is to constitute a unit of payment and account for the exchange-rate and intervention mechanisms and for the development of the credit mechanisms. It is also a limited reserve instrument. In return for depositing 20% of their gold reserves and 20% of their dollar reserves with the European Monetary Cooperation Fund (EMCF), the national central banks receive a corresponding quantity of ecus to cover their international settlements (official ecus). The ecu can also be used for international transactions and for issues and investments on the international capital markets (private ecus).

(b) The exchange-rate and intervention mechanism – the core component of the EMS – operates via a parity matrix. A central rate for each EMS currency is set in ecus and the various participating currencies are then matrixed against each other to give a full set of bilateral exchange rates; these can vary up or down within a predetermined margin. Initially the margin was set at 2.25% (up or down), with temporarily extended margins of 6% (up or down) for the UK, Italy and Spain. At the beginning of August 1993 these were widened to 15%. If rates hit the extremes, the central banks must immediately intervene by buying or selling on the foreign exchanges to even out the fluctuations. Following the Basel/Nyborg agreement of September 1987 on the reform of the EMS, central banks are also empowered to intervene within margins before extremes are reached.

The political significance of this structure is that the tighter the margins, the greater the need for convergent monetary, fiscal and economic policies in EU Member States and the corollary – less room for manoeuvre for the national central banks. The margins thus reveal the degree of integration of core policy areas in the various countries involved and their determination to achieve a community of stability. That explains why some countries were not ready to participate from the outset in the intervention mechanism (at the end of 1994 the 'outs' were the UK, Italy and Greece).

Where the central rates break out through the upper or lower margins, there must be a realignment. This is prepared by the Monetary Committee and requires a unanimous decision of the Finance Ministers. The political significance of a realignment is that the economic fundamentals of a realigned country no longer reflect the existing rate. Devaluation is consequently a blow to the Government's political prestige. After a series of realignments between 1981 and 1983, the system stabilized so thoroughly during the rest of the 1980s that there were none between the beginning of 1987 and September 1992. Then came a new series.

(c) The three credit facilities of the EMS were created between 1970 and 1972 and extended in 1979. They make provision for credit on different terms. Where a central bank is obliged to intervene but does not have adequate foreign exchange reserves, it can obtain 'very short-term financing' from the EMCF. There is also provision for short-term currency support between central banks and medium-term assistance between Member States. Credits carry differing terms as to duration and rates.

Development and assessment The EMS is now at the focus of monetary cooperation policy and operations. In the 1980s there were regular attempts to move on from the EMS to a common currency. But the world-wide recession at the beginning of the 1990s, coupled with the costs of German unification (the expansion in public debt accelerated the weakening of the mark), made it more and more difficult to coordinate economic, financial and interest-rate policies, especially as between Germany and France. As market confidence in the ecu declined, so speculative pressures against currencies seen as candidates for devaluation (lira, sterling, French franc) built up. The EMS faced its most serious crisis ever. After a long period of stability the Finance Ministers and Central Bank Governors widened the bands to 15% (up and down) in August 1993. National currencies have enjoyed wider room for manoeuvre since then. The EMS coordination mechanisms have not been withdrawn. A return to narrower bands would not require any basic political decisions, but it is not expected to happen in the near future. Monetary cooperation too has been proceeding smoothly enough.

Eckart Gaddum

European Parliament

Treaty basis: Articles 137–144, 158 and 189b of the EC Treaty.

Composition: 626 Members from the 15 EU Member States. More significant is the breakdown by political groups (see below).

Powers: Consultation and control (Article 137). Motion of censure on the Commission (Article 144). In addition (as a result of amendments to the Treaty and various agreements), rights of decision (on non-compulsory expenditure under the EC budget, pursuant to Article 203 of the EC Treaty, accession and association agreements, Article 238 of the EC Treaty and Articles N and O of the Treaty on European Union). Rights of participation (consultation on legislation pursuant to Articles 43, 100 and 130s of the EC Treaty, cooperation procedure under Article 189c of the EC Treaty, right to question the Commission pursuant to Article 140). Forms of participation not laid down in the Treaties (confidential information on the negotiation of trade and association agreements, right to question CFSP Presidency, formal consultation on the framing of legislation). Approval of the appointment of a new European Commission (Article 158), right of co-decision on certain legislative acts (Article 189b) and right to appoint an ombudsman.

Voting procedures: As a rule, by simple majority; on certain important issues (for example motion of censure on the Commission, budgetary decisions), in accordance with provisions laid down in the EC Treaty.

Literature from the European Union:
European Parliament: The European Parliament.
Luxembourg 1996 (Cat. no.: AX-94-96-857-EN-C. Free).
European Commission: Serving the European Union. A citizen's guide
to the institutions of the European Union.
Luxembourg 1996 (Cat. no.: FX-89-95-939-EN-C. Free).
European Parliament: The members of the European Parliament:
Fourth electoral period 1994–1999.
Luxembourg 1996 (Cat. no.: AX-94-96-097-EN-C. ECU 10.00).
European Parliament: Meet your MEPs.
Luxembourg 1996 (Cat.no.:AX-90-95-550-EN-C. Free).
Noel, Emile: Working together; The institutions of the European Community.
Luxembourg 1994 (Cat. no.: CC-76-92-172-EN-C. Free).
European Parliament: European Parliament: Rules of procedure.
Luxembourg 1994 (Cat. no.: AX-84-94-323-EN-C. ECU 10.00).

The European Parliament is the parliamentary institution of the EU; since 1979 it has been directly elected. Its predecessor was the Common Assembly of the European Coal and Steel Community.

The role of the European Parliament was originally limited to advising the

→ Council of the European Union and to monitoring the activities of the → European Commission. Its powers were then extended in several stages, although it has not yet acquired a range of powers comparable to those of the national parliaments.

Those calling for the strengthening of the EP as an institution repeatedly drew attention to what they saw as the need for stronger democratic endorsement for the → decision-making processes within the → European Union (EU). In its judgment of 12 October 1993 on the Treaty on European Union, Germany's Constitutional Court found that, at the present stage of unification, democratic authority derived from the feedback from the European institutions to the national parliaments. This was supplemented, however, by the democratic authority invested in the European Parliament, which was elected by the citizens of the Member States.

Article 138 sets the number of Members at 626 for the 15 Member States. The number of Members from a given country does not always reflect the size of its population: for example, each German Member of Parliament represents some 800 000 citizens, whereas his Luxembourg colleague represents only some 60 000 inhabitants.

The breakdown by country is less significant than the breakdown by political group. These groups indicate the ways in which the various European political parties have formed alliances. Following the European elections in 1995 the picture was as follows:

Table 1: Composition of the European Parliament by political group and by nationality — October 1996

	B	DK	D	EL	E	F	IRL	I	L	NL	A	P	FIN	S	UK	TOTAL
PES	6	3	40	10	21	16	1	18	2	7	8	10	4	7	63	216
EPP CD	7	3	47	9	30	12	4	14	2	10	6	1	4	5	19	173
UEG	-	-	-	2	-	16	7	27	-	1	-	3	-	-	-	56
ELDR	6	5	-	-	2	1	1	6	1	10	1	8	6	3	2	52
GUE/NGL	-	1	-	4	9	7	-	5	-	-	-	3	1	3	-	33
GREENS	2	-	12	-	-	-	2	4	-	1	1	-	1	4	-	27
ERA	1	-	-	-	2	12	-	2	1	-	-	-	-	-	2	20
EDN	-	4	-	-	-	12	-	-	-	2	-	-	-	-	-	18
NI	3	-	-	-	-	11	-	11	-	-	5	-	-	-	1	31
TOTAL	25	16	99	25	64	87	15	87	6	31	21	25	16	22	87	626

Political groups

PES: Party of European Socialists; EPP CD: European People's Party (Christian-Democratic Group); ELDR: European Liberal, Democratic and Reform Party; GUE/NGL: Confederal Group of the European United Left/Nordic Green Left; UEG: Union for Europe Group; Greens: Green Group in the European Parliament; ERA: European Radical Alliance; EDN: Europe of the Nations (Coordination Group); NI: Non attached members.

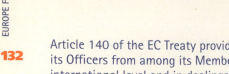

Article 140 of the EC Treaty provides that Parliament is to elect its Presidents and its Officers from among its Members. The President represents Parliament at international level and in dealings with the other institutions; he may delegate these powers. Parliament takes decisions at its plenary sessions, the preliminary work having been done by 20 committees:

- Committee on Foreign Affairs, Security and Defence Policy
- Committee on Agriculture and Rural Development
- Committee on Budgets
- Committee on Economic and Monetary Affairs and Industrial Policy
- Committee on Research, Technological Development and Energy
- Committee on External Economic Relations
- Committee on Legal Affairs and Citizens' Rights
- Committee on Social Affairs and Employment
- Committee on Regional Policy
- Committee on Transport and Tourism
- Committee on the Environment, Public Health and Consumer Protection
- Committee on Culture, Youth, Education and the Media
- Committee on Development and Cooperation
- Committee on Civil Liberties and Internal Affairs
- Committee on Budgetary Control
- Institutional Affairs Committee
- Committee on Fisheries
- Committee on the Rules of Procedure, the Verification of Credentials and Immunities
- Committee on Women's Rights
- Committee on Petitions

In principle, Parliament acts by a majority of its Members; in the case of important decisions, however, the provisions of the EC Treaty require a quorum: to be carried, a motion of censure on the Commission requires a two-thirds majority of the votes cast, representing a majority of the Members (Article 144); amendment or rejection of a common position adopted by the Council under the cooperation procedure requires an absolute majority of the Members (Article 189b or 189c); amendments to the budget require a majority of the Members; amendments to compulsory expenditure at the first reading require an absolute majority of the votes cast; amendments at the second reading (within certain limits) require a majority and three fifths of the votes cast; rejection of the budget requires a majority of the Members and two thirds of the votes cast (Article 203).

Tasks The tasks of the European Parliament cannot be compared with those of national assemblies in the Member States, since the EU has no Government for Parliament to form and oversee; moreover, Parliament has only a limited say in the framing of legislation. The tasks of the European Parliament may be defined as follows:

(i) the shaping of policy, comprising all parliamentary activities intended to influence existing EU policies; this may involve taking the initiative, involvement in the framing of legislation and the monitoring of policies themselves;

(ii) the shaping of the EU system, i.e. bringing about changes in the decision-making procedures and redistributing powers between the EU and the Member States;

(iii) interaction between the Members of Parliament and the voters, which involves voicing voters' concerns, reconciling divergent positions and mobilizing the public for important causes.

Since the first European election in 1979, Parliament has done much to shape EU policy (particularly in its initiation and monitoring of policy) and to shape the EU system itself. Its interaction with the voters has not been entirely satisfactory, however.

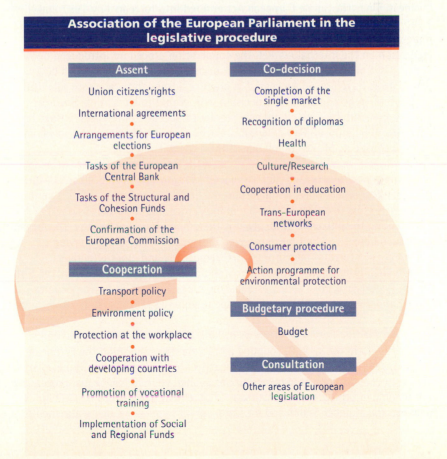

Association of the European Parliament in the legislative procedure

Assent
- Union citizens'rights
- International agreements
- Arrangements for European elections
- Tasks of the European Central Bank
- Tasks of the Structural and Cohesion Funds
- Confirmation of the European Commission

Cooperation
- Transport policy
- Environment policy
- Protection at the workplace
- Cooperation with developing countries
- Promotion of vocational training
- Implementation of Social and Regional Funds

Co-decision
- Completion of the single market
- Recognition of diplomas
- Health
- Culture/Research
- Cooperation in education
- Trans-European networks
- Consumer protection
- Action programme for environmental protection

Budgetary procedure
- Budget

Consultation
- Other areas of European legislation

Shaping policy Following the first European elections in 1979, Parliament developed a range of new activities. It adopted numerous resolutions on human rights violations throughout the world, questions affecting the Third World and current events in the EU. Given its lack of powers, however, its influence on important EU decisions in traditional policy areas remained unsatisfactory. Members of Parliament engaged in trials of strength with the Council in the context of the budgetary and legislative procedures and did not shrink from referring such matters to the → European Court of Justice. In 1980 and 1985, the EC budget was rejected, with the result that a system of 'provisional twelfths' came into operation until a new budget was drafted. Under this system, one twelfth of the previous year's budget was made available each month.

Since 1979 Parliament has expanded its role as a watchdog by making intensive use of its right to ask questions, by keeping a closer eye on EU expenditure (through the Committee on Budgetary Control) and by setting up committees of enquiry.

The multiplicity of Parliament's activities, some of which were poorly coordinated, led to criticism of the institution for not concentrating sufficiently on essential EU business. Since the Single European Act entered into force in July 1987 and the Treaty on European Union in November 1993, the situation has changed in that more and more of Parliament's time is taken up by its involvement in framing legislation on the internal market. The cooperation procedure introduced by Article 189c of the EC Treaty and the co-decision procedure introduced by Article 189b have proved successful in practice, although they are no substitute for more far-reaching powers of decision with regard to legislation. Both the Commission and the Council are now readier to accede to Members' wishes and demands. The European Parliament has placed great emphasis on the social and ecological aspects of the completion of the → single market.

Shaping the system In discussions concerning the reform of the EU, the European Parliament plays an important dual role. In the first place, it is central to decision-making in a democratic Community since it is the elected body representing the citizenry. Secondly, it is the driving force for change. This became clear even before the first European elections in 1979, Parliament having repeatedly put forward plans for a more democratic and more effective Community, for example its draft treaty on an ad hoc ECSC assembly in 1953, the Pleven Report on a draft treaty establishing a union of the European peoples (1961) and the Bertrand Report on European union (1975).

Following the first European elections in June 1979, Parliament stepped up its efforts to reform the system, adopting a draft treaty establishing the European Union on 14 February 1984. This draft treaty represented the basic framework for a European constitution. Parliament and the Council were to have equal powers over the shaping of EU legislation. There was to be a clear division of responsibilities between the Member States and the Union, great importance being attached to the principle of subsidiarity. The 1984 draft was never adopted but it provided the essential impetus towards the drafting of the Single European Act.

Once the Maastricht Treaty on European Union entered into force in November 1993, Parliament was able to play a far more significant role. It obtained the right to approve the appointment of each new European Commission, which in future would have the same term of office as Parliament, and became more closely involved in the legislative process thanks to the extremely complicated new co-decision procedure introduced by Article 189b. Under the new arrangements, Parliament can set up committees of enquiry to investigate important issues (Article 138c). An ombudsman handles any complaints from citizens of the Union (Article 138e). Parliament's powers in respect of the → common foreign and security policy and → justice and home affairs are still insufficient, however.

The → Intergovernmental Conference to review the Maastricht Treaty is of particular significance for Parliament's institutional position in that the agenda includes a review of the co-decision procedure. Essential features of this procedure include majority voting in the Council and three readings in Parliament. In practice this gives Parliament almost the same rights as the Council. The procedure can be applied only in a restricted number of cases, however (mainly on questions relating to the single market).

In Parliament's opinion the co-decision procedure should be the rule from now on, although particularly sensitive issues (amendments to the Treaty, enlargement, own resources, uniform election arrangements, additional powers pursuant to Article 235 of the EC Treaty) would still require unanimity within the Council and/or between the various national governments.
In its resolution of 17 May 1995 concerning the 1996 Intergovernmental Conference, Parliament dealt in some detail with the division of powers between the EU and its Member States. It advocated that the Community should gradually assume responsibility for the common foreign and security policy and for justice and home affairs (the second and third pillars), which until now have been the preserve of intergovernmental cooperation. The Commission and Parliament would thus be more closely involved in these matters in future. The European Court of Justice would assume responsibility for upholding the law in these areas.

For the common foreign and security policy a procedure has been proposed which would enable a qualified majority of EU Member States to carry out humanitarian, diplomatic or military operations which were regarded as 'joint action'. No country could be forced to take part in such operations against its will, but no country could prevent the majority from doing so.

In Parliament's view the Commission should retain its important role and its independence. The Commission's exclusive right to initiate legislation is not called into question; this would only lead to the renationalization of European politics, with the risk that some right of initiative would then be conferred on the Council. This stance may be explained by the fact that Parliament's political importance derives essentially from the institutional strength of the Commission, in whose appointment Parliament plays a key role.

Interactions with voters and political role/model Despite many endeavours, Parliament still has great difficulty in making the citizens of the EU aware of its role and its achievements. According to a representative poll carried out for the European Commission in the spring of 1994, only 52% of the EU population had heard or read anything recently about Parliament. Only 44% of those questioned (as compared with 52% four years earlier) hoped to see a strengthening of Parliament as an institution. Some 55% expressed the view that national considerations determined the way people voted in the European elections. All this would indicate that the European Parliament has so far failed to make its institutional role sufficiently clear to those who elect it. One explanation might be that, statistically speaking, each European Member of Parliament has to represent approximately 600 000 people.

The role of Parliament in the EU and its public image are largely the result of the peculiarities of the EU system and Parliament's institutional position in that system, but they also depend on how Parliament performs its tasks and what priorities it sets itself. A realistic image for the European Parliament might be that of an institution which helps to frame policy, since Parliament is involved in various ways in the EU's decision-making processes. Although unable to determine the procedure to be followed in each case, Parliament has so many powers and instruments at its disposal that the other parties to the decision-making process have to take its aims and interests into account, even if Parliament itself lacks the power to take decisions in individual cases.

The concept of a body which helps to frame policy provides the closest description of Parliament's institutional role within the current EU system. Such an image does not correspond, however, to the past experience of voters and MEPs with their own national parliaments. The European Parliament has still not become a European legislature; and yet its position is more in line with the classical 'separation of powers' than that of many a national parliament, since it is the European Parliament as a whole that keeps watch on the executive, and not merely the opposition, which is permanently in a minority.

Conclusions Now in its fourth term of office, the European Parliament enjoys, within the institutional framework of the Community, a position which greatly exceeds that assigned to it in the original Treaties. It has a clearly discernible influence on the framing of legislation on the single market, it can use its

budgetary powers to influence essential Community activities and can make the Community procedures more comprehensible to the general public by asking parliamentary questions, setting up investigative and *ad hoc* committees, and holding emergency debates. In addition, it influences in many ways the external policies of the Community and its 15 Member States.

All this cannot conceal the fact, however, that there is a need for further reform. Parliament still lacks essential decision-making powers. The media continue to show little interest in its work, and its public profile is none too high. Progress could be brought about by a further strengthening of Parliament's institutional position, over and above the reforms agreed in the Treaty on European Union. An opportunity to achieve such progress is the Intergovernmental Conference which is reviewing the various arrangements laid down by the Maastricht Treaty. Further reforms should show the public the way ahead, simplify the legal system and ensure greater democracy by enhancing the status of Parliament.

Otto Schmuck

European Union

The European Union has become the central concept on which public discussions on the future shape of Europe hinge. It is a typical case of a possibly useful ambiguity which has accompanied and coloured the process of integration of (Western) Europe from the very beginning. The concepts surrounding the idea of European unity were always moulded into aims and forms of European integration policy by a variety of completely different models (→ models for European integration).

History of the term: constructive ambiguity The term 'European Union' was formulated by the Heads of State or Government as a goal at the Paris summit in 1972, where they set themselves 'the major objective of transforming, ... with the fullest respect for the treaties already signed, the whole complex of the relations of Member States into a European Union'. This notion was repeated in the preamble to the Single European Act but omitted in the Treaty on European Union. Article A of the Treaty on European Union states instead that this 'Treaty marks a new stage in the process of creating an ever closer union among the peoples of Europe, in which decisions are taken as closely as possible to the citizen'. In the process the Union should organize relations among its peoples demonstrating cohesion and solidarity.

Attempts both from political and academic circles to define this concept more closely have met with only limited success. Scientific attempts to arrive at a greater degree of precision by examining the concept of 'union' or mutually-held aims and objectives have not produced a political consensus. In both the Stuttgart Declaration of 1983 and the preamble to the Single European Act of 1987 only general objectives for such a European Union were listed, such as the principles of democracy and respect for the law and human rights. Both texts outline a two-pronged strategy for the development of the European Union which is still recognizable today, namely that the Member States are resolved 'to implement this European Union on the basis, firstly of the Communities operating in accordance with their own rules and, secondly, of European cooperation among the signatory States ... and to invest this Union with the necessary means of action'. These formulations express the notion of a development of the Community system defining the existing forms of integration and cooperation as the essential elements of a European Union. A similar formulation can be found in Article A of the Maastricht Treaty: 'The Union shall be founded on the European Communities, supplemented by the policies and forms established by this Treaty'.

Other political conceptions of European Union centre on notions of federalism. In its draft Treaty establishing the European Union of 1984 (often known as the Spinelli draft), the → European Parliament lent a federal touch to its formulation of the principles, aims and institutional definitions of a European Union. However, this clear suggestion has yet to become a binding model.

Since the signing of the Maastricht Treaty and the subsequent arguments about its ratification there has been a great deal of criticism levelled at the concept of federalism. The characterization of the European Union as an association of States by the German Constitutional Court in its Maastricht judgment of October 1993 provoked a wide range of reactions but did introduce a new concept into the debate, the depths and scope of which still have to be sounded out. It remains to be seem whether the choice of a new vocabulary will enrich, and thus revitalize the discussion or whether old conflicts about the direction of integration will flare up in a new guise.

The Maastricht Treaty on European Union In 1991, at the Maastricht summit, the notions of a European Union were formally laid down in a new Treaty, which came into force on 1 November 1993, thus providing students of post-war European history with a new date to memorize. 'Maastricht' is short for a stepping stone in the process of integration and its actual meaning and implications are the subject of fierce debate.

The text which was approved by the → European Council is basically a amalgamation of several elements from different legal areas and, as such, can be difficult to get to grips with. It is perhaps easiest to understand if it is compared with a temple

European Union

European Community	Common foreign and security policy	Cooperation in justice and home affairs
Customs union, Single market, Common agricultural policy, Structural policy, Economic and monetary union		

The basic elements contained in the Treaty on European Union are:

1. common provisions;
2. amendments to the EEC Treaty to set up the European Community, including → economic and monetary union and citizenship of the Union;
3. common foreign and security policy (CFSP);
4. cooperation on matters of justice and home affairs;
5. final provisions;
6. protocols, of which the most important relate to economic and social cohesion and → social policy, as well as explanations regarding CFSP and texts produced by the Member States of the Western European Union (WEU) on the role of the WEU.

Objectives of the Union and the subsidiarity principle The overall objectives of the Union serve to set out the range of fields which are to be dealt with in the uniform institutional framework, as described above. Article B of the Treaty an European Union states that the Union sets out 'to promote economic and social progress which is balanced and sustainable, in particular through the creation of an area without internal frontiers, through the strengthening of economic and social cohesion and through the establishment of economic and monetary union, ultimately including a single currency'. The second major objective of the Union, as set out in Articles B and J of the Treaty on European Union, is to assert its identity on the international scene, in particular through the implementation of a common foreign and security policy including the eventual framing of a common defence policy. Thirdly, Article B outlines the aim of strengthening the protection of the rights and interests of the nationals of the Member States by introducing citizenship of the Union. Fourthly, under Articles B and K the Member States aim to develop close cooperation in matters relating to justice and home affairs.

Although the Union can concern itself with nearly all public political issues, it does not have exclusive competence on matters of detail. In fact, the allocation of degrees of competence is determined in many different ways. In some areas of activity the notion of a 'common policy' is used, for example in the case of → transport policy (Article 74 et seq.); in other areas reference is made only to 'a policy', such as → environmental policy (Article 130r et seq.) and → social policy (Article 117 et seq.). In yet other areas (energy, civil protection, tourism) promotion or 'measures' are the terms used without there being any provision for harmonisation of legislation or administrative action on the part of the Member States. The legal and institutional framework of the 'common' foreign and security policy is such that it cannot be compared with the 'common' agricultural policy.

The subsidiarity principle aims to prevent the EC from acquiring 'too much' influence. In accordance with this principle in 'areas which do not fall within its

exclusive competence, the Community shall take action ... only if and insofar as the objectives of the proposed action cannot be sufficiently achieved by the Member States and can therefore, by reason of the scale or effects of the proposed action, be better achieved by the Community'. (Article 3b).

The need for reform: the European Union is an ongoing process

While the ratification debate was in full swing crucial aspects of the Treaty were transformed into battlegrounds. One of the major controversies still concerns the relationship between the European Union as set out in the Maastricht Treaty and the constitutional nation State. Fears of a far-reaching shift in the balance of powers from the national to the European level, and resistance to the idea, became all too evident, the move being often depicted as a threat to nationhood and as a danger for the comprehensive guarantee of basic rights. In the eyes of some citizens and parties the European Union was transformed from a model into an enemy. As a consequence, immediately after the signing of the Maastricht Treaty, it became clear that finishing touches still had to be applied. So, in autumn 1992, the Heads of State or Government agreed a package of guidelines and measures intended to increase the transparency of the structures and procedures of the European Union.

Article N(2) of the Maastricht Treaty states there should be an examination of the progress made at an Intergovernmental Conference in 1996. The challenge posed by further accessions to the Union has increased the need for reform. Out of the discussions various possibilities have arisen as to how to reconcile the impending reforms, or, as they are often collectively known, the 'deepening' of the EU, with the expected → enlargement, so that basic points of reference for the further development of the integration process can be laid down.

One strategy aims to 'widen without deepening' the European Union, for example the number of Member States is to be increased while a status quo should be maintained as far as political and institutional aspects are concerned. In contrast the 'deeper before wider' option requires the Union to take further steps towards integration before admitting new Member States which would then join a reformed EU. The 'wider and deeper' strategy favours both processes running in parallel and reinforcing each other. The strategy of 'widening to weaken' the integration process would mean that as the number of Member States increased there would be a greater reduction of the *acquis communautaire et politique* and the EU would be less and less able to build up momentum for integration. The phased integration option proposes limited and phased steps towards integration taken at first only by certain Member States, whereby new Members would be offered the chance to catch up step by step. The overall objectives would, however, be commonly held and remain binding for all Member States. The Europe à la carte option favours *ad hoc* problem solving in individual fields by the European states involved in each particular instance. This alternative would make it

impossible to maintain a uniform direction for general development. The 'hard core' strategy is based on a relatively small group of States achieving a comparatively high degree of integration. In doing so, however, they would automatically distance themselves from the other Member States.

Both the nature and the form of the European Union are becoming increasingly controversial. The direction being taken would appear to be that of a more marked differentiation of the integration process. This will lead in future to increased tension between the acceptance of different groups of participants and the desire to maintain a uniform institutional framework and a guiding and binding model.

Wolfgang Wessels and Udo Diedrichs

Europol

Treaty basis: Article K.1(9) of the Treaty on European Union; Europol Convention.
Members and headquarters: All EU States, The Hague (Netherlands).
Organs: Management Board, Director, Joint Supervisory Body for data protection, Financial Controller, Financial Committee.
Literature from the European Union:
European Parliament: Second report on Europol. Committee on Civil Liberties and Internal Affairs. Rapporteur: Mr. Hartmut Nassauer.
Luxembourg 1996 (Cat. no.: AYC-09-60-76-EN-A).

Europol is the European Police Office provided for by the Treaty on European Union; it is a supranational body set up in the intergovernmental context.

Pending ratification of an instrument of international law setting up Europol, there was a precursor body, the Europol Drugs Unit (EDU), that operated in The Hague. It consisted of the Member States' liaison officers, who had direct access to investigation and working data of their respective sending States and exchanged personal data in drugs-related cases on a controlled basis. The EDU was already actively and successfully involved in solving international drug cases, notably by coordinating what are known as controlled deliveries (where clandestine drug shipments are kept under surveillance until they are delivered at some point where investigators can most usefully intervene). In 1995, 2 000 or so requests for information were transmitted and processed by national authorities. The number is rising. Analysis work focuses on gathering statistics, researching street prices in the various countries and investigating new smuggling routes.

A joint action dated 10 March 1995 extended the area of competence of the EDU to illegal trade in radioactive and nuclear substances, illegal immigrant smuggling and motor vehicle crime. A further extension to include trafficking in persons is planned for 1996.

The Europol Convention was signed by the Member States on 26 July 1995. An additional protocol signed at the same time gives the → European Court of Justice jurisdiction to interpret the Convention. The main points of the Convention are as follows. Europol is to pursue the objective, within the framework of cooperation between Member States pursuant to Article K.1(9) of the Treaty on European Union, of improving the effectiveness and cooperation of the competent authorities in preventing and combating serious forms of international crime. Initially this covers drug trafficking, trafficking in nuclear and radioactive substances, illegal immigrant smuggling, trade in human beings and motor vehicle crime. After two years, Europol is also to deal with terrorist violence and money-laundering in connection with all these forms of criminal activity. The Council is further empowered to instruct Europol to deal with other forms of crime (listed in an Annex to the Convention), for which purpose a unanimous decision will be required.

Europol's tasks include facilitating the exchange of information between Member States, gathering, collating and analysing information and intelligence, notifying the competent authorities of the Member States without delay via their national units of information concerning them and thereby aiding investigations in the Member States. Computerized data-storage systems are to be set up, and the following systems are to be made available to Europol. One information system contains data on persons who have been convicted of an offence within Europol's remit or are suspected of having committed or taken part in such an offence (accessible not only to Europol but also to national units and liaison officers attached to Europol). The other consists of work files held by Europol for analysis purposes. These less heavily-protected databases ('soft data') contain data on persons identified as witnesses or as actual or potential victims of criminal offences.

The financial regulation and the rules on the rights and obligations of liaison officers have been negotiated as additional instruments required for the operation of Europol. The most important legal and political aspects are the implementing rules for the work files and the staff regulations.

Europol has legal personality. Its organs are as follows: (1) the Management Board, which basically takes all important decisions outside Europol's technical responsibilities. It consists of one representative of each Member State and its decisions are taken by a two-thirds majority unless otherwise provided; (2) the Director, appointed by unanimous decision of the Council, after consulting the Management Board, for a four-year period renewable once. He is responsible for performance of the tasks assigned to Europol and for administration. He and his two deputies may be dismissed by Council decision taken by a two thirds majority; (3) the Joint Supervisory Body for data protection; (4) the Financial Controller; and (5) the Financial Committee.

Europol should not be confused with Interpol (International Criminal Police Organization), an organization currently involving the police forces of 177 countries and based in Lyons. Unlike Europol, Interpol is not bound to any particular regional grouping of States; it is a world-wide organization.

Reinhard Rupprecht

External relations

Treaty basis: Articles 3(b), (q), (r), 9, 18-29, 110, 113, 115; 130u-y; 131-136a; 228, 228a-231, 238 of the EC treaty; Article O of the treaty on European Union.

Aims: Establishment and operation of a common commercial policy based on a common customs tariff applying to non-member countries, representation of common foreign trade interests in international trade relations, continuing liberalization of the international economy, development of particularly close economic and trade policy relations with particular States or groups of States, promotion of third world development through trade and economic cooperation.

Literature from the European Union:

European Commission:The European Union's common foreign and security policy. Luxembourg 1996 (Cat. no.: CC-97-96-443-EN-C. Free).

European Commission: The European Union and world trade. Luxembourg 1995 (Cat. no.: CC-89-95-753-EN-C. Free).

European Commission: EU-ACP cooperation in 1995. What form of structural adjustment? Brussels 1996 (Cat. no.: CF-AA-96-00-42-AC. Free).

European Commission: The European Union and Asia. Luxembourg 1995 (Cat. no.: CC-92-94-691-EN-C. Free).

European Commission: Europe in a changing world: The external relations of the European Community Luxembourg 1994 (Cat. no.: CC-74-92-273-EN-C. Free).

In → European Union (EU) usage, external relations is taken to mean the relations of the EU with non-member countries and international organizations in economic and trade matters. Despite the considerable relevance to foreign policy, it is therefore to be distinguished, in both practical and legal terms, from the → common foreign and security policy (CFSP), which deals with the actual political relations between the European Union and non-member countries and international organizations. External relations, whose main components are the common commercial policy, the association policy and → development policy, constitute, together with the CFSP, the basis for a European foreign policy. They are based on the common customs tariff of the EU, the external powers assigned to the EU institutions, procedures established in the treaties, an extensive body of secondary Community legislation and an ever-increasing network of bilateral and multilateral agreements with third countries.

Origin and legal bases The common market (→ single market) of the EU and the customs union surrounding it could not have survived without unified import and export rules and a unified representation of interests in relations with non-member countries. Right from the start, the founding treaties required the six founding States of the European Communities to give the EC institutions powers to establish unified external trade relations, in contrast to foreign policy relations, which remained a matter for Member States. What really prompted this crucial decision was the aim of developing the common commercial policy (Article 113 of the EC Treaty), which, according to the Treaty, was to become the exclusive preserve of the Community after the transitional period ended in 1970.

Furthermore, the Community can also conclude agreements with non-member countries in other policy fields in which they do not have express external powers, if they have authority to legislate in these fields within the Community, as for example in the case of the → fisheries policy or the → research and technology policy. These so-called 'implied treaty-making powers' were recognized in the 1971 AETR judgment of the → European Court of Justice and are an important additional legal basis for external relations. However, there has always been disagreement over the division of powers between the EC and the Member States. This was and often is overcome by involving both the Community and the Member States in international agreements (so-called 'mixed agreements'). The fact that the Community is represented by Delegations of the → European Commission in most non-member countries and international organizations is also important for the development of external relations, as is the fact that almost all countries have diplomatic representations to the EU in Brussels.

Within the many areas of external relations, the common commercial policy still plays a central role, not only because it is by far the most integrated external relations policy but also because it has particular political significance as the external aspect of the single market and as the policy of the largest trading power in the world.

Autonomous commercial policy The autonomous commercial policy covers all the measures that the Union takes affecting imports and exports of goods, not within the framework of treaty obligations to non-member countries, but autonomously. These include common export and import rules, anti-dumping measures, measures against subsidized imports or illicit trade practices as well as limits on quantities (quotas) and foreign policy-related trade bans (embargoes, trade sanctions). Autonomous measures are of particular importance for protecting the Community economy from damage that can be caused by imports from non-member countries. Here we can distinguish between four types of measures.

(1) Anti-dumping measures, in the form of provisional anti-dumping duties, can be imposed by the Commission at the request of the Community industry affected

after the request has been scrutinized and the Member States consulted. They can then be changed by a simple majority in the → Council into definitive anti-dumping duties. The precondition, as for the other protective measures, is that damage (already existing or imminent) to the industry concerned be established.

(2) Anti-subsidy measures, unlike anti-dumping measures, are not directed against unfair trade practices by foreign industries, but against subsidized exports from non-member countries to the Community. The procedure is the same as for anti-dumping measures and can lead to the introduction of temporary or definitive countervailing duties on the products concerned. The anti-subsidy and anti-dumping measures provided for comply with GATT rules.

(3) Safeguard clause measures can be taken if 'serious damage' to a Community industry through a substantial increase in third country imports and considerable price undercutting is established. They take the form of import monitoring and quotas. Because of the very restrictive GATT rules in this field, the Community has made only limited use of this option to date.

(4) Since 1984, the Community has also had the 'New Commercial Policy Instrument', which enables it to react relatively quickly to unfair trade practices by third countries against imports from the Community. This means first using international consultation and conciliation procedures but can also subsequently lead to tougher measures such as the suspension of trade concessions, increased customs duties on imports from the countries concerned and quantitative restrictions. A special form of the autonomous commercial policy consists of foreign policy-related trade sanctions, such as the trade embargoes imposed on Iraq and Bosnia. Sanctions of this kind can, according to Article 228a of the EC Treaty, be adopted by the Council by qualified majority on a proposal from the Commission within the framework of the CFSP.

A fundamental basis for both the autonomous and treaty-based commercial policy is the common customs tariff, regulated in Articles 9 and 18-29, which gives the Community a common customs tariff *vis-à-vis* third countries. On a proposal from the Commission, the Council can decide autonomous alterations to the common customs tariff at any time.

Trade balance — Percentage share of world trade (excluding intra-EU trade)

Value 1995 (ECU billion)

Main sources of EU imports   **Main destinations for EU exports**

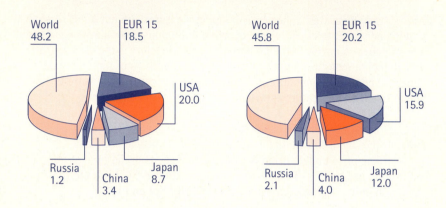

World 48.2 | EUR 15 18.5 | USA 20.0 | Russia 1.2 | China 3.4 | Japan 8.7

World 45.8 | EUR 15 20.2 | USA 15.9 | Russia 2.1 | China 4.0 | Japan 12.0

Treaty-based commercial policy The treaty-based commercial policy covers all the EU agreements with third countries relating to imports and exports of goods. These agreements can be limited to particular third countries or groups of third countries, or they may have a global dimension as, for example, in the case of the results of the most recent round of negotiations in the GATT, the Uruguay Round, which ended in December 1993.

In the field of treaty-based commercial policy the Commission has a monopoly, not just on proposals, but also on negotiating. Negotiation by the Commission is, however, subject to stringent control by the Member States through the Council, which does not allow it much room for manoeuvre. In the course of the negotiations, at which the Member States always have observers present, the Commission must stick to the Council's detailed guidelines (so-called 'negotiating mandate') and must constantly report to it on the progress and problems of the negotiations before a special Council committee (Article 113(3) of the EC treaty). The agreements are also concluded ('ratified') by the Council on a proposal from the Commission. While the → European Parliament must be consulted in the case of other agreements in accordance with the uniform treaty-making procedure of Article 228 of the EC Treaty, and must give its assent in the case of association agreements and certain other important agreements, for agreements concluded under the common commercial policy the Council is not even obliged to consult Parliament. However, Parliament is kept informed, via its competent committees, about the course of the negotiations and the content of agreements.

The Community has concluded many and extremely varied commercial agreements with third countries. Some of these agreements cover all aspects of trade relations, others only certain products or groups of products. In terms of substance these agreements contain such things as voluntary restraint of imports to the Community and the granting of trade preferences by the Community. In the last 10 years, the Community has used its commercial policy opportunities extensively to develop and integrate more closely its immediate economic surroundings, i.e. Central and Eastern Europe and the Mediterranean.

The successive major rounds of GATT negotiations which have taken place since the 1960s are of particular importance in the context of the treaty-based commercial policy. Although the Community is not formally a contracting party to the GATT or its successor organization, the World Trade Organization (WTO), it does represent the Member States there as negotiator. In the Uruguay Round, the Community successfully argued for further substantial import duty reductions, the incorporation of trade in services into the international trading system, minimum standards for the protection of intellectual property, a clearer definition of the GATT's regulatory task and a reformed conciliation procedure in trade disputes. It had to make concessions particularly on its → agricultural policy, where it had to accept substantial cuts in export refunds, subsidized exports and the internal level of support, and in the field of textiles, where it agreed to the step-by-step elimination of the quotas allowed under the Multifibre Arrangement, which expired in 1994, for the protection of its textile and clothing industry. Unresolved problems persist, particularly in the areas of services and steel, where there is still considerable potential for conflict between the Community and the US.

New initiatives in relations with the US and Asia Both the US, as the Community's biggest individual trading partner and a leading player in the world economy, and the rapidly growing economies of Asia's industrial countries, as newly emerging markets and trading powers with enormous potential, are of vital importance for the Community's external trade. The Community has recently taken major new initiatives in its relations with both parties.

In December 1995 the Community and the US agreed on a joint Transatlantic Agenda which includes not only more intensive political cooperation but also closer collaboration in implementing the results of the Uruguay Round, the gradual creation of a transatlantic market with the removal of any remaining bilateral trade barriers and the establishment of a comprehensive dialogue between the private sectors of both sides. There was already extensive cooperation in removing technical barriers to trade and harmonizing conditions of access for specific products and the Transatlantic Business Dialogue has now produced the first concrete recommendations to governments regarding the harmonization of competition rules and product standards. Success in implementing the Agenda is of particular importance in view of the differences in trade policy matters which frequently overshadowed relations with the US.

The Essen → European Council in December 1994 approved a new Asia strategy for developing relations with the Asian countries in trade, industrial cooperation, promotion of investment, inter-company cooperation and research and development both on a bilateral basis and in a broader regional framework. Major advances were made at the first Euro-Asia Summit in Bangkok in early March 1996 when the Community and Asia's 10 leading economic powers defined a market-economy approach, non-discriminatory trade liberalization and open regionalism as the bases of closer Euro-Asian partnership and agreed to step up consultations within the World Trade Organization and to mount concrete action programmes in areas such as promotion of investment and simplification of customs procedures.

Assessment Since its inception, the Community has managed, within its external relations framework, to create a vast panoply of external economic policy instruments and a dense network of global agreements. The most recent GATT round has once again shown that the Community, together with the US, plays a key role in international economic relations shared by no other economic power – not even Japan. It therefore has an extraordinary potential in world politics, which, because of its very poorly developed (in comparison with its economic external relations) foreign policy negotiating arrangements – the common foreign and security policy – has been, and indeed can only be, very inadequately exploited. In the longer term, external economic relations also need the framework of an effective common foreign policy in order to stabilize and develop further. However, as long as this is missing, external economic relations and their central element, the common commercial policy, must fill this gap as far as possible, and, by developing their instruments in line with the dynamic of international economic relations and through new and intensified agreements, further secure and develop the position of the European Union in international relations.

Jörg Monar

Fisheries policy

Treaty basis: Article 38 of the EC Treaty.
Aims: Fair standard of living for persons employed in fisheries; stable prices; availability of supplies; supplies to consumers at reasonable prices; preservation and protection of fish resources.
Instruments: Common organization of the market, support for producer organizations, determination of total allowable catches in EU territorial waters and allocation to the Member States, technical specifications for nets and minimum sizes, surveillance, agreements with non-member countries, structural measures.
Budget: 1995 = ECU 39 million (cost of market organization).
Literature from the European Union:
European Commission: How does the European Union manage agriculture and fisheries?
Luxembourg 1996 (Cat. no.: CM-43-96-006-EN-C. Free).
European Commission: Aquaculture and the environment in the European Community.
Luxembourg 1995 (Cat. no.: CU-88-993-EN-C. ECU 28.00).
European Commission: The new common fisheries policy.
Luxembourg 1994 (Cat. no.: CM-81-93-874-EN-C. Free).

'Blue Europe', as some like to call the common fisheries policy, is a relative newcomer to the European integration scene. Two EC regulations enacted from 1970 govern free and equal access to all EC fishing grounds for all EC fishermen, subject to a few exceptions for particularly sensitive coastal waters.

Enlargement of the Community northwards in 1973 substantially increased the area of Community fishing grounds and the fisheries policy obviously came up for renegotiation. The UK, Ireland and Denmark obtained a few special reserved areas (six or twelve-mile zones) valid until 1983. The problem of the allocation of catch quotas arose not only in the EC context but also internationally from the mid-1970s. At the Third UN Conference on the Law of the Sea there was, however, no agreement on fishing rights. Many countries claimed a 200-mile zone, and the EC followed suit in 1977.

The aggregate area of international fishing grounds shrank accordingly. Countries with neighbouring zones were obliged to agree on how to share out fishing rights. The EC then followed with a series of fisheries agreements with non-member countries. The technique for conserving resources was to determine annual total allowable catches and divide them into quotas.

Although enlargement southwards in 1986 further extended EC territorial waters somewhat, the number of fishermen actually doubled. Spain and Portugal were given transitional arrangements, valid until 1996, to govern access and restrict fishing rights.

Market organization By Article 38 of the EC Treaty, the rules governing agriculture and trade in agricultural produce apply likewise to fisheries. In 1970, in the process of extending the organization of agricultural markets the Council (→ Council of the European Union) issued a Regulation on the common organization of the market in fisheries products, which was amended in 1976, 1981 and 1992. Common marketing standards were first determined – classification by quality, size, weight and presentation, packaging and labelling. The aim is to ensure market transparency and exclude substandard products. Implementation of the marketing rules is the task of producer organizations. Guide prices are set annually for the different fish species. Producer organizations may determine withdrawal prices, below which they do not sell fish landed by their members but pay them financial compensation financed in part by the European Agricultural Guidance and Guarantee Fund (→ regional policy).

Non-members may also be obliged to observe the withdrawal prices (general statement of obligation). The withdrawal price for most species is between 70 and 90% of the guide price. Customs duties are levied on fish imported into the Community. In addition, reference prices are set for the different categories of fish and derived products on the basis of producer prices for the preceding three years. Imports may be made conditional on the price not undercutting the reference price. For certain products a compensatory levy corresponding to the gap between the reference price and the free-at-frontier price plus customs duties may be charged. Export refunds are payable to offset the difference between the price in the Community and the (lower) price on certain export markets.

Structures policy On 20 October 1970, a Regulation on a common policy for fisheries structures (revised in 1976) was enacted to accompany the market organization Regulation. The objective is to secure a balanced, harmonious development of the fishing industry and promote rational use of the biological resources of the sea and inland waters. For the purpose of coordinating the structures policy, the Member States undertook to report annually to the → European Commission on the nature and volume of measures planned for the year ahead and their multiannual programmes. The Commission is required to report to the → European Parliament and the Council on the structure of the fishing industry, the Community-level coordination of the structural policy, the measures taken for the purpose and Community financing.

After lengthy negotiations, multiannual restructuring programmes for fishing fleets were adopted in 1993, valid until 1996. Proceeding from the capacity targets set earlier for 1991, they envisage fleet reductions for each Member State, modulated according to fish species and fishing techniques. The reduction is of the order of 20% for trawling for demersal species, of which stocks are already seriously threatened, and 15% for flatfish. Fishing for pelagic species, where the stock situation is better, and what is known as static-gear fishing (using fixed nets and pots) is confined to the levels of the base year, 1991. In contrast to what had been done with earlier Community programmes, upper limits on fishing fleet sizes were set by multiplying catch capacities and temporary fishing activities, and objectives could be attained as to 45% by reductions in temporary activities. As reduction targets were related to earlier objectives, the rates of fleet reduction from the pre-programme August 1993 levels differed widely from one Member State to another.

In the context of the reform of the Structural Funds, the Financial Instrument for Fisheries Guidance (FIFG) was set up and earlier Community support schemes were wound up on 31 December 1993. Decisions on future financial support will be taken primarily by the Member States on the basis of the resources allocated to them and of a simplified programming system.

Conservation and rational use of fishery resources The basic concept of a single economic area (→ single market) implies that fishing grounds within it should be available for use without nationality discrimination. Initially this was not the case in practice, as the Member States' fishing industries were of uneven efficiency and coastal fisheries had to be protected against the more efficient industrial fishermen. For the initial five-year period exclusive zones of three miles were established. After exclusive fishing zones were extended from 12 to 200 miles with effect from 1 January 1970, the Community needed to reach a solution that would ensure the orderly use and conservation of fish resources.

Between 1976 and 1982 the Council was hard put to settle questions of total allowable catches, their allocation among the Member States and access to coastal waters. On 25 January 1983 the conflicts were resolved. The Member States were authorized to preserve their 12-mile zones for 20 years, subject to traditional fishing rights of vessels from other Member States. For the major fish species catch quotas were renewed for 20 years, subject to regular adaptations to take account of variations in fish stocks.

As fishermen had to compete for declining stocks, the problem of monitoring compliance with catches and the agreed restrictions on techniques became more and more acute. In 1993 the Council decided on a set of fundamental changes. The authorities of the Member States are obliged to take appropriate measures in the event of a violation, including prosecution. They are also responsible for inspections. The Commission monitors their activities here, especially by making unannounced inspections supported by new technologies for ongoing surveillance. All fishing vessels must keep a logbook so that inspectors can verify whether catches on board comply with Community rules on composition of catches in relation to types of net used.

Winfried von Urff

Health

Treaty basis: Article 129 of the EC Treaty; Agreement on social policy.
Aims: Protection of health; health and safety precautions at work.
Budget: 1996: Campaign against cancer – ECU 12 million; campaign against AIDS –
ECU 9.4 million, health protection at the workplace – ECU 10.5 million; anti-pollution and
public health initiatives - ECU 12.5 million; campaign against drug abuse – ECU 6.5 million.
Literature from the European Union:
European Commission: Health and safety at work: Community programme 1996-2000.
Luxembourg 1996 (Cat. no.: CE-90-95-518-EN-C. Free).
European Commission: European principles for health and safety at work: European week
for health and safety at work 7 to 13 October 1996.
Luxembourg 1996 (Cat. no.: CE-97-96-677-EN-C. Free).
European Commission: The European Union and the fight against drugs.
Luxembourg 1996 (Cat. no.: CM-99-96-827-EN-C. Free).
European Commission: The European Union and sport.
Luxembourg 1996 (Cat. no.: CC-95-96-617-EN-C. Free).

At the Maastricht summit, the Heads of State or Government agreed in the Treaty
on European Union to ensure a 'high level of human health protection' in the
Community Member States, with the declared aim of researching into, preventing
and combating serious widespread diseases, including drug dependence. The
Member States coordinate their policies and programmes in these fields in liaison
with the → European Commission. To implement health policy the → Council of
the European Union adopts recommendations by a qualified majority, or incentive
measures under the → decision-making procedure laid down in Article 189b of
the EC Treaty. However, actual legislative powers remain the province of Member
States.

The Treaties establishing the European Economic Community did not specifically
lay down a common health policy. In 1987 the Single European Act incorporated
into the EEC Treaty provisions on Community-wide cooperation on health
protection and the harmonization of minimum rules regarding the working
environment (Articles 100a and 118a). It was only with the Treaty on European
Union that health was defined as a separate area of European policy under Title X.
Joint action in the public health field includes a wide range of explanatory and
educational work as a basis for the general promotion of health. Further aspects of
public health protection are regulated under → environment policy (Article 130r)
and → consumer policy (Article 129a).

Specific action programmes 'Europe against cancer', one of the first, long-running initiatives, was launched by the Heads of State or Government in 1985. In 1987 the Commission drew up specific action programmes which have continued ever since. These include European support for research and education and extensive information campaigns on reducing the risk of cancer. 'Europe against AIDS' is another Community programme, launched in 1991 and directed at both sufferers and the healthy. To step up the fight against AIDS, Ministers decided to establish a Union-wide system for pooling information and experience. The most recent AIDS action plan covers the period from 1995 to 1999.

The Member States have also joined forces in the fight against addiction. Bearing in mind that drug abuse is specifically mentioned in Article 129, the Commission drew up an initial action plan in 1995 covering the period up to the year 2000. Since there are many sides to the drugs problem, the policy also concentrates on prevention, the sharing of information, experience and tried and tested methods as well as on the collection of data at Community level. It also provides support for counselling, rehabilitation and the social reintegration of addicts. In 1993 the Community launched a third action programme in one of its traditional fields of activity – the health protection of workers. The programme runs until the end of the century and emphasizes safety, ergonomics and hygiene at the workplace as well as dialogue between management and trade unions. However, in order to ensure a uniform level of protection in practice, European works councils are advocating cross-border information and consultation of workers in firms operating at Community level.

Assessment The European integration process has given the health systems which have evolved in individual Member States fresh impetus to tackle specific problems. In the frontier-free → single market, it is increasingly important that countries join forces to combat diseases, conduct research into their causes and promote health information. The Union Treaty has given greater weight to health policy and creates the conditions for Community-wide protection of public health.

Ralf Schmitt

Industry

Treaty basis: Article 130 of the EC Treaty in the main, within the limits set by Article 3b of the EC Treaty and Title V (Competition).

Aims: To foster internationally competitive, efficient and innovative firms by creating a favourable environment, in particular for smaller firms; to support research and development, cooperation between firms and restructuring in the context of 'a system of open and competitive markets'.

Instruments: Consultation and coordination between Member States on the initiative of the European Commission; support for specific measures by Member States after a unanimous decision by the Council.

Budget: In the 1995 draft budget only ECU 38.5 million was allocated directly to industrial policy activities. Impetus also comes from other budget headings (R.&D., education, information and communication, single market, trans-European networks) which were allocated a total of around ECU 3.7 billion. In 1993 the EIB granted loans totalling ECU 17.7 billion, of which ECU 4.2 billion was intended for the industrial and service sectors, including ECU 1.5 billion for small businesses, and ECU 7.2 billion for trans-European networks.

Literature from the European Union:
European Commission: Panorama of EU industry 1995-96.
Luxembourg 1995 (Cat. no.: CO-90-95-356-EN-C. ECU 130.00).
European Commission: Enterprises in Europe: Fourth report.
Luxembourg 1996 (Cat. no.: CA-94-96-170-EN-B. ECU 50.00).
European Commission: Activities in favour of SMEs and the craft sector.
Luxembourg 1996 (Cat. no.: CT-90-95-542-EN-C. Free).
European Commission: Grants and loans from the European Union.
Luxembourg 1996. (Cat. no.: CC-90-95-106-EN-C. ECU 35.00).

Unlike competition policy, which seeks to create equal, non-discriminatory market conditions for all firms, industrial policy is aimed at selective intervention in the market, either to protect old industries threatened by imports, to foster cooperation between small firms at the pre-competitive stage of production (R.&D., financing), to strengthen modern key sectors or to improve productivity and lower costs across the board. For this purpose the Union uses traditional instruments such as tax measures, financial assistance, public contracts and research aid alongside more modern instruments such as technology transfer institutions and technology councils set up as a forum for dialogue between businessmen, economists, technologists, and politicians. Thus, modern industrial policy relies very much on the wisdom of strategists, whose task is to gear the domestic production of goods and provision of services to probable future trends. Today the primary objective of industrial policy is restructuring.

Treaty basis The Paris and Rome Treaties made no provision for a common industrial policy in these terms. However, many sections of the Treaty establishing a European Coal and Steel Community (ECSC) contain very specific rules on the European mining industry, indeed on most branches of the coal and steel industries. The Euratom Treaty also focuses on a specific industry, aiming, among other things, 'to promote research and ensure the dissemination of technical information' and 'facilitate investment' in nuclear energy.

The basis for industrial policy in the EEC Treaty was less clearly defined. Until the EEC Treaty was superseded by the EC Treaty, the Community's action in this field had to be based on the general Treaty objectives, in which case Article 235 of the EEC Treaty could be used. Under the new Article 130, the Community was expressly given responsibilities in industrial policy, although its power to carry out specific measures is still subject to the principle of subsidiarity (Article 3b) and unanimity in the → Council.

Implementation of objectives For too long Community industrial policy was characterized by crisis management in specific sectors, particularly in the period after 1975 and in the early 1980s, when the → European Commission developed structural programmes for the iron and steel industries, the textile industry, shipbuilding and the shoe industry. In the case of iron and steel, these measures sometimes had a strong *dirigiste* flavour – temporarily suspending free competition in the interests of achieving an orderly capacity reduction in all firms – and were flanked by external restrictions. As the economy recovered towards the end of the 1980s, most of these measures were repealed or toned down.

In the early 1990s the Commission adopted a new approach to industrial policy. In a policy document it emphasized the importance of competition, open markets and 'horizontal' measures to increase productivity and encourage innovation, a position determined largely by the restrictions on industrial policy enshrined in Article 130. The Commission's most recent industrial policy initiative should be seen in the same light. It lays down four priorities for action: to promote intangible investment, develop industrial cooperation, guarantee a level playing field and modernize government intervention.

In the first priority area the aim is to improve vocational training, introduce new methods of organizing work, establish total quality control, explore new technologies and develop information networks. Research policy is to be more market-oriented.

In the second field the Commission proposes that instruments be developed to encourage cooperation between private initiatives in the Community interest and to boost the presence of European firms on geographically expanding markets. The Commission believes that the best way of achieving these goals is to remove legal and tax barriers, set up industrial round tables and develop a coherent legal approach to the promotion of investment abroad. The main target regions are Central and Eastern Europe (where the Union even wants to take over partial guarantees for investments), Latin America, the Mediterranean and the booming economies of Asia - where the emphasis is very much on technological cooperation.

The third priority area has both internal and external aspects. Items on the internal agenda include introducing full-blooded competition to the → single market by managing subsidies more effectively, while taking into account → regional policy and other Community policies with financial implications, and opening up sectors hitherto shielded from competition, namely gas, electricity and telecommunications. On the external front, one of the main aims is to sharpen the Community's trade policy instruments and extend them to the services sector, so that regulated international competition can be pushed beyond the results of the GATT Uruguay Round. The Community wants a more effective means of reacting to the widespread emergence of strategic alliances on global markets and to discriminatory bilateral agreements such as the agreement between the United States and Japan on semi-conductors. An industrial assessment mechanism to help uncover hidden discrimination will be established between the Commission and non-member countries in which European industry finds it difficult to gain a foothold despite its strong competitive position.

Finally, the main objective in the fourth priority area is to pursue deregulation, simplify administrative procedures and improve cooperation between national and Community authorities.

In its White Paper on growth, competitiveness and employment, the Commission sought to add a labour-market and employment dimension to Community industrial policy. It sees particular potential for growth and employment in technical know-how, culture, health, biotechnology, the environment and information and communications technologies. Innovations in these fields are to be protected against imitations by introducing better copyright and patent safeguards. The White Paper considers that trans-European networks in transport, energy and telecommunications are vital not only to make the information society a reality, but also to unlock the full potential of the single market, which includes extending its scope to Central and Eastern Europe. The Commission hopes that the investment required for these networks between now and the end of the century – around ECU 370 billion, including ECU 120 billion to be financed by the Community – will have a highly beneficial effect on the labour market, both in the construction and operational phases.

Contentious issues Industrial policy has always been the subject of dispute in the Community. German economists, rooted in the strict free-market tradition, regarded the Commission's industrial policy memoranda, action programmes and structural programmes, up to and including the recent White Paper and the attempts to establish fair competition in foreign trade, as inspired by the French philosophy of *planification* and Colbertism. It was mainly the French who drew attention to the technological gap *vis-à-vis* the United States and Japan, the strategic trade policy of the latter which threatened to monopolize key technologies, the growing mobility of capital and technology on globalized markets, the national compartmentalization of the Community market and its structural weaknesses. They argued that the process of adjustment, modernization and, inevitably, concentration could not be left to market forces alone, if Europe's economic position were not to be permanently endangered.

The differences became blurred as the single market gradually took shape, France turned its back on sectoral planning and Germany expanded State subsidies and took a more active role in industrial and technology policy. Industrial policy ideas gained much ground in Germany as the threat of de-industrialization loomed over whole regions in the east of the country. Today business cooperation initiatives and research aid are regarded as important in all Member States.

Nevertheless the old dispute has flared up again, for a variety of reasons. First, the Commission has met with only partial success in promoting its new industrial policy credo that priority must be given to a system of 'open and competitive markets'. This is evident in the disregard which some Member States have shown for rules on steel subsidies, the generous aid that has been handed out to other branches of the economy and the politicization of Council decisions on regional aid. This latent conflict between industrial and regional policy, on the one hand, and competition policy on the other will be exacerbated as expenditure on structural policy and R.&.D. increases.

More recently there have been conflicts over trans-European networks: some Member States feel that the Community should not play a major role in financing these networks, while the Commission and other Member States stress the importance of developing the networks as a general industrial policy measure. Other contentious issues include the further development of commercial policy instruments and the question of who should represent the Community in the new World Trade Organization – the Member States or the Commission.

Fritz Franzmeyer

Information society

Treaty basis: Articles 3, 52, 59, 85, 86, 90, 100a, 129a, 129b, 129c, 129d and 130 of the EC Treaty.
Aims: To increase the competitiveness of the European economy, to provide support for changes in economic and social structures, to enhance the quality of science and training.
Instruments: The creation of a Europe-wide legal, regulatory and technical framework for the information society, the promotion of pilot projects and technical innovations, the securing of equal opportunities in competition and access to new technology.
Information: European Commission: 'Europe and the Global Information Society' (the Bangemann report), Brussels 1994; 'Europe's way to the information society. An action plan', Brussels 1994; 'La préparation des européens à la société de l'information', Luxembourg 1996; 'Implications of the information society for European Union policies – Preparing the next steps', Brussels 1996; *First Annual Report to the European Commission from the Information Society Forum*, Brussels 1996; WWW: European Commission: http://europa.eu.int/; Information Society Project Office: http://www.ispo.cec.be.
Literature from the European Union:
European Commission: The Information society.
Luxembourg 1996 (Cat. no.: CC-94-96-316-EN-C. Free).

Since the beginning of the 1990s, the term 'information society' has been used to describe the many and varied challenges and opportunities which have been created by the rapid development of modern information and communications technologies in the economy, politics and society as a whole. The knitting together of digitally stored data, texts, sounds and images (multimedia) has led to widespread use of modern telecommunications systems, personal computers and electronic information services as well as a quantitative growth in the traditional media. The Internet, a worldwide data network, has established itself as a global communications platform. The actors in the industrial societies of Europe are facing the necessity of having to rethink ways of transferring information on a daily basis.

There are great opportunities: spatial and temporal constraints on communication are being reduced; information can be stored and transferred quickly and with a high usage value; the price of automated services is falling. Information society enthusiasts are discovering ways of setting up virtual communities as counterweights to the centrifugal forces of industrial society. On the other hand, sceptics bemoan the widening of the knowledge gap between an information elite and socially disadvantaged groups and criticize the poor quality of data to be found on the forever congested information highways. Individual creativity and the desire to invest on the part of the social players will therefore determine whether the information society will bring with it innovation and efficiency. The only way to obtain the acceptance of the people is through the development of media competence and democratic access to the information available.

In the 1993 White Paper on growth, competitiveness and employment the EU made explicit reference to these challenges in terms of new methods of organizing work and life and of opportunities for employment. In 1994, on the basis of recommendations in the Bangemann report, the European Commission presented the action plan entitled 'Europe's way to the information society', proposing, first and foremost, measures to create the technical, legal and regulatory standards and framework for the information society. Freedom from regulation is the aim since it should serve to offer the private sector incentives to invest in one of the most important European markets: the European Information Technology Observatory expects an annual growth rate in Europe of over 8% for information and communications products; the volume of trade in this area worldwide has already exceeded ECU 1 000 billion.

From 1994 to 1998, some ECU 3.6 billion has been earmarked for promoting a European multimedia industry in the fourth framework programme in the field of research and technological development (including Esprit, Acts and télématique). The funds are to be channelled into 10 applications-related initiatives in the fields of teleworking, distance learning, research networks, telematics, transport, air safety, health, public procurement, public administration and cabling up private households. MEDIA II serves to support the audio-visual industry and, lastly, the INFO 2000 programme, set up in 1996, promotes the development of multimedia programmes by small and new companies. As the European telecommunications markets are due to be liberalized by 1998, the EU will also have the task of guaranteeing a level playing field for the communications services market as part of its competition policy.

The Commission is assisted in its reflections on the information society by various institutions: the Information Society Project Office, set up in 1995, provides a social exchange for ideas and contacts. The Information Society Forum, comprising over 100 representatives from interest groups, evaluates EU measures and formulates strategic options. A group of experts has been commissioned to reflect on the specific effects of the new technologies and to come up with proposals to overcome any problems. A Legal Advisory Board, comprising legal experts from the Member States, is to discuss legal questions in relation to the digital age, such as the threat posed to copyright. Suggestions from these circles have already given rise to various Commission Green Papers channelling discussion on the social, economic and legal challenges posed by the information society and attention was focused on the individual by the 1996 Green Paper entitled 'Living and working in the information society: People first'.

To give the information society the necessary global perspective, the EU organized a meeting of the G7 States in Brussels in 1995 and a conference in South Africa on the information society and development in 1996. Also in 1996, a meeting was organized with Mediterranean States in Rome and there was a second meeting in Prague with representatives of the countries of Central and Eastern Europe to work out both Europe-wide and contiguity strategies. In the coming years it will be necessary to work together to flesh out the declarations made on these occasions in support of fair competition, the promotion of private investment and open access to networks. Certain challenges relating, for example, to the setting up of a global information structure, are likely to prove especially thorny problems.

Patrick Meyer

Intergovernmental Conference

Treaty basis: Articles N(2), B, indent 5 of the EU Treaty, 189b of the EC Treaty, J. 10 and J. 4 of the EU Treaty relating to revision and Declarations 1 and 16 annexed to the EU Treaty.

Aims: More efficient institutions and decision-making procedures, bringing Europe closer to the people, greater Union capacity for action in the field of foreign and security policy, further development of justice and home affairs policy.

Further reading: European Parliament, DG Research, White Paper for 1996 Intergovernmental Conference, three volumes, Luxembourg 1996.

Literature from the European Union:

European Commission: 'The EU's future shape – the 1996 Intergovernmental Conference': A new database on the 1996 Intergovernmental Conference. Luxembourg 1996 (Cat. no.: CC-97-96-136-EN-C. Free).

European Commission: Intergovernmental conference 1996. Commission opinion. Reinforcing political union and preparing for enlargement.
Luxembourg 1996 (Cat. no.: CM-94-96-356-EN-C. Free).

European Commission: Intergovernmental Conference 1996. Commission report for the Reflection group.
Luxembourg 1995 (Cat. no.: CC-89-95-357-EN-C. Free).

The Intergovernmental Conference on the review of the Maastricht Treaty was opened by the European Council in Turin on 29 March 1996 and will probably continue well into 1997. The personal representatives of the Foreign Ministers meet once a week and the Foreign Ministers themselves once a month. The European Council monitors the progress of the Intergovernmental Conference, if necessary by holding extraordinary meetings. The European Parliament is kept regularly informed and is entitled to express its views.

Background The Intergovernmental Conference is a response to the terms of the Treaty which require all the newly introduced procedures and policies to be reviewed in 1996. The review agenda has been extended to include proposals from individual Member States and a list of reforms compiled by the European Council at its meetings in Brussels, Corfu, Madrid and Turin. Another factor which has a bearing on the Intergovernmental Conference is the next wave of Union enlargement, which has to be preceded by a deepening of the integration process.

A reflection group set up by the Heads of State or Government to prepare for the Conference (July to December 1995) produced a report setting out options for the revision of the EU Treaty. This was preceded by reports by the Council and the Commission on the operation of the EU Treaty and by two resolutions of the European Parliament. The Commission made a clear statement of its expectations before the Conference began.

Main areas of discussion The Conference is focusing on three main areas. The first concerns the general public and the European Union, or, more precisely, the consolidation of citizens' rights and fundamental rights in the Treaty on European Union, greater openness in the workings of the Union and greater internal security in the Union. The second area concerns greater procedural efficiency, possibly involving an extension of majority voting, a redistribution of votes in the Council (so as to improve the balance between the larger and smaller Member States) and the simplification of procedures with particular consideration for the co-decision powers of the European Parliament. The third area concerns greater EU capacity for action in the field of foreign and security policy based on the establishment of a planning and analysis unit, possible changes to the decision-making system, the improvement of the Union's external representation and further development of defence policy. More recently, the high levels of unemployment in the Union have propelled the subject of a European employment policy into the foreground. Another potential topic for consideration is a Franco-German proposal for the introduction of more flexible procedures enabling a group of Member States to move ahead in the integration process.

Assessment So far the progress made at the Intergovernmental Conference has been only very sporadic. Particular problems have arisen not only because of the obstructive attitude of the present British government but also because of disagreement between the other Member States concerning the practical scope of amendments or additions to the Treaty despite the fact that a clear majority of Member States have the same interests in reform. Given the need to ratify the results of the negotiations, the most likely outcome will be consolidation and cautious advances.

Mathias Jopp

Justice and home affairs

Treaty basis: Articles 7a, 8-8c and 100 of the EC Treaty; Articles K1-K9 of the Treaty on European Union.

Aims: To extend citizenship of the Union, movement across internal frontiers without checks being carried out; increased cooperation between the signatories of the Schengen accords and EU States in matters relating to justice and home affairs, including the setting up of common institutions.

Literature from the European Union:

European Commission: Intergovernmental conference 1996.
Commission opinion. Reinforcing political union and preparing for enlargement.
Luxembourg 1996 (Cat. no.: CM-94-96-356-EN-C. Free).
European Commission: Intergovernmental Conference 1996. Commission report for the Reflection group. Luxembourg 1995 (Cat. no.: CC-89-95-357-EN-C. Free).

In 1985, at a village called Schengen, where the borders of Germany, France and Luxembourg meet, these three States, together with Belgium and the Netherlands, signed an agreement to phase out checks on the movement of persons at their common borders. In a further agreement, the Convention applying the Schengen Accords of 14 June 1990, the following security measures were adopted to offset the loss of security suffered as a consequence of the abolition of border controls.

- A joint automated search system, the Schengen Information System (SIS), which allows Member States, in accordance with clearly laid-down criteria, to set up and maintain data files on persons and certain objects (firearms, blank documents, identity documents, registered bank notes and vehicles which have been stolen, misappropriated or lost). The police forces of other Member States can then access to the files as well as their national investigation sections. A technical support unit in Strasbourg ensures that the data files are kept completely up to date.

- Close checks at all crossing points on external borders of the Schengen Community (and, if possible, at all external borders of the → European Union), to be carried out in as uniform a manner as possible.

- Increased cooperation among the police forces in the region around the internal borders through the building up of a communications structure, joint exercises, cross-border observation and right of pursuit.

- The obligation to supply other Member States with any information that may be of assistance in crime prevention.

- Increased cooperation in the fight against drugs and drug-related crime.

- Harmonization of the laws governing the possession of firearms in the Member States.

Justice and home affairs policy in the EU 'Schengen' is seen as a pilot project for the integration of justice and home affairs in the European Union. Until 1992, all cooperation between the security forces of the EC States took place within the framework of informal meetings held by the Trevi group of the Justice and Interior Ministers of the EC States and had no legal basis in any multilateral Treaty. Six-monthly meetings at ministerial level and preparatory working parties were able to increase, above all, the exchange of information, and cooperation in matters regarding terrorism, serious crime, civil aviation safety measures, nuclear safety, conflagrations, natural disasters, police technology and equipment. The Maastricht Treaty on European Union of 7 February 1992 brought about a quantum leap in the integration of justice and home affairs. In the context of the 'first pillar' of the EU, Article 7a describes the → single market, which is to be progressively established as 'an area without internal frontiers in which the free movement of goods, services and capital is ensured'.

The second part of the EC Treaty, specifically Article 8 *et seq.*, the notion of citizenship of the Union is introduced, giving every citizen of the Union the right to move and reside freely within the territory of the Member States under Article 8a(1). Article 8b(1) also confers on citizens of the Union the right to vote and stand as candidates at municipal elections in the Member State in which they reside.

Article 100c sets out a common visa policy, whereby the → Council of the European Union, acting unanimously on a proposal from the → European Commission and after consulting the → European Parliament, determines the non-member States whose nationals must be in possession of a visa when crossing the external borders of Member States.

All other matters relating to justice and home affairs in the European Union are dealt with under Article K. Asylum policy, rules governing the crossing of external borders, immigration policy and policy regarding nationals of third countries are all characterized as matters of common interest, as are combating illegal entry, residence and work, combating drug addiction and international fraud, judicial cooperation in civil and criminal matters, customs cooperation and police cooperation for the purposes of preventing and combating serious forms of international crime, including the setting up of a European police office, → Europol. In the above areas the Council – in the composition of Interior and Justice

Ministers of the Member States – can adopt joint positions. As long as it takes the principle of subsidiarity into account, it can also adopt joint measures and formulate agreements. In principle, the Council's decisions are arrived at unanimously, the meetings having been prepared by working parties, steering committees and, under the provisions of Article K of the Treaty an European Union, by a Coordinating Committee. The Committee's tasks also include giving opinions for the attention of the Council and, within the framework of the 'first pillar', contributing to the preparation of justice and home affairs policy under Article 100c.

The Commission plays a full part in areas within the framework of the 'third pillar'. The European Parliament must be regularly informed by the Presidency and the Commission about activities carried out and must be consulted on the most important aspects of those activities.

On 8 February 1993, the Council adopted a Regulation on the establishment of a European Monitoring Centre for Drugs and Drug Addiction, which commenced operations in Lisbon in 1994. On the basis of an action plan put forward by the Commission the Council is currently working on a new strategy in the fight against drugs, involving both prevention and penalization.

In 1994, in view of the sharp increase in vehicle theft, the Council in Essen declared itself in favour of examining ways of fitting all new vehicles with immobilizers. They are to be made obligatory on all new models as of 1997 and on all new vehicles as of 1998.

Aliens and visas As a result of the pressure faced by most EU Member States owing to the marked increase in immigration, the Maastricht report on the harmonization of immigration and asylum policy emphasizes the need for basic restrictions: apart from granting the right of abode for humanitarian reasons, immigration is basically to be limited to family reunion. With the exception of those seeking certain specified forms of temporary work, nationals of non-Member States wishing to pursue an occupational activity will generally be refused entry. Self-employed people are only granted entry to pursue a commercial interest if the economy of the State admitting them benefits from their entry, be it through investment, innovation, technology transfer or job creation. A further Council resolution has made it easier for students from non-Member States to gain entry, and schoolchildren from non-Member States who are residing in one Member State can make class trips to other Member States without needing a visa.

Previously simply a working party, Cirefi, the Centre for information, discussion and exchange on the crossing of frontiers and immigration has been transformed into an operative instrument in the fight against illegal entry and the smuggling in of illegal immigrants.

Progress has been made in inserting visa policy in the Community framework. Regulation (EC) No 2317/95 laid down the list of non-member countries whose nationals must be in possession of visas to enter the Union. Regulation (EC) No 1683/95 laid down a uniform format for a forgery-proof visa. On 23 November 1995, the Council reached agreement on a recommendation on consular cooperation regarding visas which contains a common list of non-member countries whose nationals require a transit visa. The conditions governing a visa to be valid in all Member States are to be specified in the external frontiers convention, which is still under negotiation within the Council.

On 23 November 1995, the Council also approved a resolution on the status of third-country nationals residing on a long-term basis in the territory of the Member States.

Refugees and asylum Owing to the large number of asylum-seekers, refugees and emigrants fleeing from civil wars, policy on refugees and asylum have dominated meetings of the Interior Ministers of the EU States in recent years. After several years' negotiation, on 23 November 1995 the Council agreed on a joint position on the definition of the term 'refugee' in Article IA of the Geneva Convention of 28 July 1951 relating to the status of refugees.

In a resolution dated 20 June 1996 the Council called for help to be given to refugees locally and in the regions from which they come, especially by the creation of safe zones. The EU States agree on the need to create rules allowing refugees in emergency situations to be taken in quickly and on an equitable basis by the Member States. However, no agreement has yet been reached as to whether the percentage of foreigners already living in the Member States or the unemployment rate within a given State should be among the criteria when deciding how to apportion the burden fairly. The Centre for information, discussion and exchange on asylum (IDEC) has laid down guidelines for joint status reports and a common statistics system.

The fight against racism and xenophobia In the context of European integration, the fight against racism and xenophobia has a particular significance, given the large number of xenophobically motivated acts of violence, some of which are antisemitic in nature, and other offences in recent years. According to a survey carried out by the Council working party on terrorism, 25 xenophobically or racially motivated homicide offences (of which 15 were attempts), 100 attacks and 468 cases of unlawful wounding were reported in EU Member States in 1995.

In Cannes in June 1995, a Consultative Commission on Racism and Xenophobia set up by the European Council presented its findings. These included a total of 107 recommendations and suggestions in the fields of education, information and the media, police and justice. The European Council called on the Council to examine the legal and financial aspects of setting up a European Monitoring Centre on

Racism and Xenophobia and to see what relations the Monitoring Centre would have to establish with the Council of Europe.

The Council and the Member States have decided to make 1997 the European Year against Racism, to bring home to the public the threat that racism, xenophobia and antisemitism pose for the respect of fundamental rights and unity in the Community. At the same time action to combat this threat should be considered in the form of exchanges of experience and information should be given about the advantages of integration measures in individual Member States. The projects for the European Year against Racism include conferences and seminars, information campaigns, and sporting and cultural events. A logo, slogan and posters will make it clear that all the projects are an individual country's contribution to a joint Union measure. The European Commission's strategy is to design the European year in such a way that it becomes firmly established in people's minds and has an impact well into the future by achieving tangible results that are widely publicized and so help to bring about more effective strategies for combating racism. Alongside the Community-level measures, which will be supported by an *ad hoc* group of Member States representatives, national projects are to be mounted by central and local authorities and NGOs in national coordination committees.

Justice Prior to the Maastricht Treaty, attempts had already been made to increase cooperation between Union States on matters of justice. The Convention applying the Schengen Accords is one shining example. The Treaty on European Union regards judicial cooperation in criminal matters as a question of common interest. Since then discussions have led to progress on the simplification of the extradition procedure (extradition is facilitated as long as the person being sought agrees) and on combating fraud against the European Union. In 1993, an agreement was signed on the protection of the financial interests of the Union.

All in all, integration in matters of justice and home affairs is a slow process. There are fundamental differences as to how to interpret 'intergovernmental cooperation'. Some Member States do not recognise any obligation under Article K.1 *et seq.* to put any flesh on the bones of a common security policy, preferring instead to view it as an opportunity to make use of the organizational assistance of the Union to solve problems of justice and home affairs. The instrument set up under Article K.8(2), whereby the Council may decide unanimously that operational expenditure is to be charged to the budget of the European Communities, is generally rejected by some Member States.

Progress can be expected if, at the Intergovernmental Conference, justice and home affairs are incorporated more fully into the Community from a procedural point of view and the supranational competence of the EU is extended in this area.

Reinhard Rupprecht

Media policy

Treaty basis: Reference to Articles 59 and 60 (freedom of services), 130 f-q (research and technological development) and 128 (culture) of the EC Treaty.
Aims: To create a European media market, to encourage and develop a competitive programme industry, to introduce a standard for high-definition television.
Individual programmes: Media II to promote the development of the European audio-visual industry, Eureka 95 to create the HDTV standard, audio-visual Eureka to promote the audio-visual infrastructure.
Literature from the European Union:
European Commission: Strategy options to strengthen the European programme industry in the context of the audio-visual policy of the European Union: Green Paper.
Luxembourg 1994 (Cat. no.: CC-83-94-620-EN-C. Free).
European Commission: Report by the think-tank on the audio-visual
policy in the European Union.
Luxembourg 1994 (Cat. no.: CC-83-94-733-EN-C. Free).

The mass media make communication possible. As the central distributor of culture, entertainment and information it fulfils an important social function. Any policy on the media must tread a very fine line between economics and culture. As producers of economic goods, the media are subject to the Community regulations governing the → single market. Culture, on the other hand, is a national matter; the cultural role of the → European Union (EU), which has only had a treaty basis under Article 128 since the Treaty on European Union, basically comprises the right to make joint recommendations and to supplement and support the action of Member States. In the case of the print media, the principle of the free flow of information in EU States has been taken for granted for years and required no joint regulation. Against this background, EU policy on the media has concerned itself almost exclusively with audio-visual media. In hardly any other sphere has there been so much change over the last 10 years. Originally, national regulations and the shortage of frequency space dictated a narrow framework for media policy. Then there came the breakthrough of cable and satellite, causing a veritable explosion in the number of the programmes that could be received while greatly limiting the scope for a national media policy as supranational broadcasts became increasingly normal.

From the point of view of the programme makers there developed a parallel necessity: to cover rising production costs by broadcasting to a wider area. European film and television productions are only profitable to a limited extent,

with 80% not going outside their country of origin. American productions in particular cover their costs on their home market and then swamp the European market at far lower prices.

The European media market Since the beginning of the 1980s the EC has been trying to create a media market. By harmonizing the regulations governing the activities of the suppliers, the basic idea has been to ensure that transnational broadcasting of television programmes – which *de facto* can hardly be prevented – does not violate the regulations in the States to which they are being broadcast.

On 3 October 1989, following lengthy preparation, the → Council of the European Union adopted the EC 'Television without frontiers' Directive, allowing audio-visual programmes to be broadcast freely throughout the EU as long as minimum guidelines are observed and cultural policy aims are taken into account. The Directive contains limitations on advertising time, rules regarding the protection of minors and a right of reply, as well as highly controversial rules governing the promotion, distribution and production of European television programmes, according to which over 50% of broadcasting time should be reserved for European productions. What is more, at least 10% of broadcasting time or the programming budget should be devoted to the work of independent producers. These quotas are to be applied 'where practicable', and are therefore not enforceable by law. Additional protocols grant Member States the right to impose stricter rules on domestic television organizations.

The → European Commission's endeavours to develop the television guidelines further has only served to revive fundamental criticism of them. Whereas France in particular has been pushing for years for a binding quota to be laid down for European productions to support the European film industry, at least for a transitional period, other Member States describe this move as pointless, easily circumvented protectionism. In March 1995 the Commission presented a proposal for a revision of the 'Television without frontiers' Directive. One provision was for a binding quota arrangement for a 10 year period. Unlike the European Parliament, the Council was unable to find a consensus on this. In June 1996 it adopted a common position extending the flexible quota arrangement for a further five years. A future revision of the Directive will have to take account of the far-reaching impact on the audio-visual industry of technological change (teleshopping).

Furthermore, doubts have repeatedly been expressed about the EU's powers in matters relating to media policy. The Union justifies it on the grounds that television is a service. The establishing of quotas, however, represents interference in programme planning, which, in Germany, for example, is a matter for the Federal *Länder*.

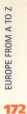

In recent years some supporting measures have further defined the European media market. In 1993 two guidelines were issued relating to the harmonization of copyright law in the case of transnational broadcasts and, since the appearance of the Green Paper in 1992, there has been furious discussion throughout the Union as to whether European regulations are a sensible method of maintaining pluralism within the media and preventing organizations from acquiring a dominant market position.

Support for the audio-visual infrastructure Within the Union, film and television productions are seen as extremely important instruments for the dissemination of culture and identity. In view of the difficult market situation the European Commission presented a Green Paper in 1994 discussing strategic options for the programme-making industry, from which there should emerge a plan for the competitive, future-oriented development of the media. Carefully targetted support is intended to offset the effects of the fragmented market, as much as anything to emphasize cultural variety within Europe. This is the object of the Media programme, which has been running since 1987. In order to improve the competitiveness of the European production industry, funds have been made available for professional training programmes, on the one hand, and dubbing, cooperation, distribution and marketing, on the other. The Media programme aims to help create a favourable environment for European film production without interfering with the production process itself. Since the most serious problem related to this programme was lack of funds, the budget for the second stage of Media (1996-2000) is to be doubled to approximately ECU 400 million.

Technical standardization In addition to language barriers Europe faces the problem of differing television systems. The introduction of cinema-quality high-definition television (HDTV) was therefore seen as a means of bringin about technical standardization. The Community's approach to HDTV was to prove a disaster in terms of industrial policy, however. The compulsory introduction of the D2-MAC standard, which was intended as the precursor to high-definition television, was a failure. Both consumer and producers found it expensive and unattractive at a time when direct transmission by satellite was becoming increasingly popular. Despite bitter resistance the planned introduction of D2-MAC had to be abandoned as unmarketable. At the same time and at great expense, a Eurpean HDTV system was developed as part of the Eureka initiative and was originally intended for establishment as a wordwide standard. Although America had developed a digital HDTV system which could be received by means of an antenna, the EC persisted with its own analogue system until the end of 1992 although it had become technically obsolete. Determined resistance from the United Kindgom finally led to the abandonment of the project. In 1994 work began on a digital standard within the Eureka framework. Over the next few years, therefore, various standards and formats will compete with each other until the introduction of high-definition television in 16:9 format. Since the success of the

new technology will depend essentially on the range of programmes available, the Council adopted in July 1993 a four-year action plan with a budget of ECU 228 million. As an incentive to production, compensation is provided for the extra costs incurred in making programmes for wide-screen television.

Prospects On the threshold of the digital age, the world of the media represents one of the greatest European markets of the future. Interactive services, individual programmes on demand and links to global data networks will pose challenges for European policy on the media. In Brussels the step into the multi-media information society is regarded as a great opportunity. However, in future, leaving aside the commercial aspects, the role of the media in shaping identity must not be overlooked. In spite of joint regulations a European media policy must play a part in maintaining the variety of systems in Europe. Then joint projects, such as Euronews, the five-language news channel, and Arte, the European cultural affairs channel, together with transnational specialist programmes can help ensure that the European dimension to our daily lives is easily comprehensible.

Olaf Hillenbrand

Mediterranean and Middle East policy

Treaty basis: The future of relations between the Community and the Maghreb, SEC (92)401, April 1992; Future relations and cooperation between the Community and the Middle East, COM (93)375, September 1993; Strengthening the Mediterranean policy of the European Union: Establishing a Euro-Mediterranean partnership, COM (94)427, November 1994; Conclusions of the 1994 Essen and 1995 Cannes European Councils, in supplement 2/95 to the *Bulletin of the European Union.*

Aims: To support the Middle East peace process and social and political stability in the most strategically important region after Eastern Europe.

Instruments: Financial cooperation, the establishment of stable trade structures to further economic development.

Literature from the European Union:

European Commission: The European Union's common foreign and security policy. Luxembourg 1996 (Cat. no.: CC-97-996-443-EN-C Free).

Euro-Mediterranean Partenship. Barcelona Declaration and work programme. Brussels 1996. Available from: European Commission. DG I/B. External Relations. Rue de la Loi 200. B-1049 Brussels.

European Investment Bank: Fostering a Euro-Mediterranean Partnership. Luxembourg 1996. Available from: EIB-Information and Communications Department. Luxembourg 100, Bld. Konrad Adenauer. L-2950 Luxembourg.

The real roots of the European Union's Mediterranean and Middle East policy go back to the 1970s. After the Yom Kippur War between Israel and her Arab neighbours and the subsequent oil embargo imposed by Arab oil suppliers, the Member States adopted a resolution within the framework of European political cooperation in November 1973 calling for a speedy end to the Middle East conflict. Furthermore, at the Copenhagen summit in December 1973 they decided to open a Euro-Arab dialogue. As part of the 'overall Mediterranean policy', in 1976 and 1977 cooperation agreements of indeterminate duration were signed with all the southern and eastern Mediterranean States. Attached to the agreements were what are known as financial protocols. These protocols covered a five-year period, providing financial aid to further the economic development of the Treaty partners. In all, four waves of finance protocols have been implemented up to 1996.

In 1980 the European Council adopted the Venice declaration, aiming to strengthen the dialogue between the PLO and Israel and find a middle way in the conflict between the two parties. Since the beginning of the 1990s there has been far greater European involvement in the region. The Arab-Israeli peace process, at times dynamic, offered new opportunities to make economic and political

progress. To support the process, the Union played a special part in multilateral aspects of the peace process, which began in this form with the Madrid conference in 1991.

EU trade with Mediterranean third countries

In ECU billion - 1994 - EUR 12

Imports

- Other 5%
- Morocco 10%
- Turkey 21%
- Malta Cyprus 5%
- Algeria 16%
- Tunisia 8%
- Libya 16%
- Egypt 8%
- Israel 11%

Exports

- Other 11%
- Morocco 10%
- Turkey 19%
- Algeria 10%
- Malta Cyprus 10%
- Tunisia 8%
- Libya 4%
- Egypt 8%
- Israel 20%

Source: Eurostat

However, new threats to Europe's security have also been identified. In comparison with Europe, the economies are underdeveloped, the annual per capita income ratio being 1 to 10. The population is growing rapidly, from 146 million in 1990 to what is expected to be more than 230 million in 2010. These developments can lead to social tension and further strengthen Islamic fundamentalism.

In response to these challenges, a new three-stage EU Mediterranean policy has been developed. In 1992 the Commission formulated the aim of a Euro-Maghreb partnership, following that up one year later with the formulation of the aim of long-term cooperation with Israel and their Mashreq Arab neighbours. Both initiatives led to the concept of an all-embracing Euro-Mediterranean partnership, which in turn provided the framework for the negotiations on association agreements with Israel, Morocco and Tunisia in 1995. The first concrete achievement of this concept of partnership was the Barcelona Conference of 27 and 28 November 1995, which was attended by all the EU Member States and the Mediterranean-rim countries (with the exception of Libya, Albania and the countries that were formerly part of Yugoslavia), together with Jordan and the autonomous Palestinian authorities. The Conference adopted a comprehensive programme to restructure Euro-Mediterranean relations grounded on three pillars.

The first pillar establishes a security partnership between the participating States based on peaceful dispute settlement mechanisms, arms control and other principles. The second sets out the aim for closer inter-regional economic relations, the key element being the establishing of a Euro-Mediterranean free-trade area by 2010. From then on, it will be possible to trade industrial products duty free on the trans-Mediterranean market, thus creating the largest free-trade area in the world, with over 600 million potential consumers. Finally, the third pillar adds social and cultural components to the partnership.

European involvement is being supported by financial aid amounting to ECU 4.6 billion for the period 1995-96. Moreover, the European Investment Bank has granted long-term loans on a similar scale. This financial assistance is intended to make possible the economic and political structural reforms in the southern partner countries necessary for the free-trade agreement. In 1992, average per capita GNP in the southern Mediterranean States was USD 1 500; in the EU, it was about USD 20 000. For income to be effectively raised in the partner region, economic growth of 6% would have to be achieved in the next 20 or 30 years. The EU is attempting to attain this goal by restraining the public sector and strengthening the private economy. With the help of special financial instruments, as well as the partnership agreements, the Union is also trying to encourage trade in goods within the region, which at present makes up only about 7% of the regional trade volume.

Sven Behrendt

Models of European integration

Literature from the European Union:
Klaus-Dieter Borchardt: European Integration. The origins and growth of the European Union.
Luxembourg 1995 (Cat. no.: CC-84-94-355-EN-C. Free).
Pascal Fontaine: Europe in Ten Points.
Luxembourg 1995 (Cat. no.: CC-90-95-623-EN-C. Free).

Since European policy has deliberately kept open the question as to the form the finished article should take, the significance of models for the development of the → European Union is based on four factors. Firstly, models bundle together participants' expectations regarding integration in a loose form which is easily adaptable to new conditions. They also justify the role of the Community institutions in terms of the process of building the Community (this is particularly true of the → European Parliament). They have an effect on European public opinion, permitting identification of the stage of development of the European Community with the political values and expectations of the citizens. Finally, models are an expression of the political recognition of the value of the integration process; they lend importance to European policy and have a stabilizing effect during periods when European decision-making becomes controversial.

Both the effects and the limits of the role of models became evident during the public debate on the ratification of the Treaty on European Union. In Germany, as in other Member States, the ideal of a federal European State turned into the nightmare of a 'superstate'. At the same time other traditional images, such as that of the Europe of sovereign states, experienced a revival in popularity, mainly, but not exclusively in the British debate on Europe. The effectiveness of the old models as guiding lights declined owing to increasing insecurity and doubts about the future shape of Europe, the degree of integration and the relationship between integration and the nation. Under stable conditions concepts such as European Union, which are open to interpretation, can serve to reinforce consensus. However, the degree of integration arrived at in Maastricht and the easing of external pressure following the end of the East-West conflict seemed to cause the opposite reaction; in the debate on the deepening of integration the concept only served to polarize opinion.

There are three strains of argument currently colouring the debate about models of the integration process. The first strain incorporates a gradual farewell to the idea of a 'United States of Europe' moving instead towards the much-lauded formula of an association of nations which emphasizes the continuing intermeshing of national sovereignty and supranational integration in a unique system. The second strain gains its intellectual nourishment from the change in the attitude of the citizens of Europe to the progress of integration, as documented by opinion polls. The way the people received the Treaty on European Union would indicate that their desire for integration has been satisfied. What, from a federalist point of view, appeared to be a stepping stone now seems to be more or less the end of the journey for many.

To a certain extent the third line of argument does not fit in with the other two, dealing as it does with the question of the pan-European value of an integration model. The prospect of → enlargement of the European Union to the East would cause the principle and the organizational forms of western European integration to be extended to cover large areas of the whole of Europe. The costs involved, the expected shift in the political balance of power and political consensus could, if linked to foreseeable consequences for the institutional structure, jeopardize the earlier development of the integration process. These are the reasons that have sparked off the fresh discussions about making Europe more flexible and differentiated, on variable geometry or a multi-speed Europe or even on concepts of a 'hard core' within Europe. These different levels of debate are simply many of the old arguments about models for European integration in new guises. None of the old models seem to have been consigned to the history books; they just reappear in a new form.

Federal State – Association of States – Confederation of States

Since work first started on the building of a European community at the beginning of the 1950s, a federal Europe or an association of European States have been the two basic terms used to describe completed integration. The ideal of an organization with supranational decision-making powers, as represented in all its various forms by the image of a federal State, was the light guiding the European policies of Italy, Germany and the Benelux States in particular. This was contrasted by the French view of a Europe of nation States, as expressed by de Gaulle, with intergovernmental cooperation between sovereign States providing the basis for integration.

The development of the European Community has moved beyond a simple division between these two models. In fact its structure displays characteristics from both. Although British policy towards Europe in the late 1980s deliberately returned to de Gaulle's rhetoric to justify the rejection of monetary union, a common foreign and security policy or a Community → social policy, Margaret Thatcher's great aim, and that of her successor, John Major, was to limit supranational growth, not reduce it. The nature of the State is more central to the current debate about the final form the Community should take. The federal tendency within the integration process, actually outlined in the Treaties of Rome, can be seen in a series of defining terms; throughout the last 30 or 40 years the image of a 'United States of Europe' has been sketched out, and another analogy has been the concept of the 'Federal Republic of Europe'. The model of the federal State and its various definitions imply the application of western democratic constitutional norms to the integration process. Federalist notions, of the division of responsibilities between the Union and the Member States, of the democratic quality of decision-making and of the guaranteeing of civil and individual rights resound as demands in the picture painted of a federal State.

Since the 1970s the concept of 'European Union' has been found in European communiqués and decisions as a way of bringing these models under one roof. Subsequent attempts to lend the concept substance, for instance in the Tindemans Report and the draft constitution prepared by the European Parliament in 1984, have proved to be political failures. On the face of it, by establishing the European Union the Maastricht Treaty achieved a long-held aim of European policy. However, the form of the Union has not resolved the conflict surrounding the concept. On the one hand, the changes in the Treaty, in particular, for example, the introduction of a new → decision-making procedure (co-decision) or rather of subsidiarity, have laid the model of European Union open to a more federal interpretation, whereas, on the other hand, the preamble describes the EU as, among other things, a 'union among the peoples of Europe'. What is more, the EU lacks the quality of international law of the European Community. The European Economic Community has become the more comprehensive European Community, yet the raising of three pillars in the EU Treaty underlines the parallel nature of supranational and inter-governmental structures. The → common foreign and security policy is substantially based on unanimity among the Member States; the option of taking qualified majority decisions on joint action has not yet been used. Similarly, by 1995 no permanent institution had been set up under the third pillar of the Treaty, apart from the Europol drugs unit, the forerunner of → Europol. By contrast, the introduction of citizenship of the Union and the right to participate in local and European elections at the place of residence have strengthened the idea of the EU as a State. The complaint frequently made by those working in European institutions that the replacement of the term 'Community' by the term 'Union' has obscured, linguistically speaking, the collective element of the integration process from the outside world is also part of this ambivalence. Thus the Maastricht Treaty and its controversial ratification have not produced a clearly defined model. The Community continues to be divided between the choice of supranational or intergovernmental development and this would seem to be the basis for any future construction. With the millenium beckoning the European Union will not fall apart, nor will it develop into the Federal State of Europe, as previously conceived.

Motives Since the 1950s there have been four aims underlying the formation of a Community: security, peace, freedom and prosperity. These are accompanied by the notion of economic growth, the desire for balanced convergence in economic and social matters and for integration to enable a European organization to make a contribution to civilization. As a consequence of the enlargement to the South in the 1980s the governments added the concepts 'democracy' and 'political stability'. These goals, underpinning the treaties and referring to traditional areas of State activity, indicate one underlying motive for integration. The retention of sovereignty, in the sense of the ability to act, appears to be the basic aim of the governments of the Member States. It is the attempt to confront involved international problems at a new level of capability, given the loss of power and substance of European politics following the two World Wars. Different facets of this motivation can be seen, in the world of the media, in the desire for 'self-assertion' or for the 'Europeanization of Europe'. Notions such as 'the Third Power' between the superpowers or the image of the 'civilian power' offered a direction, corresponding, at the same time, to the desire for a European identity which is supposed to result from the activities of the Community and its institutions. Other basic explanations view the unity of Europe as the response to the disintegration of and conflict between nation States. After 1989 these expectations of integration proved to be the guiding force behind the foreign policies of many of the former eastern bloc States of Central and Eastern Europe, being in effect the reverse side of the equally magnetic attraction of the economic and political success of western integration. Membership of the European Union became the crucial element of the 'return to Europe'.

European governments' reactions to the radical changes in Europe, German unification and the prospect of enlargement to the East are suffused by two differing motives. On the one hand, the radical changes have strengthened determination to 'advance European integration', as it says in the preamble to the EU Treaty, and thus to strengthen the links tying all Member States into the process of integration, thereby counteracting centrifugal tendencies following the break-up of the blocs. In this light the further deepening of the EU is seen as a prerequisite for its enlargement.

The process of European unification As well as offering statements of intent and motives, certain procedural concepts function as models lending a direction to any activity which extends beyond the situation at a given time. Some of the strategies listed below show that the path itself can become the goal of the unification process. This is true, particularly and most clearly, of the concept of integration itself.

The self-assessments of European movements often feature a conception of integration which, from a normative point of view, is very highly charged. Integration is viewed as the only contemporary response to the destructive powers

of ultranationalism. The analytical version of this is functionalism, which views integration as a problem-related response to a complex international structure. The overriding significance of functional integration lies in the forecasts regarding Europe made by its exponents, namely that the results and experiences of certain sectors intertwining will have a spill-over effect, building up momentum for a political community. Other procedural concepts have more of a supportive function, by increasing the plausibility of the statements of intent. Consequently, they become more attractive whenever the actual process of integration is stagnating. In this context two procedural strategies are especially important, both of which, it can be claimed, rank as concepts.

The pragmatically experimental strategy, which is a politico-administrative formulation rather than an academic formula, makes a case for a flexible approach to integration policy, if necessary outside the legal framework, so as to overcome impasses in the decision-making process. European Political Cooperation and the → European Monetary System are held up as shining examples of successful pragmatic experiments, with CFSP and cooperation on → justice and home affairs following in their footsteps, albeit from a position secured within the framework of the EU Treaty.

The second strategy, favouring integration conducted either in phases or by a part of the Community as a method of overcoming stagnation seems even richer in terms of concepts. 'Flexible integration' sets out to avoid the Community being modified by external forces while enabling integration to be deepened by a part of the Community as and when the time is right. This is the intellectual home of the notion of a 'hard core' of European States, which, starting from the founding members of the Community, envisages a ring of less integrated States around a highly integrated central structure. Other theories favour a graduated system with the degree of integration increasing as the States move towards the middle (the 'concentric circle' system), a solution based on a confederation around the EU or the restructuring and transformation of the European Economic Area (EEA) into a sort of waiting room outside full membership of the European Union. Both of these models attempt to view the enlargement and the integration of the European Union as parallel processes. By doing so they maintain the dynamism of the integration process, notwithstanding the great differences there would be within a European Union of as many as 25 or even 30 States.

Josef Janning

People's Europe

Treaty basis: No specific basis in the Treaty, this being an expression covering a wide range of measures in various policy areas with direct effect for the citizen; citizenship of the Union (Article 8) and Articles 8a–d of the EC Treaty; subsidiarity (Article 3b of the EC Treaty).

Aims: Freedom of establishment and residence; reducing the negative effects of the integration process; building up a positive image; identification with the European Union; encouraging mobility.

Instruments: Instruments for the appropriate policy areas; public information; support programmes.

Literature from the European Union:

European Commission: The European Union-What's in it for me?
Luxembourg 1996 (Cat. no.: CM-43-96-001-EN-C. Free).
European Commission: Citizens first. Information programme for the European citizen.
Luxembourg 1996 (Cat. no.: C1-99-96-229-EN-C. Free).
European Commission: Serving the European Union. A citizen's guide to the institutions of the European Union.
Luxembourg 1996 (Cat. no.: FX-89-95-939-EN-C. Free).

The citizens' relationship with the European Union is not easy to understand: on the one hand, people feel a social and psychological unease regarding a remote so-called 'superbureaucracy', whose actions seem impossible to control and direct in accordance with their own interests. On the other hand, they have high expectations of the Community's ability to take action, which – to judge by the state of progress on integration – are occasionally misplaced, as the conflict in the former Yugoslavia shows. Confusing abstract concepts, impersonality and the difficulty of assigning responsibility for Community action add to the public's sense of remoteness. There seems to be no way of hacking through the 'Euro-jungle'.

Present mood The discussions on the Treaty on European Union and the problems of finding bearings in a world no longer typified by bipolarization have revealed a downward trend in support for the process of European integration in the Member States. The high levels of support seen from the mid-1980s onwards, which can be explained partly by the vast information and publicity campaigns launched in connection with the completion of the European → single market and the favourable economic circumstances, began to tail off in the early 1990s. Whether this decline really reflects a rejection of the idea of integration – and hence an important turning point for further efforts towards European integration – or is just a cyclical low, will only emerge for certain in a few years when trends in public opinion are studied. On average, moves towards European integration continue to be supported by over half the population (*Source*: Eurobarometer).

In the beginning, moves towards integration were sustained by a consensus of the elite and the basic consent of the people. With the advance of European integration, ever more redistribution decisions were taken and the number of people noticeably affected by Community regulations increased. The rising tide of Community-level legislation created a greater need for people to be given more detailed information about European policy decisions and more influence over these decisions. The European level was seen as the level at which policy was made. Different positions and opinions in the political debate led to a differentiation of public attitudes to European integration. This is a normal democratic process, part of the culture of democratic discussion, which is a necessary part of the development of an informed opinion and increasingly involves a European dimension.

UNION CITIZENSHIP

What benefits does the Maastricht Treaty offer the general public? In particular new rights and freedoms. They derive from Union citizenship, which is automatically enjoyed by all nationals of Member States.

★ The right to reside anywhere in the EU is substantially enhanced

★ Since 1994 Union citizens are entitled to vote and stand for election in whichever Union country they reside. The same rights are gradually being extended to cover local council elections.

★ In countries outside the European Union, Union citizens can seek diplomatic and consular assistance from any other EU Member State if their own country does not have a representative there.

★ The right to present petitions to the European Parliament and the right to apply to the Ombudsman are now enshrined in the Treaty.

★ The European Union must respect fundamental and human rights as guaranteed by the European Human Rights Convention and as deriving from the constitutional traditions common to the Member States.

European integration – in the interests of the citizen from the outset

The history of European integration is marked by the search for the most effective instruments and mechanisms for the peaceful coexistence of States and the people who live in them – especially where there is a clash of interests. The idea of a people's Europe was the force behind the creation of the European Community. The rather simplistic view that the EEC was created primarily to serve the world of business ignores the fact that the basic concept was concerned with achieving a steady improvement in living and working conditions for the ordinary person. Once the initial stages of integration were complete, every effort was made to give a codified form to the attempts to achieve a people's Europe. Milestones along the way included the Tindemans Report (1974), the introduction of direct elections to the → European Parliament (1979), the Adonnino Committee which paved the way for the Single European Act, the many programmes to promote mobility and exchange, the concept of citizenship of the Union as laid down in the Maastricht Treaty and a whole series of regulations to guarantee a special level of protection for the citizen (e.g. health protection, consumer protection, etc.).

Specific measures on Union citizenship

The relationship between the citizen and the European Union is a mutually dependent process. There are a whole series of regulations which define the relationship between the Union and its citizens. Free movement of persons and freedom of establishment and residence are established, at the latest, with the completion of the internal market – although this is not yet completely finalized. In a bid to create a genuine people's Europe, the Maastricht Treaty has rationalized existing regulations and introduced some new aspects. It also specifies what rights citizens of the Union should enjoy: the right to live where they wish (Article 8a); the right to vote and stand for election to the European Parliament and in municipal elections irrespective of the country of residence (Article 8b); diplomatic or consular protection in a non-member country by another Member State of the Union if their own Member State is not represented there (Article 8c); the right to petition the European Parliament on matters coming within the Community's fields of activity (Article 8d); and the possibility of complaining to an ombudsman appointed by Parliament on matters affecting the administration of the Union (Article 138e). The Treaty on European Union also refers for the first time to political parties, which, among other things, should contribute to forming 'a European awareness' (Article 138a).

The introduction of the concept of citizenship of the Union into the Treaty is an attempt to create a more direct link between the citizen and the Union, which often seems to its people to be just an abstract concept. To be a Union citizen it is necessary to be a citizen of a Member State; however, it is an interesting fact that only the rights of Union citizenship are set out in so many words, and none of the duties.

The principle of subsidiarity, which was established in the Maastricht Treaty (Article 3b), is also intended to bring the European Union closer to its people.

Conclusions: the problem of democratic legitimacy Policies which fail to take account of the interests of the people have no legitimacy. However, a political process which carries a large number of citizens with it and displays geographical and cultural diversity will make heavy weather of creating structures to which the people can relate directly. So to begin with, the political system of the European Union was based on the Member States as decision-makers. As the integration process increased in scope and intensity, particularly in the 1980s and 1990s, the power of decision shifted towards the European Parliament. The Maastricht debate lamented above all the lack of democratic legitimacy.

Decisions on European policy have hitherto had a dual basis for their legitimacy: the European Parliament and national parliaments. The European Parliament has been directly elected by the people of the Union since 1979. However, at present it has only limited rights to share in decision-making on European legislative acts. Moreover, Members of the European Parliament are recruited on the basis of national structures, and voting reflects national issues. Links between MEPs and their constituencies and feedback between European party officials and national decision-making processes are also difficult to organize, if only because of the scheduling of plenaries and committee meetings.

The European Union's political actions are still in many cases dominated by the → Council of the European Union, the second line of democratic legitimacy. The increase in the number of areas in which majority decisions could be adopted in the Council and hence in which Member States' representatives could be overruled in a vote, and the greater powers of co-decision awarded to the European Parliament, heightened the problem of the democratic legitimacy of Community action (→ decision-making process). The question of how national elected representatives could better bring their influence to bear on Community legislation, and ways of strengthening the European Parliament, are therefore also topics for discussion in the run-up to the 1996 Conference. European political power will have to be kept in check – at least until further notice – by these two legitimizing pillars. The 1996 → Intergovernmental Conference will count among its tasks the striking of a better balance between the pillars on which legitimacy is based.

The European Union is in a period of transition. The European Parliament still does not really have enough powers in the legislative process to provide the European citizen with a direct source of legitimacy and national parliaments can only claim to do so indirectly. Moreover, it is one of the sacrosanct principles of democracy that the perception of the duties of the State and the exercise of the authority of the State are matters for the people (German Constitutional Court discussing

Maastricht). Attempts to strengthen the powers of the European Parliament are occasionally countered with the argument that as yet there is no European people.

Prospects: the citizen still at the heart of unification The Maastricht Treaty led to a hotting up of the debate about the European Union's relations with its citizens. The present discussions add a further three points.

1. How can the European Union's decision-making system be made more open, easier to understand and hence more transparent for the ordinary person? European policy should be made less impersonal. The distribution of responsibilities at national or European level needs to be rationalized.

2. Should a list of basic rights be included in a constitution or similar document, to guarantee the citizen certain rights?

3. The European bodies need to provide better information. The steady advance of integration, the encroachment of European politics on the life of the people, and the differentiation of the integration process also demand different approaches to information.

Melanie Piepenschneider

Regional policy

Treaty basis: Preamble, Articles 2 and 3, Article 39, Articles 123–125 and 130a–e of the EC Treaty.

Aims: Strengthening the economic and social cohesion of the Union, particularly by means of regional, structural, social, agricultural and labour-market measures.

Instruments: The three Structural Funds (the European Regional Development Fund (ERDF), the European Social Fund (ESF) and the European Agriculture Guidance and Guarantee Fund (EAGGF, Guidance Section); the Financial Instrument for Fisheries Guidance (FIFG); the Cohesion Fund for Member States whose per capita GDP is less than 90% of the EC average, to provide funding for projects in the fields of the environment and trans-European transport networks; European Investment Bank (EIB); the European Coal and Steel Community (ECSC).

Budget: Planned for 1994 (commitments): Structural Funds: ECU 21.3 billion (29% of the EU budget), comprising ERDF: ECU 9.0 billion, ESF: ECU 6.5 billion, EAGGF Guidance Section: ECU 3.3 billion, FIFG: ECU 0.4 billion, Community initiatives: ECU 1.7 billion, other measures: ECU 0.4 billion, Cohesion Fund: ECU 1.9 billion (2.5%). EIB (not forming part of the EC budget): loans within the Community in 1993: ECU 17.7 billion.

Literature from the European Union:

European Commission: Europe at the service of regional development.
Luxembourg 1996 (Cat. no.: CX-94-96-300-EN-C. Free).
European Commission: The European Union's Cohesion Fund.
Luxembourg 1995 (Cat. no.: CC-85-94-753-EN-C. Free).
European Commission: Women, players in regional development.
Luxembourg 1996 (Cat. no.: CX-95-96-099-EN-C. ECU 7.00).
European Commission: Structural Funds and Cohesion Fund 1994-99:
Regulations and commentary.
Luxembourg 1996 (Cat. no.: CX-88-95-121-EN-C. ECU 1.00).
European Commission: Europe 2000+: Cooperation for European territorial development.
Luxembourg 1994 (Cat. no.: CX-86-94-117-EN-C. ECU 16.00).

The economic and social disparities within the → European Union (EU) are considerable. Dominant among the structural problems are regional imbalances. These are reflected in major income differences between the regions of the European Union and in large-scale unemployment problems. As well as the regional differences within individual Member States there may be huge differences in the performance of the relevant national economies. As the Community expanded southwards the prosperity differential widened considerably, since the new Member States included some much less economically developed regions. Since then, eastern Germany, with its major economic and structural

problems, has also become part of the EU. Finland, Austria and Sweden, members of the EU since 1995, are by contrast prosperous countries although they do have some structural problems. The Union's economically less developed regions include Greece, Portugal, large parts of Spain, southern Italy and Sardinia, Ireland, Northern Ireland, Corsica, the French overseas *départements* and the new German *Länder*. The problem of regional backwardness is made more difficult in the Union by the particular difficulties of what were formerly prosperous areas struggling to manage the necessary restructuring process to move from declining industries – such as coalmining, steel, shipbuilding and textiles – to industrial and service branches of the economy which have a future. Again, the three new Member States present, on a Union scale, only isolated instances of poorly-developed regions.

Per capita gross domestic product 1993 in purchasing power standards

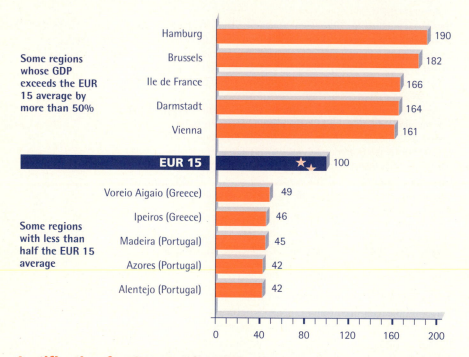

Some regions whose GDP exceeds the EUR 15 average by more than 50%

Hamburg	190
Brussels	182
Ile de France	166
Darmstadt	164
Vienna	161

EUR 15 100

Some regions with less than half the EUR 15 average

Voreio Aigaio (Greece)	49
Ipeiros (Greece)	46
Madeira (Portugal)	45
Azores (Portugal)	42
Alentejo (Portugal)	42

0   40   80   120   160   200

Justification for Community action There was very early recognition that there was a need, on the one hand, to cushion the impact of economic integration on workers and particularly hard-hit economic sectors and, on the other, to achieve a financial balance between prosperous and disadvantaged regions. As early as the Treaties of Rome, it was noted that measures should be taken to combat the adverse social and agricultural consequences of integration. The need for specific regional-policy instruments became more apparent with the accession of Denmark, Ireland and the United Kingdom to the Community in 1973, leading finally in 1975 to the introduction of the Community's regional policy.

Structural policy approach The Community's structural policy has a dual approach of offering financial incentives and coordinating the policy of Member States. Regional policy also involves monitoring the subsidies provided at national level to ensure that there is no distortion of competition. The Structural Funds are the heart of European structural policy. The European Social Fund (→ social policy) was established as early as 1960 and over the years has become an ever more powerful instrument of European labour-market policy. The EAGGF (→ agricultural policy) followed in 1962, its Guidance Section having the role of stimulating structural adjustment. In 1975, the European Regional Development Fund (ERDF) was founded, a major consideration being to prevent the new Member State, the United Kingdom – an importer of agricultural produce not confronted with the severe structural problems in agriculture plaguing other countries – ending up as a net contributor to unsuccessful agricultural policies. Ever since then, the Community has provided financial aid for the development of disadvantaged regions.

In addition to the Structural Funds, there are a number of other Community financial instruments for implementing structural policy: the Cohesion Fund for economically weak Member States (since 1993), the Financial Instrument for Fisheries Guidance (FIFG) created in 1993 and the loans provided by the → European Investment Bank (EIB) and the European Coal and Steel Community. From very early on, these structural-policy funds were to a very large degree allocated independently from each other and it was therefore not possible to ensure that one subsidy did not duplicate or cancel out another. For a number of years now, the Community has sought to intermesh all structural-policy measures more closely in order to produce a 'homogeneous' structural policy placing considerable emphasis on the regional policy objective.

The → European Commission was required under the 1986 Single European Act to present an appropriate comprehensive proposal. The Council (→ Council of the European Union) approved this reform of the Structural Funds after consulting the → European Parliament and the → Economic and Social Committee: this decision required unanimity. In the light of experience gained thereafter, the provisions were again reformed in the summer of 1993 and, in the shape of the FIFG, a separate financial instrument was created for → fisheries policy. Individual implementing decisions on grants under the Structural Funds are proposed by the Commission in cooperation with the European Parliament and adopted by the Council of Ministers by a qualified-majority vote.

In the Treaty on European Union, the Member States decided in February 1992 to establish by the end of 1993 a Cohesion Fund to benefit Spain, Portugal, Greece and Ireland. By providing subsidies for environmental and transport projects (in the latter case, trans-European networks) it was intended to boost regional development and enhance links between the periphery and the centre. In the spring of 1993, the Fund was established on the basis of a provisional regulation. The Treaty also laid down, in a structural-policy context, explicit consultative rights to be enjoyed by the then still to be created → Committee of the Regions.

Unemployment: marked regional disparities

Unemployment rates in regions of the Union (%, 1994)

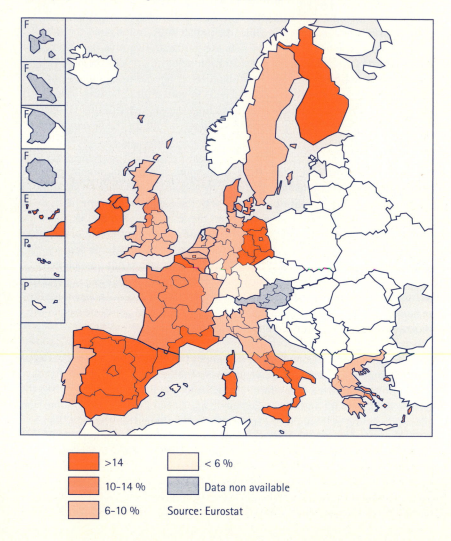

🟧	>14	⬜	< 6 %
🟧	10-14 %	⬛	Data non available
🟧	6-10 %	Source: Eurostat	

Principles of structural policy Following the 1988 reform of the Structural Funds on the expanded basis established by the Council in July 1993 to cover the years 1994-99, the Community's structural policy continues to concentrate on five priority areas, although some of the objectives have changed since 1988:

1. Stimulation of regions lagging behind in development. A region is considered to be inadequately developed if per capita GDP is below 75% of the EC average.
2. Conversion of regions, border regions and smaller areas badly hit by industrial decline. In such areas, the originally dominant industrial activity is clearly in decline and unemployment is above the EC average.

3. Combating long-term unemployment and easing the entry into the labour market of young people and those at risk of exclusion.

4. Facilitating workers' adaptation to industrial change and changes in the production systems.

5. Stimulating the development of rural areas by accelerating the adjustment of agricultural structures and using structural adjustment including adaptation of fisheries structures. The preconditions for the granting of aid are that the area should be characterized by a low population density, a high proportion of the labour force employed in agriculture, low levels of agricultural earnings and a below average overall regional economy. A result of the accession negotiations with the four EFTA countries was the addition of a sixth objective to stimulate regions with extremely low population densities. This criterion applies where the population density is below eight persons per square kilometre. The regions concerned – in Scandinavia – are to be assisted in the same way as Objective 1 regions. This objective will be re-examined when the Structural Fund regulations are reviewed in 1999.

Community action is subject to the subsidiarity principle whereby measures may only supplement national, local and other action taken and must be restricted to cases in which the initiator's own resources are inadequate.

Implementation of accepted measures EC structural incentive measures must comply with the applicable Community support framework (CSF). CSFs are drawn up by the Commission in negotiations with national authorities and are based in the case of Objectives 1, 2 and 5b on regional development plans compiled by national governments in cooperation with the competent regional and local bodies. They must contain socio-economic and environmental impact analyses for the region/subregion concerned, the strategy to be followed, the main aspects to be assisted and an assessment of the expected effects on employment and the environment, together with details of how the requested Community funds are to be spent, broken down by individual finance institutions. In the case of Objective 1 regions, they must also include details of national funding made available. With regard to Objectives 3 and 4, national action plans drawn up by the Member States form the basis of the CSF. These plans also contain a description of the situation, a review of the appropriate labour-market policy strategies, the use to be made of the requested funding and the effects expected. CSFs cover the objectives and main emphases, the nature and term of intervention by the Community and a financing plan showing the extent and source of Community funds. In most cases, they are put into action by means of so-called operational programmes grouping together a range of projects – provided that these supplement one another. These programmes may be drawn up by national authorities or developed at the initiative of the Commission (Community initiatives).

CSFs may, however, also involve individual major projects or call for global grants. In the latter case, a special body may be entrusted with monitoring the implementation of certain measures.

Measures The ERDF is involved in particular in productive investment and in economically relevant investment and infrastructure projects in fields which include health and education, and the trans-European networks for transport, telecommunications and energy. In order to exploit the local development potential of a given region, to stimulate innovation and tourism, and to provide service facilities, the ERDF can support small businesses with both investment and operating aid and take part in research and development activities. The first priority for the ESF is combating unemployment and this includes measures to make it easier to enter the labour market, to encourage equality of opportunity, to develop vocational qualifications and to create new jobs. In Objective 1 regions, expansion and improvement of general and vocational training – particularly training of instructors – can also be subsidized. The Guidance Section of the EAGGF encourages structural measures in agriculture as well as the restructuring of agricultural production and secondary activities for farmers.

As specific instruments of structural policy, and in line with a proposal by the Commission, 13 approved Community initiatives in seven different problem areas are receiving aid from the Structural Funds: inter-regional cooperation and cross-border networks, rural development, most remote regions, employment and improvement of qualifications, industrial change, urban crisis areas and restructuring of fisheries. Using the Cohesion Fund, the Community aids investment to improve the environment and to expand the trans-European transport networks in Greece, Spain, Ireland and Portugal. The FIFG not only funds special structural measures in the field of fisheries itself, but also supports projects involving agriculture and the processing and marketing of the relevant products. In Objective 1 areas, the Structural Funds and the FIFG usually cover up to 75% (in properly justified exceptional cases, up to 85%) of overall costs and at least 50% of public-sector expenditure. In the other regions, the Union pays up to 50% of the total cost but this must represent at least 25% of public expenditure on stimulatory measures. To this end, regions are classified in terms of the severity of the regional problem and the financial resources available to the Member State concerned. The EIB provides loans for infrastructure investment, usually at commercial rates. At the request of the Commission, the EIB also provides loans drawn on the funds of the new Community instrument (NCI) (→ budgets) for which interest subsidies may also be provided by the Commission in order to make the loan cheaper. The 'Edinburgh facility' called for additional funding to be made available for infrastructure projects in 1993 and 1994 in order to achieve an economic upturn in Europe, particularly in the fields of transport, telecommunications and energy – preferably relating to trans-European networks – and in the fields of environmental protection and urban renewal.

Financial resources After the February 1988 decision of the → European Council, the structural resources of the Community were doubled in real terms between 1987 and 1993. At the Edinburgh Summit in December 1992, it was decided again to greatly boost these funds between 1993 and 1999. At 1992 prices, it was intended that the Structural Funds (including the FIFG) should be able to commit ECU 24 billion in 1997 and ECU 27.4 billion in 1999. Of the above, about 70% is destined for Objective 1 regions. These resources are supplemented by the Cohesion Fund which controlled ECU 1.5 billion in 1993 and is due to have resources of ECU 2.5 billion in 1997 and ECU 2.6 billion in 1999. Structural-policy funding is distributed on an indicative basis by individual Member State and by objective. This distribution shows that the problems of regional under-development continue to be accorded the greatest priority.

Assessment There can be no doubt that more concentrated and better coordinated measures have made Community structural policy more efficient. More recently, the grant procedure has again been somewhat simplified and the Commission is encouraging Member States to make greater use of the option of simplifying the procedure by compiling a single document covering strategies and programmes. The considerable increase in the resources available to the Funds is also a better reflection of the severity of the problems. However, doubts are increasingly being voiced that the ability of the regions being stimulated to absorb these funds may already have been exceeded and that the intensity of stimulation activities does not give enough incentive to local initiative. Criticism has also been heard that the Commission, through Community initiatives, is increasingly influencing the shape of regional policy and thus violating the subsidiarity principle, particularly since a series of initiatives could also be included in the common support frameworks. Finally, there is concern about the establishment of ever more new funds and financing instruments, given that this hampers the transparency of structural-policy action. Moreover, it does not solve the fundamental problem of the EU's entire structural policy: in the final analysis, it is merely a substitute for an efficient system of general regional financial adjustment. Such a system, however, would require a level of consensus and political integration which is probably not achievable in the foreseeable future.

Bernhard Seidel

Research and technology

Treaty basis: Article 55 of the ECSC Treaty; Articles 2a and 4-11 of the Eurotam Treaty; Articles 41(a) and 130f-130p of the EC Treaty.

Aims: To improve the industrial and technological competitiveness of European industry, especially in the technologies of the future. This initially entails agreeing on common R&D objectives. To promote economic development in the European Union on a targeted basis, there is to be greater concentration and coordination of R&D policy in future. In the long term, R&D objectives are to be aligned on the objectives of the 1993 White Paper on growth, competitiveness and employment.

Instruments: Framework programme for research, technological development and demonstration; Joint Research Centre; European Commission's special research programmes; Eureka.

Budget: The resources allocated to the fourth framework programme for research, technological development and demonstration for the period from 1994 to 98 are ECU 12.3 billion plus a reserve of ECU 1 billion.

Literature from the European Union:

European Commission: Inventing tommorrow. Europe's research at the service of its people. Preliminary guidelines for the Fifth Framework Programme.
Luxembourg 1996 (Cat. no.: CG-NA-16961-EN-C. Free).

Cannell, William/Dankbaar, Ben: Technology management and public policy in the European Union.
Luxembourg 1996 (Cat. no.: CG-93-95-217-EN-C. ECU 36.00).

European Commission: EC research funding: A guide for applicants.
Luxembourg 1996 (Cat. no.: CG-NA-16-729-EN-C. ECU 20.00).

European Commission: Dissemination and optimization of the results of research activities.
Luxembourg 1996 (Cat. no.: CD-94-96-073-EN-C. Free).

European Commission: Research and technology: The fourth framework programme (1994-98).
Luxembourg 1996 (Cat. no.: CG-NA-16-620-EN-C. ECU 7.00).

European Commission: Community research and technological development policy: The main issues at stake in the European Union's fourth framework programme for research and technological development (1994-98).
Luxembourg 1995 (Cat. no.: CG-NA-15-637-EN-C. Free).

The → European Commission has attached top priority to research and technological development since 1993. Given the growing technological gap in relation to our American and Japanese competitors, a major research effort is felt to be vital for international competitiveness. The weakness of European firms on world markets are manifest not only in traditional industries but also in high-tech industries. The background to action by the → European Union is low growth and a structural unemployment problem, exacerbated in the early 1990s by a Europe-wide recession. And visibly not enough was being done about all this. The formal backdrop to the new policy on research and technology was provided by the 1986 Single European Act and the Treaty on European Union; as a result of these, Articles 130f to 130p prescribed an objective of reinforcing the economic and technological basis of European industry. Accordingly, both the European Commission and the Member States are keen that Europe's potential should be better exploited. At the end of 1993, as a practical reaction to the economic situation, the Commission published its White Paper on growth, competitiveness and employment to provide food for thought and pointers for action for economic development at local, national and Community level so that Europe's economies can be ready to face international competition and generate the millions of missing jobs. In this connection the White Paper attaches great importance both to research and technology and to telecommunications, seen as having major significance for the future and requiring considerable expansion in support of industrial competitiveness. The Commission set out its stance in the fourth framework programme for research, technological development and demonstration (1994-98), approved by the → European Council and the → European Parliament in December 1993 with resources of ECU 12.3 billion plus a reserve of ECU 1 billion. Following on from the third framework programme (1990-94), the resources of which were boosted from ECU 5.7 billion to ECU 6.6 billion in December 1992, this has raised the resources devoted to research to unprecedented levels.

Development With the establishment of the European Economic Community and the European Atomic Energy Community, research and technology acquired the status of a fully-fledged Community policy. This was particularly important in the nuclear field, where the objective was to use Community policy on research and uranium supplies to develop a nuclear industry that was both competitive and autonomous on the international scene. A Joint Research Centre and a Euratom Supply Agency were also established. At the Hague Summit in 1969, the Heads of State or Government agreed to broaden the research policy in order to avoid competitive weaknesses and dependence. In 1974 the European Community, acting under Article 235 of the EEC Treaty, introduced research programmes on a shared-cost basis, involving research centres and industrial firms. The adoption of the 1984 Esprit programme (European strategic programme for research in information technologies) to promote basic research in micro-electronics was a qualitative leap forward in European research policy. In the 1990s R&TD gained in significance as a result of the accelerating pace of technical progress and worldwide competition. As the → single market approached completion, so the concept of a European Technology Community attracted growing attention. Despite occasional wide differences of opinion between the Commission and some of the Member States, which prompted both Community action and the establishment of Eureka (based on technology initiatives combining the private sector and individual States), policy here was formalized in the 1986 Single European Act and in the parts of the 1993 Maastricht Treaty on European Union devoted to the Community as such. Community action and financing have been provided for by the framework programmes for research, technological development and demonstration since 1984.

New horizons The new horizons mapped out by the Commission in the fourth framework programme and the White Paper on growth, competitiveness and employment call more energetically than ever before for efforts to promote international technological development. The fourth framework programme in particular sets out to make up Europe's research deficit, which in the European Commission's view stems especially from lack of funds and lack of coordination. Telecommunications, information technology and innovation hold the keys to Europe's economic future, and the Commission is putting priority focus on them through a variety of initiatives, programmes and financial mechanisms. To boost the competitiveness of European industry and secure growth and employment, the Commission's White Paper calls for the establishment of trans-European networks not only for transport and energy but also for telecommunications and information. Innovation and the creation of trans-European telecom networks will open up new markets. The aim is to extend the common information area on which the European internal market truly depends for its success.

To sum up The dramatic challenge to Europe's efficiency thrown down by the rapid pace of technological change, international competition in high tech and competitive inadequacies raised the need for a qualitative reorientation of the European Union's efforts in the field of research and technology policy. Past mishaps such as the failure of the JESSI programme (which was to develop Europe's semi-conductor manufacturing industry) and of the HDTV initiative must not be allowed to recur, and small businesses must be more closely involved in the research effort.

Another important factor in the Community perspective is that a promising research and technology policy must be backed up by political initiatives in other areas, and especially competition, industrial, social and labour-market policies. Unfortunately, political friction is generated when measures in these areas are linked up to each other. The key point is that research and technology initiatives, often chastised as being *dirigiste* industrial-policy measures, cannot be reconciled with fundamental competitive free-market convictions. Against the backdrop of decades of dispute between free marketeers and the proponents of the command economy, the necessary efforts to modernize the European economy are liable to get bogged down in pro- and anti-subsidy arguments, and all sense of direction and dynamism is lost. It follows that the thing that matters most is to bolster Europe's technological strong points with a common strategic effort combining every form of political action and every form of instrument in a properly coordinated manner.

Jürgen Turek

The single market

Treaty basis: Article 2 of the EC treaty (establishment of a common market);
Article 3(a) of the EC treaty (elimination of customs duties, quantitative restrictions and
other trade measures with equivalent effects); Article 3(c) (abolition of obstacles to the free
movement of goods, persons, services and capital); Articles 7a–7c (establishment of the
internal market by 1992, procedural rules and derogations); Articles 3(d) and 100c (entry
and movement of persons in the internal market and uniform visa arrangements); and
Article 8a (right of Union citizens to live anywhere in the Union).

Literature from the European Union:
European Commission: The single market and tomorrow's Europe.
London, Luxembourg 1996 (Cat. no.: C-1-01-96-010-EN-C. ECU 12).
European Commission: The single market.
Luxembourg 1996 (Cat. no.: CC-95-96-318-EN-C. Free).
European Commission: Services of general interest in Europe.
Luxembourg 1996 (Cat. no.: CM-98-96-897-EN-C. Free).

The 'official' deadline for the completion of the single market expired some time ago
– on 31 December 1992. But this chapter in the history of European integration is
far from closed; the achievement of the 'four freedoms' (free movement of people,
goods, services and capital in the single market) is an ongoing process.

In the period following the setting up of the EEC, significant progress was made in
terms of negative integration, i.e. elimination of customs duties and quantitative
restrictions. However, only slow progress was made towards achieving the free
movement of goods characterizing a common market, and securing the four
freedoms. The free movement of goods and production factors was often hindered
by national regulations designed to protect consumers, public health or the
environment. Only a very small fraction of these regulations were harmonized by
the procedure for approximation of laws (provided for by Article 100 of the
EC Treaty), which required unanimity. Differences in diplomas showing vocational
qualifications further restricted freedom of movement for people, a diverse array
of supervisory and other regulations presented an obstacle to the provision of
services across national borders, and restrictions on capital movements distorted
investment flows and decisions.

Commission White Paper In June 1985, in response to what appeared to
be a relative standstill in integration initiatives and fears, in some cases backed by

evidence, about Europe's inability to compete with Japan and the United States, the European Commission presented its White Paper on completion of the internal market. This was a detailed and precise programme-cum-timetable for 270 legislative measures deemed essential for the completion of the internal market. The White Paper was divided into three main sections on physical, technical and (indirect) tax barriers. The greater part of the measures were aimed at eliminating technical barriers. None of the proposals concerned topics which were addressed at Maastricht and which are closely related to the internal market project, such as social Europe, convergence of economic and monetary policies or harmonization of direct taxes.

Majority voting Speeding up the legislative process was also of central importance to the attempt to build a genuine single market. Accordingly, under Article 100a of the EC treaty, the → Council of the European Union adopts most single market legislation by qualified majority vote. In many cases, the fear of being outvoted is enough to make individual Member States more willing to compromise. However, some key areas, such as freedom of movement (in part at least) and, in particular, tax harmonization, are explicitly excluded, which means that unanimity is still required.

The → European Parliament's role in the → European Union's legislative process has been considerably expanded through the introduction of two new → decision-making procedures: the 'cooperation' procedure (Article 189c of the EC treaty) and the 'co-decision' procedure (Article 189b of the EC treaty). Parliament may now, with an absolute majority of its members, reject a common position adopted by a qualified majority in the Council. Parliament may then be overruled only by a unanimous decision in the Council if the procedure laid down in Article 189c is used, and not at all if the Article 189b procedure is used. Thus, in March 1995, the Directive on the patenting of bio-technological inventions was thrown out by Parliament, despite agreement in the Conciliation Committee, and the Council was powerless to overturn its decision.

Costs and benefits The single market relies for its impact on a series of 'knock-on effects' at a number of levels. For example, the abolition of border controls and formalities reduces operating costs for businesses. Economies of scale are possible thanks to the sheer size of the single market; increased competition between firms leads to rationalization and greater specialization, increasing the EU's international competitiveness.

In preparation for a comprehensive evaluation report on the effects of the single market programme and as a basis for the establishment of a new 'single market agenda', the Commission presented 39 sectoral studies in 1996. The 1993 White Paper on growth, competitiveness and employment already contained the interim results: the completion of the internal market had led to the creation of nine million new jobs between 1986 and 1990; GDP had grown half a percentage point faster than it would have done otherwise and trade in the hitherto 'protected' industries had doubled. The problem with such figures is that it is difficult to know exactly what can be attributed to the completion of the single market. What is more, regional variations, ecological costs and social effects have to be taken into consideration as well as the overall consequences. For instance, the flanking policies and large amounts of money for the Structural Funds and Cohesion Fund that are needed to offset, or at least cushion, the negative effects of the single market, are also important factors in the calculation. However, apart from financial transfers, the staggered entry into force of directives and the introduction of derogations are also important considerations.

Strategies The single market project uses two complementary strategies to create one big common market. One strategy involves the rejection of 'institutional' harmonization in favour of approximation of a minimum number of laws to enforce the basic safety standards required to protect public health, the environment and the consumer – activities which by and large used to be the preserve of the Member States. The other strategy involves increasing the amount of 'functional' harmonization, based on 'mutual recognition' – a principle which has been endorsed by the → European Court of Justice on a number of occasions.

Since the end of the transitional period, there has been a conflict of interests in non-Community areas between the Member States' residual powers on the one hand and free trade in goods on the other. While Article 30 of the EC treaty has always prohibited 'all trading rules enacted by Member States which are capable of hindering, directly or indirectly, actually or potentially, intra-Community trade' (ECJ judgment in *Dassonville*, 1974), such measures may be allowed on grounds of public health, consumer protection, public morality, public policy or public security, or the environment. However, recourse to Article 36 of the EC treaty, allowing national measures which may restrict trade, is possible only if such measures are not applied in a discriminatory fashion, are necessary and proportionate, and constitute the least interventionist means of achieving the desired effect.

Mutual recognition Trade between the Member States is often restricted by deliberate obstructions masquerading as safety regulations. In the dispute over the imports of the French liqueur *Cassis de Dijon,* the Court of Justice found the import ban was an excessively restrictive way of protecting consumers – the declared aim of the measure – and ruled that clear labelling, providing information on the alcohol content in this case, was sufficient. This ruling introduced mutual recognition as one of the guiding principles for the creation of the single market – and not only in goods. It also applies to goods from non-member countries, once they are already in free circulation in one of the Member States. The Court has since confirmed the *Cassis de Dijon* judgment in numerous other cases concerning the purity of beer, milk products, sausages and durum wheat pasta, for example. However, it has not always given priority to free movement of goods. In some cases, it has attached greater importance to 'mandatory requirements' (e.g. deposit-bottle judgment).

In cases where the principle of mutual recognition cannot be applied, the 'new approach to technical harmonization and standards', introduced by the Commission in 1985, takes precedence. This means that the Council adopts directives laying down basic and relatively general safety requirements designed to protect public health, the environment and the consumer. Technical details are dealt with through European standards ($\rightarrow$ consumer policy).

European standards The two organizations dealing with European standards, CEN for general standards and Cenelec for electro-technical ones, are composed of members of the national standardization organizations. As in the Council, a qualified majority is needed to adopt a decision. And, like the Member States in the EU's legislative procedure, they are required to withdraw national standards which are not compatible with European standards. The 'new approach' assumes that a product manufactured in accordance with European standards must meet the basic safety requirements laid down in the directive. Manufacturers may still choose not to observe European standards, but in that case, the burden of proof is reversed: it is up to them to prove that their product is safe. Thus, like national standards, the standards established by CEN and Cenelec are not binding; compliance is voluntary. Almost 300 technical committees are currently working on 10 000 standardization projects.

To prevent the emergence of new trade barriers and promote mutual recognition, the Member States have undertaken to give the Commission prior notice of all draft technical regulations and standards. This is laid down in Directive 83/189, which has been extended on numerous occasions.

Progress with implementation All but 11 pieces of the legislation proposed in the Commission's White Paper have been passed – a total of 259 measures, spread over 275 legal instruments. While the dismantling of technical barriers went smoothly and a satisfactory temporary solution was found to the problems posed by taxation, eliminating the physical barriers is still proving to be difficult.

Amongst the successes in relation to core single-market issues are: the 'new approach' directives referred to above, the removal of restrictions on capital movements, the opening up of public procurement (building and supply contracts, accounting for 8% of the EU's GNP) and the extension of EU regulations to cover hitherto excluded industries (energy, water, transport and telecommunications), liberalization of financial services (e.g. banks and insurance) and transport (road cabotage and air transport), mutual recognition of higher education diplomas and vocational qualifications, the long-awaited establishment of a European type-approval procedure for motor vehicles, the establishment of a European Agency for the Evaluation of Medicinal Products in London and an Office for Harmonization in the Internal Market (trade marks and designs) in Alicante.

Provisional solution for taxes The White Paper's approach to eliminating tax barriers in the single market has proved not to be politically feasible in the medium term. The approach involved starting to tax in the country of origin rather than the country of destination with input tax deductible on international transactions, setting bands for national taxes and continuing to distribute tax revenues according to the country-of-destination principle by means of a clearing system. However, so that border controls could be eliminated on schedule, some very effective transitional arrangements were introduced. Under these arrangements, due to expire at the end of 1996, private transactions (excluding purchases of motor vehicles) were already to be taxed in accordance with the land-of-origin principle, while corporate international transactions continued to be taxed in the country of destination on the basis of the importer's and exporter's delivery records. By and large, the country-of-destination principle also continues to apply to excise duties. Minimum rates for the various excise duties and for VAT have been set – 15% for the standard rate and 5% for the reduced rate.

Physical barriers: the last hurdle Significant progress has been made towards dismantling physical barriers to the free movement of goods: the transit advice note and the single administrative document have been abolished; a new system has been introduced for gathering statistics on intra-Community trade; veterinary and vehicle checks have been shifted away from border posts to other sites (e.g. factories); and a provisional solution has been found for indirect taxes. However, only partial answers have been found to the problems posed by highly political issues such as terrorism, drug-trafficking and other forms of crime, and immigration and asylum policy, all of which must be resolved if controls on people are to be eliminated. At least an encouraging start has been made with the Dublin and Europol Conventions (→ Europol) and, since March 1995, the free movement of people brought about by the Schengen Agreement has delivered real results to the people, even though it is outside the EU legal framework. The Commission presented three proposals for directives in July 1995 with a view to clearing up the remaining difficulties once and for all and achieving complete freedom of movement for people.

The introduction of a general right of residence, irrespective of employment status, for students, pensioners and those not in gainful employment, and the right of Union citizens to reside wherever they choose (Article 8a of the EC treaty) is, however, more relevant to the creation of a → people's Europe.

Problems with implementation As the deadline came and went, attention increasingly turned to transposition and management of the single market. The Community measures, mostly directives, had to be transposed into national law and applied with due respect for time limits and content. On average, the Member States have transposed 92.9% of the single market legislation. Denmark and the Netherlands lead the field with 99.1%, followed by the United Kingdom, Sweden and Luxembourg, while Austria, Finland, Italy and Germany bring up the rear. A purely quantitative assessment can be misleading, however, as it ignores the shortcomings of the relevant national legislation. The Commission is making slow progress with the task of checking the legislation.

Transposition of single market legislation									Situation at 16 September 1996					
	NL	DK	UK	S	L	E	IRL	P	F	EL	B	D	I	FIN	A
Measures notified	217	215	210	208	207	204	204	200	202	194	198	196	196	191	181
In percentage	99.1	99.1	95.9	95.5	95.4	95	94.1	94.1	92.2	91.3	90.4	90.4	90.4	87.7	83.1
Not applicable	0	2	0	2	4	0	2	3	0	3	0	2	2	1	1
Derogation	0	0	0	0	0	0	0	3	0	3	0	0	0	0	0
Measures not notified	0	0	3	8	5	5	6	6	8	16	10	14	14	21	31
Partial transposition	1	0	2	1	0	5	2	0	4	1	2	2	0	6	6
Infringement of Treaty through inadequate transposition	1	2	4	0	3	5	5	7	5	2	3	5	7	0	0

275 measures are now in force. 219 require transposition into national law.
Source: European Commission.

Consequences The danger of creating a 'Fortress Europe', of which there was so much talk from non-member countries at the beginning of the single market project, has largely proved to be unfounded. Instead, the completion of the single market had the effect of filling the remaining gaps in the Union's common commercial policy; since the elimination of border controls, Member States have no longer been able to take advantage of the protection afforded by Article 115 of the EC treaty. The last such gap was closed with the introduction of the controversial market organization for bananas.

Not for the first time, the debate on Maastricht demonstrated that the creation of the single market was a means to an end as well as an end in itself; the credibility of the single market project finally paved the way for further integration and for the idea of creating an → economic and monetary union.

Kristin Schreiber

Social policy

Treaty basis: Preamble, Articles 2 and 3(i), (j) and (p), 48-51, 117-125, 130b and 130d of the EC Treaty, Protocol on social policy.

Aims: Improving living and working conditions, stimulating employment and equality of opportunity, minimum social protection.

Instruments: European Social Fund, programmes, legal measures to improve equality and to supplement national regulations and legislation.

Budget: ECU 6 233 million (1994), of which ECU 5 819 million for the European Social Fund (in total, 9% of the 1994 EU budget).

Literature from the European Union:

European Commission: Community social policy: Current status 1 January 1996.
Luxembourg 1996 (Cat. no.: CE-93-95-306-EN-C. ECU 44.00).
Social dialogue: The situation in the Community in 1995.
Luxembourg 1996 (Cat. no.: CE-AA-95-002-EN-C. ECU 24.00).
European Commission: Working on european social policy: a report
on the forum, Brussels, Palais des Congres, 27-30 March 1996.
Luxembourg 1996 (Cat. no.: SY-94-96-566-EN-C. ECU 7.00).
European Commission: Social portrait of Europe.
Luxembourg 1996 (Cat. no.: CA-79-93-437-EN-C. ECU 35.00).
European Commission: Social protection in Europe.
Luxembourg 1996 (Cat. no.: CE-92-95-013-EN-C. ECU 12.00).
European Commission: The European Social Fund: employment and
human resources development across the European Union: 1994-1999.
Luxembourg 1995 (Cat. no.: CE-86-94-739-EN-C. Free).

Following on from the social policy provisions of the Treaty founding the European Coal and Steel Community (1951), the Treaty establishing the EEC also set as an integration objective the improvement of living and working conditions. This was intended to be achieved in particular by the European Social Fund and through the coordination and cooperation of the Member States. As part of the realization of free movement for workers, one of the key objectives of the → single market, a system to ensure that social security benefits were available to persons working in another Member State had already been put in place by 1970.

Development Until the adoption of the first 'social action programme' in 1974, which marked the real beginning of EU social policy, the latter had been limited to the activities of the European Social Fund. Social policy after the mid-1970s focused on specific action programmes such as safety and protection at the workplace (→ health) and improving the equality of opportunity for women

(→ women's Europe) and the integration into working life of disadvantaged groups. Only a few of these social policy activities could boast a specific legal basis. Social policy programmes relied on the general competence provisions (Articles 100 and 235 of the EC Treaty) and always required unanimous decisions in the → Council of the European Union. Nevertheless, there has been a basic acceptance since 1974 that the EC is competent to issue regulations in social policy fields.

The Single European Act did not bring with it any significant increase in the social policy powers of the EC: the new Article 118a of the EEC Treaty provided only for measures to protect health and safety at the workplace which can be adopted by the Council, in cooperation with the → European Parliament (→ decision-making procedures), by qualified majority. A significant indication of the continuing refusal of some Member States to provide the EC with greater scope for passing social legislation and developing a European social policy was that Article 100a of the EEC Treaty, designed to facilitate harmonization of legal provisions in order rapidly to complete the internal market and which was also introduced by the Single European Act, does not apply to provisions concerning 'the rights and obligations of workers'.

During the negotiations for the Treaty on European Union, social policy threatened – as a result of the British Government's refusal to agree to any extension of EC responsibilities – to become an obstacle to agreement. The → European Council in Maastricht (December 1991) eventually came to a compromise by which the social policy provisions of the EEC Treaty were left unchanged but the Union Treaty would have added to it a binding 'social policy protocol' empowering the remaining Member States to exploit the bodies, procedures and mechanisms of the Treaties to achieve a more extensive common social policy without the United Kingdom. In an agreement attached to the protocol, the objectives of a social policy without the United Kingdom are set out, but only in the matter of workers' rights do they clearly exceed those of the EC Treaty. Extensive fields of labour law (association, strike and lock-out law) and remuneration are explicitly excluded. Moreover, decisions concerning workers' rights and social protection, or the social security of workers, continued to be subject to unanimity. For the first time in the history of the Community, the application of the social protocol has given rise to secondary EC legislation which applies to only some of the Member States, and at the same time creates a competitive advantage for the United Kingdom. The first example of its being invoked – the Directive on 'Euro works councils' adopted on 22 September 1994 after some 20 years of intense controversy – does, however, show that other Member States are determined to make use of this option and, in key areas, to create a foundation of minimum standards of European social policy.

The European Social Fund The Treaty states that the European Social Fund (ESF) has the role of improving the job prospects of workers. The ESF has had a

very turbulent history: established in 1960, it initially served to fund resettlement and retraining measures and benefited in particular the 'richer' Member States more skilled at making out the applications; up to 1972, half of these funds went to the Federal Republic of Germany. Later on, in the 1980s, most of the resources were channelled towards helping unemployed young people to find a job. Stringent national quotas have applied since 1972 to ensure that a large proportion of the Fund's resources go to the 'poorer' Member States.

Completion of the internal market was associated with wide-ranging reforms to the ESF. According to the provisions of the Single European Act – left virtually unchanged by the Treaty on European Union – the ESF together with the Regional Fund (→ regional policy) and the 'Guidance' section of the EAGGF (→ agricultural policy), has the role of 'strengthening [....] economic and social cohesion' in the Union (Article 130b). In accordance with the decisions grouped into the Delors Package (1988) and the Delors II Package (1992) (→ budgets), the resources available to the Structural Funds were augmented up to 1999 to reach an annual total of approximately ECU 27 billion (at 1992 prices). Over the period 1994-99, this meant ECU 141.5 billion, of which some ECU 40 billion was allocated to the ESF. Under the terms of the framework directive covering the Structural Funds, which was adopted in July 1993, the ESF is required to direct its funding primarily towards measures under Objectives 3 (combating long-term unemployment and facilitating integration of young people) and 4 (adaptation of workers to industrial modernization processes) of the Structural Funds, but also to fund action under Objective 2 (renewal of traditional industrial regions). These efforts are supplemented by the so-called 'Community initiatives' covering certain projects or groups of persons.

'Social dimension' of the single market and 'social dialogue'

The term 'social dimension' of the single market refers to the efforts made to give the internal market and the → European Union as a whole, a more humane and more 'social' dimension and to combat the 'social dumping' feared by the trade union movement. The term therefore involves not only fundamental integration aspects but also specific rectification measures.

An important element in the 'social dimension' is the 'social dialogue'. Forerunners of this attempt to get the 'social partners' at European level to sit together around one table and to arrive at a consensus between them were, as early as the 1970s, the 'Standing Committee on Employment' and the so-called 'Tripartite Conference'. These attempts to achieve concerted action were unsuccessful at the time because of insufficient willingness to compromise and because neither the Community nor the 'umbrella organizations' possessed the necessary competence in this field.

The concept of the 'social dialogue' was introduced by the Single European Act (Article 118b) and, as further defined by Article 3 of the Maastricht Social Protocol, means that the social parties should cooperate in completing the single market and giving it a social dimension. Where representatives of the European umbrella organizations (ETUC, UNICE, ECEP) come together in summit-style meetings or events concentrating on individual policy fields or economic sectors, it is the intention that these should serve to discuss general guidelines for EU policy and to formulate common priorities.

Overall, the 'social dialogue' can be seen as an attempt to create a kind of 'social partnership' at European level. However, such a thing is unknown at national level in many Member States and a further precondition for its success would be the presence of a much more integrated array of European associations.

Social security: wide variations between Member States
Social security expenditure as % of gross domestic product (1993[a])

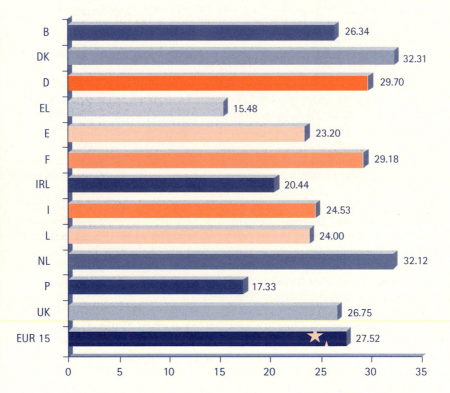

(a) Provisional figures, except for Denmark. Data non available for Austria, Finland and Sweden.

Source: Eurostat.

Social charter The 'Community Charter of the Fundamental Social Rights of Workers', adopted by the European Council in December 1989 despite a vote being

lodged against it by Britain, was intended as a major contribution to give a 'social dimension' to the single market. However – principally because of stubborn British resistance – the ambitious initial goal of a charter setting out binding and legally enforceable fundamental rights was watered down in Council negotiations after the proposal was submitted in April 1989 by the → Economic and Social Committee and became merely a non-binding political declaration of intent with regard to a number of fundamental social rights. These ranged from vocational training and freedom of association to the information, consultation and co-decision rights afforded to workers.

In order nevertheless to be able to push forward with social policy, the Commission put forward in that same month an action programme comprising 47 specific measures to implement the charter. Work on these initiatives, which have to be approved by the Council, has been largely completed. They include directives on collective redundancies, proof of employment relationships, maternity protection, juvenile labour protection and working hours. The drafting of the remaining measures will probably be conducted in part without the United Kingdom, as provided for in the Social Protocol.

Towards a social union? Although in recent years – predominantly through the pressure exerted by the single market – clear progress towards a European social policy has been made, and individual aspects of national legislation increasingly overtaken or supplemented by European minimum requirements, a 'social union' is still a very long way off. Important sectors of labour and social law remain purely in the national preserve. Similarly, it will only be in the long term, if at all, that greater market integration will be associated with greater mobility of the workforce and fewer disparities in living conditions, thus leading to harmonization of what has up to now been purely national education and training and social security systems, or even to solutions applied Europe-wide. In the meantime, it must be assumed that the different systems will continue to compete.

Discussion about the future of European social policy is, though, in full sway. The relevant consultation document submitted by the Commission in November 1993, and the White Paper on European social policy published in July 1994 on the basis of that Green Paper and the over 500 responses received to it, offer exciting prospects, as does the White Paper on growth, competitiveness, employment. What is significant here is not only the comprehensive nature of the issues tackled – ranging from the primary task of combating unemployment to the future of the welfare state – but the fact that for the first time there is an open discussion at a European level of the existence and future of a European model of society. Launching the discussion about its continued existence at a European level is an important step towards a possible agreement on the objectives and comprehensiveness of a European social policy.

Christian Engel

Transport policy

Treaty basis: Articles 3(f) and (n), 74-84, 129b-129d of the EC Treaty; common transport policy, establishment and development of trans-European networks.

Aims: Overall policy for mobility of persons and goods in the European internal market and from and to third countries; optimization of technical and organizational transport arrangements to facilitate personal travel and freight haulage between all regions and across frontiers; environment-friendly transport. These aims require action to improve safety in transport, to reduce noise and pollution and promote conservation of the countryside, fauna and flora when building transport networks.

Instruments: European legislation, financial support, coordination of national policies and measures, promotion of transport research and technological development, treaties with third countries.

Budget: Annual budget for transport safety about ECU 7 million and for promotion of combined transport about ECU 4 million. Medium-term funding (1995-99) for financial support of transport infrastructure projects of common interest about ECU 1.8 billion and for promotion of research and technological development ECU 240 million.

Literature from the European Union:

European Commission-European Investment Bank: infrastructure for the 21st century. Trans-European networks for transport and energy.
Luxembourg 1996 (Cat. no.: IX-01-96-002-EN-C. Free).
European Commission: Towards fair and efficient pricing in transport (factsheets).
Luxembourg 1996 (Cat. no.: C-39-79-65-40-EN-C. Free).
European Commission: Trans-European networks.
Luxembourg 1994 (Cat. no.: CC-82-94-399-EN-C. Free).
European Commission: The citizen's network: fulfilling the potential of public passenger transport in Europe: European Commission Green Paper.
Luxembourg 1996 (Cat. no.: C-39-39-55-64-EN-C. Free).
European Commission: The future development of the common transport policy:
A global approach to the construction of a Community framework for sustainable mobility.
Luxembourg 1993 (Cat. no.: CM-NF-93-003-EN-C. ECU 6.00).

Since the end of the 1980s, the common transport policy has developed considerably in terms of its objectives as the single market has been established. Since 1993, there has been a common transport market, throughout which the transport operators of the → European Union (EU) can offer their services freely without frontier restrictions. European integration in this field thus first benefits the transport sector itself, which now accounts for about seven million jobs and 6% of gross domestic product. Integration also contributes to the functioning of the single market: free movement of persons, goods and services in an area

without internal frontiers can be ensured only if passenger and freight transport by land, water and air operates smoothly. The common market in transport now needs to be further developed in order to keep the ever-greater volumes of traffic moving – where they cannot be avoided – and to safeguard residents' quality of life and the natural environment. What is required is to progress from removing economic barriers to developing integrated traffic systems for the Union.

The common transport market The action taken so far by the EU to set up the common transport market and enable it to function has been concerned primarily with transport as a business activity. In accordance with the principle of free movement of services, commercial services provided by road transport companies, railways, barge operators, air carriers and maritime shipping lines have been freed from discrimination based on nationality and are now subject to the common free-market conditions created by the transport regulation policy.

Before the process of European integration began, the governments of many Member States conducted their regulatory policy from a national perspective. The aims included protecting the national railways from the expansion of road transport, providing employment for the country's barge operators, promoting its seagoing merchant fleet, maintaining the national airline's position on the international market, fostering the country's basic industries, and so on. These national systems protected the national markets and made international transport dependent on a host of bilateral and multilateral agreements with extensive frontier controls. The resulting discrimination on the basis of nationality was unacceptable in itself and in addition led to increased costs, that is to say, obstacles to the operation of the common market, which had to be eliminated. In order to do this, the EC/EU, after a hesitant start, opted for an approach based on dismantling State price regulation and quota restrictions (liberalization). The Union has thus adopted the free exercise of entrepreneurs' initiative as the approach most beneficial for the economy as a whole, making the necessary changes in the regulatory environment and restricting its scope to matters of genuine public interest: real costs, international freedom of navigation, safety, technical standards, social safeguards for workers, town and country planning to ensure adequate transport coverage, noise and other environmental aspects. National regulations have been harmonized more in the interests of ensuring a level playing field; and frontier controls have been eliminated with the establishment of the single market. In addition, the transport market is also subject to the general rules of the EC Treaty which apply to all areas of the economy: freedom of establishment, free movement of workers, prohibition of anti-competitive agreements and State aid, and so on.

The new challenge: sustainable mobility As the transport sector has been integrated, however, it has become clear that liberalization and harmonization alone do not produce an efficient overall system for passenger and freight transport throughout Europe. The inherited corporate structures, especially in the railways and internal waterways sectors, are often an obstacle to competition. Moreover, optimum logistics require not only competition between transport operators but also close cooperation to form transport chains.

The common transport policy thus includes various structural measures, for example, for the inland waterways sector (scrapping arrangements to eliminate overcapacity) and the railways (separation of track ownership and service operation to allow the emergence of private and supranational operators). The Community also promotes combined transport, in particular rail/road transport, to exploit the relative advantages of these modes in freight haulage (rail for large volumes over long distances, road for local distribution). The intention is that competition should be not so much between means of transport as between transport operators who offer a broad range of services using the various transport modes for door-to-door delivery.

Finally, the problems arising as traffic exceeds capacity in the central transit areas of Europe and in conurbations are becoming increasingly apparent, mainly on the roads but also in the air. The figures speak for themselves: in the 15 Member States the roads carried about 70% of the goods transported in 1995 (in t/km) and nearly 80% of passengers (in p/km). This dominance of the truck and the motor car in today's transport system causes perennial congestion and is detrimental to the quality of life and the environment.

The EU cannot ignore these issues. It takes action supplementary to that of the Member States where the problems are of a transnational nature. This applies not only to transport on a commercial basis but also to private use of the motor car. The → European Commission has proposed an overall approach to a Community strategy complementary to the single market to create a better and more rigorous environment for travel, including private travel. This policy primarily comprises fiscal measures to redistribute infrastructure and environmental costs and more stringent technical pollution standards for vehicles. However, the overall approach also includes action to develop Europe-wide integrated transport systems.

In order to develop trans-European transport networks, the Community is promoting the interconnection of national systems by eliminating bottlenecks, creating missing links and aligning technical standards (interoperability). The EU subsidizes investment in infrastructure projects of common interest, for which budgetary resources and loans from the → European Investment Bank are available, with the aim of multimodal integration. In the central areas of Europe, EU spending is geared to making up the leeway of railways and waterways as compared with road transport.

The EU research programme (fourth framework programme 1994-98) promotes

research and development projects with the aim of acquiring aid to decision-making in the areas mentioned and using new technology to help transfer traffic insofar as mobility is desired and necessary to environment-friendly means of transport and improve the overall traffic flow. Better signalling systems and faster trains, for example, can increase railway capacity. Telematic systems (combining data processing and telecommunications) can also be used to avoid congestion on motorways and in cities and to plan travel and freight haulage better.

European transport policy has thus not come to an end with the completion of the single market: it must contribute to mastering the traffic problems of modern society, not only within the EU but also with respect to neighbouring countries, with which the EU as such and its Member States are increasingly establishing treaty relations.

Jürgen Erdmenger

Treaties

Treaty basis:
ECSC Treaty (entered into force on 23 July 1952)
EEC Treaty (entered into force on 1 January 1958)
Euratom Treaty (entered into force on 1 January 1958)
Merger Treaty (entered into force on 1 July 1967)
Single European Act (entered into force on 1 July 1987)
Treaty on European Union (entered into force on 1 November 1993).

European integration actually began with international treaties between Germany, France, Italy and the Benelux countries – the treaties establishing the European Coal and Steel Community (ECSC), the European Economic Community (EEC) and the European Atomic Energy Community (Euratom). The effect of these treaties was to transfer only very limited powers to the three Communities. This served nonetheless to lay the foundation for what, as subsequently substantiated in landmark judgments by the Court of Justice of the European Communities, was to become a legally independent supranational authority. The Community's legal order was thus founded on international law from the very outset. Furthermore, an enormous potential for integration was inherent in the treaty basis. The preamble to the EEC Treaty expressed the resolve of the partners to create 'an ever closer union among the peoples of Europe'. The ultimate objective of comprehensive political integration has been implicit in the nature of European integration and determined its progress from the very beginning. The creation of a → European Union was an objective explicitly laid down by the Community Heads of State and Government in 1972. The main driving force for integration was generated by the EEC. Its initial goals of establishing a common market and common → agricultural, → transport, → competition and → economic policies were gradually followed by new fields of activity such as → the environment, → social, → regional, → education, and → research and technology areas. The original treaties were subjected to fundamental revisions by means of the 1986 Single European Act and the 1992 Treaty on European Union, which provided a legal basis both for the substantive and institutional developments which had already taken place and for further steps towards integration. The European Union treaties have in many respects come to be regarded and even referred to as the Union's constitution. However, despite any similarities discernible from the point of view of scope and effect, binding character and efficacy, the primary law of the supranational Union remains fundamentally different from national constitutional law.

By establishing a common market in coal and steel, the ECSC, which, as the first European supranational organization, was founded on the initiative of Jean Monnet and Robert Schuman in Paris in 1951, was primarily intended to ensure peace in Europe and lay 'the bases for a broader and deeper Community' (preamble). The ECSC Community, which entered into force on 23 July 1952, is the only one of the three founding treaties with a limited lifespan. It was concluded for 50 years and will expire in 2002, after which it will probably be incorporated into the EC Treaty. After the failure in 1954 of the plans to continue integration with a European Defence Community and a European Political Community, the ECSC States agreed in Rome in 1957 on the establishment of the EEC and Euratom. The Treaties of Rome entered into force on 1 January 1958. These treaties served to set up a Joint Parliamentary Assembly and a Court common to all three Communities. Lastly, with effect from 1 July 1967, the Merger Treaty of April 1965 brought about the merger of the Councils of Ministers of the three Communities and of the High Authority of the ECSC with the Commissions of the EEC and the EAEC.

This was followed by 20 years of crises and reform discussions. Declarations of intent by the Heads of State or Government concerning the creation of a European Union such as at the Paris summit in 1972 and in the Solemn Declaration on European Union of 1983 alternated with more or less comprehensive proposals for reform such as the Tindemans Report on the establishment of a European Union (1975), the Draft Treaty of the → European Parliament on the establishment of the European Union (1984) and the Dooge Report on the reform of the EC institutions (1985). Lastly, an intergovernmental conference convened in June 1985 drew up the Single European Act, which was signed by what had by then become 12 Member States in February 1986 and entered into force on 1 July 1987. It contained amendments and additions to all three founding treaties but focused above all on the political and institutional development of the EEC. The Single Act provided for the completion of the → single market by the end of 1992 and, most notably, introduced the cooperation procedure for this field (→ decision-making procedures) by virtue of which the European Parliament has become more closely involved in the legislation process; the → European Council was given a legal basis; the powers of the EEC were expanded or officially confirmed in some areas such as social, environment and research and technology policy; cooperation in the field of → economic and monetary policy was placed on a legal basis as was cooperation in the field of foreign policy, which had developed outside the confines of the treaties as European political cooperation (EPC). The term 'single' arises from the fact that the Single Act brought the European Communities and EPC, still operating outside these confines, under a single legal superstructure.

The second and by far the most comprehensive revision of the treaties came about with the Treaty on European Union which was adopted in December 1991 in

Maastricht, signed in February 1992 and entered into force on 1 November 1993. The Treaty had been drawn up by two intergovernmental conferences, one on political union and the other on → economic and monetary union. The ratification procedure was held up in Denmark by what was first of all a 'no' vote in a national referendum and then in Germany owing to a number of constitutional objections which the Federal Constitutional Court dismissed in October 1993. With the entry into force of the Maastricht Treaty, the EEC Treaty was officially restyled as the EC Treaty. The new EC Treaty, enshrining the objective of the completion of economic and monetary union by 1999; the provisions concerning the common foreign and security policy (CFSP) – an extension of EPC; and cooperation in the fields of justice and home affairs, form the three 'pillars' of the European Union. The Maastricht Treaty contains institutional innovations such as the co-decision procedure (Article 189b), which further increases the powers of the European Parliament. It also serves to limit or expand the powers of the EC in various fields. At the same time, the subsidiarity principle was laid down as a formula for an appropriate distribution of powers between the EC and its Member States (Article 3b). In addition, the principle of Union citizenship was introduced. The Maastricht Treaty makes changes to the texts of the ECSC and Euratom Treaties. All in all, we are now faced with an extremely complex European legal entity in which various procedures for supranational integration and intergovernmental cooperation exist side by side. In addition, the Maastricht Treaty contains a number of fundamental opt-outs such as that granted to the United Kingdom under the Social Protocol attached to the Treaty.

The law will also play a central role in the process of European integration in the future. It serves as the basis, means and vehicle of integration. The new revision of the Treaty due to be adopted in June 1997 will have to lay the legal bases for the deepening and → enlargement of what has meanwhile become a Union of 15 Member States. The new version of the Treaty must safeguard the present heterogeneous nature of the EU whilst creating a Union which is comprehensible and acceptable to the citizen.

Anita Wolf-Niedermaier

Women's Europe

Treaty basis: Article 119; Articles 2 and 6 of the EC Treaty (social policy); various decisions of the Court of Justice of the European Communities.
Aims: Equal opportunities for men and women in their social, professional and political lives; assistance for disadvantaged women; measures to increase awareness.
Instruments: European Parliament Committee on Women's Rights; Equal Opportunities Unit of the European Commission; advisory committee on equal opportunities, information for women section of the General Public Unit of the Directorate-General for Information, Culture and Audiovisual Media.
Literature from the European Union:
European Commission: Employment–NOW. New opportunities for women.
Social Europe-Special Report no. 4.
Brussels 1996 (ISBN 92-827-6149-5. Free).
European Commission: The information society: A challenge for women.
Luxembourg 1996 (Cat. no.: CC-AG-96-002-EN-C. Free).
European Commission: Community social policy: Programmes, networks
and observatories.
Luxembourg 1996 (Cat. no.: CM-93-95-362-EN-C. ECU 26.00).

There is no reference in the → European Union's founding treaties to women's affairs policy as such. Nevertheless, since its foundation in 1957, the European Economic Community has developed a whole range of programmes relating in one way or another to women's issues. These activities on the part of the European Union can be seen to have two central thrusts: adding a socio-political dimension to regulations relating to economic policy, and taking steps to mitigate the consequences of the structural crisis in the job market for women. However, it is also important to bear in mind the change in women's social roles, for there can be no denying that over the years women have moved into an increasing number of spheres of activity and the demands made on them have similarly increased. Women's personal needs have also altered. Women's career patterns cannot be compared with men's, as a woman's life is still pulled about between the polarities of family and career.

The beginning: Article 119 EEC The question of women in Europe was already indirectly dealt with in the Treaty of Rome. Article 119 of the EEC Treaty – now the EC Treaty – advises the Member States of their obligation to ensure that men and women receive equal pay for equal work. As European integration has progressed the principle of 'equal pay for equal work' has provided the foundations for further discussions on equal opportunities and the dismantling of indirect discrimination against women.

In the 1970s the Commission reacted to the continued failure by some Member States to comply with Article 119 of the EEC Treaty by making a number of proposals for directives. By interpreting the above-mentioned Article broadly and consistently applying the directives the → Court of Justice of the European Communities has proved itself to be the driving force behind the concept of equal opportunities. At the meeting of the → European Council in Maastricht in 1991, moreover, an agreement on → social policy was signed, which was attached to the Treaty on European Union, providing a legal basis for equal treatment and the equal opportunities for men and women at the workplace. 'Equal pay without discrimination based on sex' is required under Article 6 of the Social Policy Agreement. Member States are not, however, prevented from maintaining or adopting measures providing for specific advantages for women (positive discrimination). In the 1994 White Paper on European social policy, against a background of structural problems within the labour market, the → European Commission produced a series of proposals aimed at improving the possibilities for women to reconcile family and working life. One of the proposals was that, starting in 1996, an annual 'Equality report' should be published to serve as a monitoring instrument for the implementation of the policy.

The work of the EU institutions The 'situation of women in Europe' provided the basis for setting up the first committee of inquiry in the history of the → European Parliament. Since 1984 this committee has been known as the Committee on Women's Rights. Its members produce reports, conduct hearings, represent the interests of women in the budgetary consultations in the EU and comment on a wide variety of topics directly or indirectly affecting women.

The Commission has an Equal Opportunities Unit assigned to the Directorate-General for Employment, Industrial Relations and Social Affairs. This unit supervises the implementation by the Member States of EU directives. It aims to support women, dealing with EU measures which have an impact on women, such as vocational education, adapting to new technologies, the setting up of companies by women and education for young girls. In 1982 the Advisory Committee on Equal Opportunities for Women and Men was set up. It meets regularly and its aims are to coordinate measures taken by individual States and to support Commission policy. In addition, an informal Council of Ministers for Women's Affairs has been meeting since 1988. It demands and aims to obtain greater commitment at European level to measures facilitating the reconciliation of the demands made by family and career.

Future challenges Women are particularly affected by the structural problems in the European labour market, and increasingly so. Consideration of new working time arrangements, of reduced working hours in the context of a general redistribution of work can provoke two contrasting outcomes. On the one hand, the reduction in working hours, and the concomitant fall in real wages can lead to more women seeking employment in order to bolster the family income. On the other hand, when times get hard women are excluded from the labour market before men, or they are forced into accepting 'atypical conditions of employment', such as fixed-term temporary work. Against the background of an increasing number of single households and one-parent families, protection standards are essential, particularly those relating to old age provision, and they must not just be aimed at people in full-time employment. Until now many of the demands made by the European Parliament and the directives proposed by the Commission seeking to get to grips with this issue have failed either for structural reasons or for reasons of content. The new Members of the European Union, especially Sweden, are expected to bring new approaches and a new impetus to the debate.

New challenges are also posed by the pace of modernization, not only in Western but also in Eastern Europe. The pulse of technological development beats ever faster while expertise and skills become ever more rapidly obsolete. This has lasting consequences, especially for women. Traditional education needs to be constantly supplemented by further qualification, but, seen in the context of the traditional distribution of roles between men and women regarding family and career, this represents a serious problem.

Conclusion European Union activities on women's rights by the EU have so far been carried out in four stages. Firstly, it was established as a socio-political requirement that Member States treat men and women equally on matters of pay. Secondly, the principle of equality was extended to cover other political spheres, whereby a whole series of employment protection standards were made binding. Thirdly, the role of women was altered so that, rather than being the objects of political decisions, they became the subjects, active participants in the political process instead of having rules made for them. The increase in the number of women MPs is an illustration of this new development, even if there is still a great deal of catching up to be done in this area. Fourthly, as a consequence of the structural problems in the labour market, questions regarding the distribution of work and working time models are discussed under the heading of employment policy and not social policy as used to be the case. This new approach finds expression in passages in the Commission White Paper on growth, competitiveness and employment, even if there was little room for matters relating specifically to women's issues.

Some points still need to be cleared up. For a start, there is a great deal of work to be done regarding increasing awareness of possibilities, rights, prospects in the labour market, qualifications for the future and further education opportunities.

Up to now, information has for the most part been directed at working women. The quality of the regulations improving the situation of women depends on the degree to which there is a general awareness of the need for the development of such a policy. What is decisive is that the issues in question acquire their own intrinsic value and are not dealt with as if they were by-products of regulations on social and employment policy. One idea would be to enshrine the principle of equality in a catalogue of basic rights for the European Union. However, one cannot help but have the impression that the measures taken by the European Union in relation to women's affairs have so far had little effect on developments in the employment situation and job prospects for women. It seems to be time to evaluate EU measures and their implementation in the Member States as well as the structures available for dealing with matters of concern to women.

Melanie Piepenschneider

The ABC of Europe

The ABC of Europe

Olaf Hillenbrand

ACP countries: Altogether 70 developing countries in Africa, the Caribbean and the Pacific are linked with the EU under the fourth Lomé Agreement (→ development).

Acts of the Community institutions (legal instruments): The acts adopted by the Council and the Commission can take various forms. A regulation has the direct force of law in all the Member States. A directive requires the Member States to adopt appropriate rules, but the choice of form and method to achieve the aims laid down are left to them. Decisions relate to specific individual cases and may be addressed to Member States, firms or individuals. They have direct effect in law. Recommendations and opinions are not binding. The same also applies to Council resolutions.

ADAPT: ADAPT is a Community initiative to further growth and employment and increase business competitiveness. The programme contains training measures and employment premiums for industrial sectors facing change. The main objective is to co-finance projects with a transnational dimension in all regions. (⇒ CSF).

For further information, contact:
European Commission, DG V/B.4, Rue de la Loi 200, B-1049 Brussels, Tel.: (322) 299 40 75

Agricultural levies: These are a kind of duty charged on farm products imported into the EU from non-member countries to offset the difference between lower world market prices and price levels inside the Community. The levy rates vary in line with changes in world market prices. These import levies guarantee high prices for EU farmers and are a major source of income for the Union. The counterpart to agricultural levies are export refunds, which make up the price difference on trade in the other direction.

Amendment of the Treaties: The Member States or the European Commission may submit proposals to amend the Treaties to the Council (Article N of the EU Treaty). After consulting the European Parliament and, where appropriate, the Commission, the Council can call an intergovernmental conference of the Member States to finalize the amendments. The amendments must be ratified by all the Member States in accordance with their respective constitutional requirements. On 7 February 1992 the Treaty on European Union was signed in Maastricht. After the Single European Act, the Treaty of Maastricht was the second major revision of the Treaties of Rome. Under Article N of the Treaty a further intergovernmental conference was set for 1996 to review and, if necessary, revise the Treaty on European Union.

Anti-dumping and countervailing duties: Anti-dumping duties are imposed on goods that are imported at a lower price than that which would apply on the exporter's home market. If the goods are backed by subsidies, countervailing duty are charged. These two types of duty have gained in importance with the widespread dismantling of customs

duties in recent years. They can only be imposed on imports that are incompatible with the common market because they distort competition and give an unfair advantage to certain firms or types of goods (→ single market).

Approximation: Approximation is the means used to overcome the disruptive impact on the common market of differing national provisions laid down by law, regulation and administrative action. Article 100a of the EC Treaty provides for the approximation of provisions which have as their object the establishment and functioning of the single market. As a rule the Council uses directives to achieve approximation.

Ariane: This programme extends the scope of the EU pilot programme on books and reading to incorporate translation. The main aim is to support the translation of contemporary literature, giving priority to lesser known languages. Ariane also provides grants for translators and supports the pooling of experience and expertise among professional translators. (⇒ Kaleidoscope)

For further information, contact:
European Commission, DG X/D.1, Rue de la Loi 200 , B-1049 Brussels, Tel.: (322) 299 92 51

ASEAN (Association of South East Asian Nations): A political cooperation agreement has existed between the EU and the ASEAN States (Brunei, Indonesia, Malaysia, Philippines, Singapore, Thailand and Vietnam) since 1978 and led to the establishment of a biennial conference of EU and ASEAN Foreign Ministers. Numerous committees and a permanent bureau (ASEAN Brussels Committee/ABC) ensure continuous contact beyond the ministerial conferences. Trade is also of major significance, the EU being the second biggest export partner of the ASEAN States.

Assent procedure: An act adopted under the assent procedure can only come into force if the European Parliament has approved it by a majority of its members. The procedure applies in various areas, including decisions relating to Union citizenship, the Structural and Cohesion Funds, rules governing direct elections, international agreements and the accession of new members to the Union (→ decision-making procedures).

Association of European chambers of commerce and industry: Founded in 1958, the association comprises 24 member organizations. Through its members the Association in Brussels speaks for over 1 200 chambers of commerce and industry, which in turn represent more than 13 million businesses across Europe. Address: 5 rue Archimède, boîte 4, B-1040 Brussels.

Barcelona Conference: At a conference in November 1995, the EU States agreed the Barcelona declaration with 12 adjoining Mediterranean States. Aiming to guarantee security in the Mediterranean region, they established three pillars. The first pillar provides for a political and security partnership, guaranteeing human rights and basic political freedoms. The second pillar aims to establish a Euro-Mediterranean free-trade area by 2010. The third aspect of the declaration refers to furthering of social and cultural matters, including mutual respect for culture and religion. The Barcelona Conference represents the start of deepening relations between the EU and the southern Mediterranean-rim States (→ Mediterranean and Middle East policy).

BC-Net/Business Cooperation Network: Set up in 1988, the Business Cooperation Network links some 600 business consultants from the public and private sector. Through a central computer system at the Business Cooperation Centre in Brussels, they help small and medium-sized businesses in the EU and a number of other countries to find partners for cooperation. Cross-border cooperation enables small firms to overcome their limited capacity and so participate in EU research and development programmes. Address: Business Cooperation Centre, 80 rue d'Arlon, B-1040 Brussels.

BCC: By means of a simple form the Business Cooperation Centre makes it possible to find business partners in over 60 countries worldwide. There are more than 500 approved liaison offices providing information on the offers held centrally in Brussels.
⇒ EIC, BC-NET, EEIG.

For further information, contact:
European Commission, DG XXIII/B.2, Rue de la Loi 200, B-1049 Brussels,
Tel.: (322) 296 50 03

BEUC: The BEUC (European bureau of consumers' unions – Bureau européen des unions de consommateurs) is an umbrella organization of national consumer associations, working to promote consumer interests in the EU. Address: 36 avenue de Tervuren, bte 4, B-1040 Brussels.

Border controls: Because national laws and tax, health and safety regulations differ, there have to be controls of goods and persons travelling from one country to another. Under the plan for the → single market, the EC Member States were to align their various national rules through harmonization or mutual recognition so that border controls between them could be dismantled by 1 January 1993. This was successfully done for goods traffic. But because of national reservations and unresolved security problems, controls on persons were not completely dismantled until 26 March 1995, and then only between the countries that have signed the Schengen Agreement (→ justice and home affairs, → Europol).

Cabotage: Cabotage is the provision of commercial transport services inside a country, where no frontier crossings are involved. Only domestic carriers used to be allowed to do this. In road transport a cabotage permit allows a haulier from one Member State access to the goods transport market in the others for two months. The issuing of cabotage permits began in 1990. Because of tax differences between the Member States, it proved impossible to liberalize cabotage fully by 1 January 1993. Following agreement in the Council on the introduction of a regional vignette and agreements on the taxation of heavy goods vehicles, the number of cabotage permits was set at 30 000 for 1994, rising by 30% each year. From 1998 EU hauliers will be able to transport goods in other Member States without any restrictions. Cabotage in air transport is also being liberalized in stages and is due to be completed in 1997.

Cecchini Report: The 1988 Cecchini Report was a study carried out at the request of the European Commission on the plan to establish the → single market by 1992. The report analysed the economic consequences of the single market, forecasting long-term economic growth and improved competitiveness for the EC. It calculated that the removal of existing barriers (frontier controls, technical and tax barriers, and so on) could produce savings of around ECU 200 billion, leading to lower consumer prices, greater economic growth and the creation of at least 1.8 million jobs in just a few years.

Cedefop: This is the European Centre for the Development of Vocational Training (Centre européen pour le développement de la formation professionelle), which serves to promote European cooperation on vocational training. Address: Cedefop, P.O. Box 27, GR-55102 Thessaloniki (Finikas), Tel. (3031) 490 111, fax (3031) 490 102.

CELEX: Celex is a continuously updated multilingual EU database. Besides official EU legislation, it contains a large number of other documents such as Commission proposals, questions by MEPs, opinions of the Court of Auditors. Altogether it contains some 50 000 to 60 000 pages per language.

CEN/Cenelec: CEN (European Committee for Standardization – Comité européen de normalisation) and Cenelec (European Committee for Electrotechnical Standardization – Comité européen de normalisation électrotechnique) are the European bodies responsible for standards. With their seat in Brussels, they work as a joint European standards organization, embracing both EU and EFTA national standards institutions. In the EU the Commission and the Council define profiles of requirements for products (e.g. common rules on health and safety requirements, minimum standards for consumer protection), which the European standards committees then issue as official standards. The European standards replace national ones, resulting in greater uniformity in product regulations.

Central (exchange) rates: The central rate is the exchange rate set for a currency in the → European Monetary System (EMS). As currencies diverge, they move away from their central rates. Once a currency's divergence from the central rate reached 2.25%, the EMS intervention mechanism came into play to push it back towards the central rate. The central rates can be changed with the agreement of all the participants in the EMS. This was not done, however, and from the autumn of 1992 the EMS came under heavy pressure on several occasions. After the severest crisis in August 1993 the Council agreed to allow currencies to diverge from their central rates by up to 15% in either direction without triggering intervention.

CERN: CERN (European Organization for Nuclear Research – the acronym comes from the earlier French title: Conseil européen pour la recherche nucléaire) is a European international organization for nuclear research founded in 1954, with its headquarters in Geneva. Its aim is to promote cooperation between the countries of Europe in purely scientific, fundamental research on nuclear energy and related areas.

Co-decision procedure: The co-decision procedure was introduced by the Treaty on European Union (Article 189b), giving wider powers to the → European Parliament. Legislation is adopted in a multi-stage procedure involving both the → Council and Parliament. If there is disagreement between the two institutions after Parliament's second reading, the Council can call on a Conciliation Committee, made up of an equal number of members from either side. If no agreement is reached, an act cannot be adopted against Parliament's will. The procedure under Article 189b applies to decisions on the single market (Article 100a of the EC Treaty), free movement, the right of establishment, freedom to provide services, education, culture, health, consumer protection as well as the adoption

of guidelines or programmes covering trans-European networks, research and the
environment (→ decision-making procedures).

Cohesion Fund: Under the terms of Article 130d of the EC Treaty, the Cohesion Fund
was set up in 1993 to provide financial help for projects in the fields of environment and
transport infrastructure. Finance from the Fund goes only to the four poorer Community
countries (Ireland, Greece, Spain and Portugal), the aim being to reduce the disparities
between EU members' economies. In 1994, funding went to 51 projects. From 1993 to 1999
the amount of financing available through the Fund each year ranges between
ECU 1.5 billion and 2.6 billion, adding up to a total of ECU 15.1 billion.

Committee of inquiry: The Treaty on European Union gave the European Parliament
the new power to set up committees of inquiry to investigate infringements of Community
law. Under Article 138c of the EC Treaty these temporary committees can be set up at the
request of a quarter of Parliament's members.

Committee procedures ('Comitology'): Under the EC Treaty, the → European
Commission is normally responsible for implementing decisions adopted by the → Council
of the European Union (Article 145). The Council monitors the Commission's executive
activities through advisory, management or regulatory committees of national experts,
depending on the sensitivity of the sector in question. Advisory committees only have the
power to make non-binding recommendations to the Commission. Management
committees, by contrast, can refer the Commission's implementing measures back to the
Council for a decision within a given time limit, the measures being suspended in the
meantime. If the Council fails to reach a decision in the time allowed, the Commission can
go ahead and implement the measures. Regulatory committees can also suspend
Commission measures and refer them back to the Council; but where the Council has not
taken a decision within the time limit, the Commission can only adopt the measures if the
Council has not rejected them, which it can do by a simple majority. To the Commission's
annoyance the Council tends to prefer the regulatory committee procedure which, under
the Decision of 18 July 1987 (Decision on committee procedures) it is free to choose
whenever it likes. The term 'comitology' is often used to refer to this restrictive approach by
the Council to the Commission's executive powers.

Common position: The two non-Community pillars of the European Union – the
→ common foreign and security policy and cooperation on → justice and home affairs –
involve intergovernmental cooperation between the EU Member States. The governments
inform and consult one another and can also adopt common positions and joint action.
Through a common position the Member States define and defend an EU approach that is
as closely coordinated as possible and in tune with national policies (CFSP: Article J.2; JHA:
Article K.3 of the EU Treaty).

Community initiatives: These are aid or action programmes set up to complement
Structural Fund operations in specific problem areas. Community initiatives are drawn up
by the Commission and coordinated and implemented under national control. In 1994 the
Commission proposed draft guidelines for 15 Community initiatives up to 1999, involving
finance from the Structural Funds totalling ECU 13.45 million. The initiatives cover cross-
border cooperation (Interreg, REGEN II), rural development (Leader II), the most remote

regions (REGIS II), human resources (NOW, Horizon, Youthstart), industrial change/employment (ADAPT), industrial change (Rechar II, coal-mining areas; Resider II, steel areas; Konver, defence industry conversion; RETEX, textile areas, Portuguese textile industry), encouraging small and medium-sized firms (SMEs), urban crisis areas (URBAN), and fisheries (PESCA).

Compensatory amounts: Compensatory amounts are levied on imports of certain farm products to offset price differences in the Community caused by exchange rate fluctuations, so helping to keep common prices stable.

Convergence criteria: The convergence criteria laid down in the Maastricht Treaty are the conditions for entry into the planned European → economic and monetary union. To qualify for EMU a country must (1) have achieved sustained price stability, (2) avoid excessive budget deficits, (3) have avoided severe exchange-rate tensions in the EMS for the previous two years, and (4) have kept its long-term interest rates down to no more than 2% higher than in the countries where prices are most stable. The criteria have deliberately been made strict in order to guarantee the stability of the planned single currency (Article 109j of the EC Treaty).

Convertibility: Convertibility is the extent to which one currency can be exchanged for another. A currency is convertible if the monetary authorities allow foreigners to exchange it for gold or foreign currency and their own nationals to exchange it for foreign currency.

Cooperation procedure: The cooperation procedure under Article 149 of the EEC Treaty was a new form of cooperation between the Community institutions that was introduced by the Single European Act in 1987. It gave the European Parliament a bigger share in decision-making. The procedure was widely used for the decisions required to complete the single market. A key factor in boosting Parliament's influence was the introduction of a second reading in both Parliament and the Council. The Treaty on European Union extended the use of the cooperation procedure, which now comes under Article 189c (→ decision-making procedures).

COPA: This is the Committee of Agricultural Organizations in the European Community (Comité d'organisations professionnelles agricoles), which is one of the largest lobbying groups in the Community. It is in constant contact with the EU institutions and delivers opinions on the development of the Community's common agricultural policy (→ agricultural policy). Founded in 1958, its main aim is to secure decent living and working conditions and better incomes for farmers. Address: 23-25 rue de la Science, B-1040 Brussels.

COST: European Cooperation on Scientific and Technical Research involves over 20 countries. The basic aim is the joint planning of research projects financed by individual countries in the fields of information technology, telecommunications, oceanography, metallurgy and material science, environmental protection, meteorology, agriculture, food technology, medical research and health.

Council of Europe: The Council of Europe was founded by 16 European States in 1949 with the aim of promoting unity and cooperation in Europe. Based in Strasbourg, it now has

40 Member States. The Council of Europe has developed an especially high profile on matters regarding human rights, social affairs, education and culture. Its most important instrument is the adoption of conventions. As the institutional organs of the Council of Europe cannot lay down legally binding norms, the individual Member States have to ratify the decisions. The European Human Rights Commission and the European Court of Human Rights were set up to enforce the European Council's Convention for the Protection of Human Rights.

Country-of-destination principle: Under the country-of-destination principle, exported goods are exempt from VAT in their country of origin (i.e. the tax is deducted) and the tax due in the country of destination is then charged. With the establishment of the single market, the European Commission is seeking to switch from this principle – the one currently in use – to the country-of-origin principle by 1997. Exporters will simply be charged the VAT due in the country of origin, regardless of the destination, so eliminating the need to deduct tax on exports and add it on imports. The resulting tax revenue will have to pass through a 'clearing house' to be shared out among the EU Member States according to the flow of trade.

Country-of-origin principle: The country-of-origin principle governs the customs treatment and status of imported goods. Under this principle, imports are subject to rules agreed with the country of origin. However, the principle does not apply to taxation. Indirect taxes in the EU have not yet been harmonized. So in trade between two States, goods being exported are exempt from tax at the border and taxed on import – in other words, they are taxed in the country of destination. With the dismantling of border controls after 1 January 1993, a reporting system had to be set up to switch controls to firms' premises. After 1996 VAT on most goods will be charged in the country of origin. Private consumers will then be able to purchase most goods on the terms applying in the country of origin and then import them.

CSF: The Community support frameworks (CSFs) coordinate EU regional activities, occasionally involving the four Structural Funds (ERDF, ESF, EAGGF, FIFG) and the EIB. In each case, however, the projects must be incorporated into plans already developed by national authorities, regional authorities and their economic partners (⇒FIFG, EAGGF, ESF, ERDF, EIC, BCC).

Customs union: A customs union is the merger of several customs area into a single one. Customs duties between the members are lifted. Unlike in a free trade area, members are not allowed to levy their own customs duties on imports from outside countries. Instead a common external tariff is imposed. The EC was able to complete the establishment of the customs union for industrial goods by 1 July 1968, one and a half years ahead of schedule, while the final arrangements for agricultural products were completed by 1 January 1970. Later entrants into the EU have been allowed a transitional period before the customs union applies fully in their territory.

Danish special arrangement: After the 'No' vote in the Danish referendum of 2 June 1992 on the Treaty on European Union, the Edinburgh European Council of December 1992 agreed a formula allowing Denmark to ratify the Treaty after a second referendum in May 1993. Under the resolution agreed, Denmark is not obliged to participate in the third stage of → economic and monetary union and the introduction of a single currency; participate in drafting and implementing a common defence policy; restrict national citizenship under the plans for Union citizenship. Lastly, any transfer of powers to the Community in the field of → justice and home affairs will require the approval of the Danish Parliament by a five-sixths majority or a further referendum. It was also made clear that each country could continue to maintain and improve its own incomes policy, environmental goals and social welfare benefits.

Delors I package: This was a package of reform proposals put forward by the Commission in 1987 to overhaul the financing of the EC, rein in spending on agriculture, boost the EC's Structural Funds and revise the rules on budget management. They formed the basis for the decisions taken by the Brussels European Council in February 1988 and, together with the Single European Act, were crucial for implementing the single market programme.

Delors II package: In February 1992, after the Treaty on European Union had been signed, the Commission presented the Delors II package aimed at securing the medium-term financing of the EU. Budget resources were to be increased to allow the decisions taken in Maastricht to be implemented, in particular with a view to boosting competitiveness, strengthening economic and social solidarity between the Member States (cohesion) and extending the EU's international role. In December 1992 the package was approved by the Edinburgh European Council, allowing a gradual increase in the EU's own resources from 1.2 to 1.27% of GNP by 1999, a further increase in the resources of the Structural Funds and the creation of a Cohesion Fund.

Directives: A directive is a legal instrument by which the Council or Commission can require the Member States to amend or adopt national legislation by a specified deadline in order to achieve the aims set out in the directive.

ECHO: Set up in 1992, the European Community Humanitarian Office provides help and support for the victims of disasters or wars. ECHO offers assistance free of charge to any country outside the EU. Some of the most notable beneficiaries have been people in former Yugoslavia, Rwanda, Burundi, Sudan, Angola, Haiti, the Caucasus region, Afghanistan and Cuba.

For further information, contact:
European Commission, European Community Humanitarian Office (ECHO),
Rue de la Loi 200, B-1049 Brussels, Tel.: (322) 295 44 00

ECIP: The European Community Investment Partners programme (ECIP) promotes EU investment in Asia, in non-member States in the Mediterranean region and Latin America. The ECIP programme supports four complementary procedures: the identification of suitable projects and partners, preparatory measures and the setting up of a Community company, financing capital requirements and management training and assistance with the running of the Community company. Approximately ECU 300 million has been allocated for the period 1992-97 (⇒MED).

For further information, contact:
European Commission, DG I ECIP programme, Rue de la Loi 200, B-1049 Brussels,
Tel.: (322) 299 02 04

Ecu (European currency unit): The ecu is the European accounting and currency unit. It is a 'basket' made up of different, fixed portions (agreed unanimously) of → European Monetary System (EMS) members' currencies. The ecu is the cornerstone of the EMS. It is the basic reference value for calculating the margin of fluctuation between the Community currencies. It also serves as an accounting unit for claims and liabilities and is used by the Member States' central banks for settling trade balances and as a reserve currency. The Community uses the ecu for its budget and the various funds, for setting farm prices and for customs duties and similar levies. The ecu can also be used for private business. Since it is calculated from the average value of the EU currencies, using the ecu reduces the risk from exchange rate fluctuations.

EEC Treaty: The Treaties establishing the European Economic Community and the European Atomic Energy Community were signed in Rome on 25 March 1957 by Belgium, France, Germany, Italy, Luxembourg and the Netherlands. The EEC Treaty, as the most important of the Treaties and the broadest in scope, constitutes the core of the European integration process. It has twice undergone major revision, through the Single European Act and the Treaty on European Union. With the entry into force of the Treaty on European Union on 1 January 1993, the EEC Treaty was renamed the EC Treaty.

EEIG: Since 1 July 1989 companies in the Community have been able to make use of the European Economic Interest Grouping (EEIG), a first instrument for transnational cooperation. The object of the EEIG is to look after the interests of its own members; unlike a company, it is not directed at third parties. By registering in the State where it is based (a notice also being published in the *Official Journal of the European Communities*), the EEIG acquires full legal capacity (⇒BCC, BC–NET, EIC).

EFTA: The European Free Trade Association (EFTA) was founded in 1960 as a reaction to the founding of the EEC, in order to prevent economic discrimination. Over the years, the two organizations developed close economic links resulting in the establishment, in 1984, of the European Economic Area (EEA). EFTA has lost much of its importance owing to the fact that, in several rounds, many of its members joined the Community. When Austria, Finland and Sweden joined the EU in 1995, the only remaining EFTA members were Iceland, Liechtenstein, Norway and Switzerland.

EIC: The Euro-Info Centres have been set up especially to provide information companies and other economic operators on the functioning of the → single market, Community R&D programmes, the Community's structural instruments, the Union's foreign relations and the awarding of public contracts. They also aid cooperation and contact between companies Europe-wide (via the BC-NET) to forge links between the EICs themselves (⇒BCC).

For further information, contact:
European Commission, DG XXIII, Project: Euro Info-Centres, Rue de la Loi 200, B-1049 Brussels, Tel.: (322) 296 13 50

Erasmus (European Community action scheme for the mobility of university students): The Erasmus programme has been under way since 1987, supporting student and teacher exchanges and cooperation between European universities. In 1994/95 some 127 000 students in the EU took the opportunity to complete part of their studies in another Member State (→ education and youth).

Eurathlon: The Eurathlon programme provides support for sporting events that develop understanding between the citizens of the Community, especially young people and women involved in popular sport and sport as a leisure activity. It also promotes measures relating to sports training for participants and officials (trainers, coaches, instructors and referees) in the form of joint courses. Linked to Eurathlon there is also the programme 'Sport for the disabled', which has special measures to integrate people with disabilities into the world of sport (⇒Helios).

For further information, contact:
European Commission, DG X/B.5, Sport section, Eurathlon/Sport for the disabled,
Rue de la Loi 200, B-1049 Brussels, Tel.: (322) 295 66 59

Eureka (European Research Coordination Agency): Launched in 1985, Eureka is a European research initiative, aimed at improving Europe's competitiveness in key areas for the future through closer industrial, technological and scientific cooperation. It involves the European Commission, the 15 EU Member States and seven other countries. The projects undertaken (some 700 altogether) are all purely civilian and are selected by industry, the scientific community and the governments of the countries taking part. They are organized as private initiatives and are eligible for grants totalling up to 50% of the cost (→ research and technology).

Eurocontrol: The European Organization for the Safety of Air Navigation was established in Brussels in 1960 by the International Convention relating to Cooperation for the Safety of Air Navigation. Its members include not only the EU countries but also Cyprus, Hungary, Malta, Norway, Switzerland and Turkey. Eurocontrol directs and monitors civil and military air traffic at altitudes above 25 000 feet and outside national airspace.

Europe agreements: This is the name given to the association agreements concluded since 1991 between the EU and the countries of Central and Eastern Europe. The aim is to enable them to participate fully in the process of European integration in political, economic and trading terms. The agreements include plans to set up a free trade area for industrial products within ten years and the EU is already moving more quickly than its partners to dismantle trade restrictions put in place to protect its own industry. The first Europe agreements were signed with Poland, Hungary and Czechoslovakia in December 1991. The agreements with Poland and Hungary came into force on 1 February 1994, followed by agreements with Bulgaria, Romania, the Czech Republic and Slovakia a year later. Agreements were signed with Estonia, Latvia and Lithuania on 12 June 1995 and with Slovenia on 10 June 1996.

European Agricultural Guidance and Guarantee Fund (EAGGF): The EAGGF finances the EU's common agricultural policy. Its purpose is to provide market support and promote structural adjustments in agriculture. The EAGGF is divided into two sections: the Guarantee Section finances price support measures and export refunds to guarantee farmers stable prices, while the Guidance Section grants subsidies for rationalization schemes, modernization and structural improvements in farming (→ agricultural policy).

European Atomic Energy Community (Euratom): Euratom was founded on 1 January 1958 at the same time as the EEC. Its aim is to conduct research and develop nuclear energy, to create a common market for nuclear fuels, to supervise the nuclear industry so as to protect health and prevent abuse. Since 1967 the institutions of the European Atomic Energy Community, the ECSC and the EEC have been merged.

European Bank for Reconstruction and Development: Set up on 14 April 1991 in London, the EBRD, like the EIB, grants loans for private and commercial ventures and infrastructure projects to promote the transition to a free market economy in Central and Eastern Europe. The Bank's financial resources total ECU 10 billion. As the Bank's founders, the European Union and the Member States have a 51% majority shareholding. In 1994 the Bank financed 91 new projects with a total value of ECU 1.87 billion.

European Coal and Steel Community (ECSC): The ECSC was founded in 1951 by the Federal Republic of Germany, France, Italy and the Benelux States as the first of the European Communities. One of the functions of the creation of a common market for coal and steel products was to tie Germany into post-war Europe and guarantee peace in Western Europe. The institutions of the ECSC, the EEC and Euratom were amalgamated in 1967 under what became known as the Merger Treaty.

European Convention on Human Rights (ECHR): The ECHR was signed on 4 November 1950 by the members of the Council of Europe, who undertook to protect essential fundamental rights collectively. These include the rights to life, liberty and security of person, the right to a fair trial, the right to respect for private and family life, the right to freedom of thought, conscience, and religion, the right to freedom of expression and assembly, the prohibition of torture, slavery and forced labour. Anyone whose rights and freedoms under the Convention are violated has the right to effective remedy before a national authority. A European Commission and Court of Human Rights were set up in Strasbourg to ensure that human rights are observed.

European Development Fund: Set up in 1957 by the Community and the Member States, the EDF finances measures to promote economic and social development in the ACP countries. In addition to investment schemes in these areas, it funds technical cooperation projects, schemes to promote export marketing and sales as well as emergency aid in special cases. The EDF's resources are partly devoted to stabilizing export earnings from certain products under the Stabex system. Each fund has a five-year lifespan. The seventh fund, covering 1990-95, totals ECU 10.7 billion.

European driving licence: The European driving licence was introduced on 1 July 1996. The categories have changed (A – motorcycles, B – cars, C – lorries, D – buses, E – trailers over 750 kg) and drivers have to have a health check every 10 years. Under the new scheme, a licence no longer has to be changed on moving to another EU country.

European eco-label: First awarded in 1994, the European eco-label is intended to encourage consumers to buy environment-friendly products and so increase demand for them. The criteria for awarding the eco-label are laid down by the EU, but the awards are made by the national authorities. The label is in the form of a flower with star-shaped petals.

European Economic Area (EEA): Under the EEA Treaty signed in 1992, the European Economic Area comprises the territory of EFTA and the EU. Inside this area, with

its 380 million inhabitants, goods, services, capital and workers can move freely in the same way as in a → single market with no national frontiers. To make this possible, the EFTA countries agreed to take over some 80% of the EC rules relating to the single market. Switzerland, however, was prevented from joining after a referendum there returned a 'no' vote, which delayed the ratification process. As a result, the EEA Treaty did not enter into force until 1 January 1994. The importance of the EEA was diminished somewhat with the entry of three EFTA members into the EU on 1 January 1995.

European Energy Charter: Launched at The Hague in 1991, the European Energy Charter currently has 51 signatories. It offers a code of conduct laying down the principles, objectives and ways of achieving pan-European cooperation in the field of energy. The aims include enhancing security of energy supplies and encouraging a single European energy market, taking account of environmental protection requirements. After more than three years of negotiations the European Energy Charter Treaty was signed in Lisbon on 17 December 1994 (→ energy).

European Environment Agency: The decision to set up a European Environment Agency and a European environment monitoring and information network was taken by the Council on 7 May 1990. This reflected the growing importance attached to environmental protection in the EU. The Agency's main task is to compile the more detailed and accurate environmental data that are essential for an effective environmental policy. After years of disagreement over the Agency's location, it finally started work in 1994, with its headquarters in Copenhagen. Address: 6 Kongens Nytorv, DK-1050 Kobenhavn, Tel. (45) 33 14 50 75, fax (45) 33 14 65 99.

European Investment Fund: Faced with a worsening economic situation and rising unemployment, the European Council decided in 1992 to launch an initiative for growth and employment. With the Commission taking the lead, the European Investment Fund was established in June 1994. With capital totalling ECU 2 billion, the Fund will help to promote economic recovery in the Member States by financing the development of trans-European infrastructures and providing support for small and medium-sized businesses through loan guarantees.

European Patent Office: The European Patent Office is an international organization with its headquarters in Munich. It helps to promote uniform patent protection in Europe by offering a single procedure for issuing and protecting patents that are valid in all the countries that have signed the European Patent Convention. Although the European Patent Office is not an EU institution, in 1975 the nine EC countries adopted a Community Patent Convention, under which EPO patents would be valid for the common market. A single patent application suffices to obtain a patent for each of the 17 signatory States. Address: Erhardtstraße 27, D-80298 Munich.

European political cooperation (EPC): European political cooperation was a system for foreign policy cooperation and coordination by the EC Member States that began in 1970. Through permanent contacts between their governments, the Member States seek to act in unison on the foreign policy stage. Incorporated into the Treaty in 1987, EPC was expanded under the Treaty on European Union into a → common foreign and security policy (CFSP).

European Regional Development Fund (ERDF): The ERDF is intended to help reduce imbalances between regions of the Community. The Fund was set up in 1975 and grants financial assistance for development projects in the poorer regions. In terms of financial resources, the ERDF is by far the largest of the EU's Structural Funds.

European Social Fund: Established in 1960, the ESF is the main instrument of Community social policy. It provides financial assistance for vocational training, retraining and job-creation schemes. Around 75% of the funding approved goes towards combating youth unemployment. With the increase in budget resources under the Delors II package, changes were made in the Social Fund and the focus moved to the new goals of improving the functioning of the labour markets and helping to reintegrate unemployed people into working life. Further action will tackle equal opportunities, helping workers adapt to industrial change and changes in production systems ($\rightarrow$ social policy).

European Space Agency (ESA): The ESA was founded in 1975 to coordinate the European efforts in the field of space exploration and technology and European cooperation with the American space agency, NASA. Its work is solely directed towards peaceful ends. It has successfully developed its own satellite technology, the European Ariane rocket and the Spacelab laboratory. The ESA's 14 members are: Austria, Belgium, Denmark, Germany, Finland, France, United Kingdom, Ireland, Italy, Netherlands, Norway, Spain, Sweden and Switzerland. Address: 8-10 Rue Mario Nikis, F-75738 Paris Cedex 15, Tel. (33 1) 53 69 76 54.

European symbols: One of the ways to get people to identify with a complex political entity such as Europe and the European Union is by using symbols. Since 1986 the European Communities have used the flag adopted by the Council of Europe, with a circle of 12 gold stars on a blue background. The number of stars, incidentally, has nothing to do with the number of Member States; it symbolizes perfection. Borrowing again from the Council of Europe, the EU uses the 'Ode to Joy' from Beethoven's Ninth Symphony as its anthem. Other symbols used by the EU are annual awards of European prizes, European signs in place of the customs signs at internal frontiers, the European passport, the uniform driving licence and Europe Day on 9 May.

European Trade Union Confederation: The ETUC was established in Brussels in 1973. Its members include 41 trade union confederations from 23 European countries and 16 industry associations. Its aims are to represent the social, economic and cultural interest of workers in Europe and to watch over the preservation and strengthening of democracy in Europe. ETUC representatives have seats on several EU and EFTA committees. Address: 37 Rue Montagne aux Herbes Potagères, B-1000 Brussels.

European University Institute: The European University Institute, sited at Fiesole near Florence, was set up by the EU Member States and opened in 1976. Its aim is to contribute to the development of the cultural and academic heritage of the EU through teaching and research in the humanities and social sciences. Some 200 graduate scholarship students study in the four faculties (History and civilization, Economics, Law, Political and social sciences). Address: Via dei Roccettini, Badia Fresolana, I-50016 San Domenica di Fiesole.

European works councils: In September 1994, after years of opposition, the Council of the EU finally agreed on a Directive on the establishment of European works councils.

Once the Directive is incorporated into national law, firms with at least 1 000 workers in the Member States and employing at least 150 people in each of two or more Member States will have to set up a company-wide works council within three years. Works councils have a right to be heard and must be informed about major company decisions. By virtue of the social protocol, the United Kingdom is excluded from the application of this arrangement.

European Youth Centre: The European Youth Centre was set up by the Council of Europe in Strasbourg as an international training centre and meeting place. Seminars and courses are held there for European youth associations to help them organize at European level, pursue cooperation, exchange information and express their views. Address: European Youth Centre, 30 rue Pierre de Coubertin, F-67000 Strasbourg Wacken.

European Youth Forum: The EU's European Youth Forum is an association of youth organizations in the Community that was founded in 1978. It serves as a platform for youth organizations to put across policy ideas to the EU institutions and seeks to promote the involvement of young people in the future development of the EU. Its members are national youth committees and international youth organizations that meet the criteria laid down in its statutes. Address: European Youth Forum, 112 rue Joseph II, B-1040 Brussels.

Eurostat: Eurostat is the Statistical Office of the European Union. It produces and publishes regular statistical analyses and forecasts, supplying the EU institutions with valuable data on which to base their decisions and action and putting out information for national administrations and the public at large on EU-related issues that lend themselves to statistical analysis. Where possible, it also acts as a centralization point, coordinating and integrating differing national statistics into a uniform, comparable system. Address: Eurostat Information Office, JMO, B3/089, L-2920 Luxembourg.

Eurovision: Eurovision is the organizational and technical centre of the European Broadcasting Union, which was founded in 1950. Its aim is to foster cooperation between radio and television broadcasters and promote exchanges of programmes and broadcasts. Over the years there has been a considerable increase in programme exchanges in order to cut costs. The main focus is on relaying news and sporting broadcasts.

Eurydice: Set up in 1980, Eurydice is an EU information network enabling national and Community authorities to exchange questions and answers and so build up a basic stock of information about Europe's widely differing education systems ($\rightarrow$ education and youth).

Export refunds: Farmers exporting their products to non-member countries receive export refunds to offset the difference between high prices in the EU and lower world market prices. Export refunds, then, are variable subsidies designed to guarantee farmers minimum prices and enable the EU to sell its agricultural surpluses on the world market. Export refunds are the counterpart of the levies charged on imports of farm products into the EU ($\rightarrow$ agricultural policy).

External tariff: With the phased introduction of the customs union in the EEC by 1968, the separate customs territories of the member countries became a single common customs area. The existing customs duties were replaced by a common customs tariff the 'common external tariff'. Since 1975 all revenue from the common external tariff has gone to the EC budget.

Failure to act, proceedings for: If the → Council or the → European Commission fails to act and thereby infringes the Treaty (Article 175 of the EC Treaty), proceedings can be brought against it in the → European Court of Justice. Any Member State or EU institution or any natural or legal person can start proceedings if the institution concerned has not acted two months after being called upon to do so. For example, in 1985 the Court of Justice found in favour of the European Parliament in its case against the Council (Transport Ministers), ruling that it had failed to act to implement the freedom to provide transport services, which the Treaty required it to do.

FIFG: Since 1994, the FIFG (Financial Instrument for Fisheries Guidance) has grouped together the Community instruments for fisheries. It is applied in all coastal regions, its main task being to increase the competitiveness of the structures and develop viable business enterprises in the fishing industry while striving to maintain the balance between fishing capacities and available resources (⇒CSF).

Flexible integration: Flexible integration refers to a unification process moving at different speeds. The concept of a two-speed Europe means that closer integration of the Community will initially involve only the Member States which are prepared to move further. The advantage of this approach is that the pace of unification is not dictated by the slowest or least enthusiastic member. On the other hand the danger with flexible integration is that the common integration process may fall apart. Examples of flexible integration are to be found in the provisions on → economic and monetary union and on → social policy. EMU is a common objective in which only some Member States will take part to begin with, while the United Kingdom has opted out of the social policy provisions. A variation of flexible integration is the hard-core concept, in which a specific group of Member States presses ahead with the integration process.

FORCE: FORCE is an EU action programme to encourage further training.

Four freedoms: The primary aim of the EEC Treaty was to eliminate economic barriers between the Member States as a first step towards closer political ties. The Treaty therefore sought to establish a common market within the Community, founded on four freedoms – free movement of goods, persons, services and capital. After almost 30 years this objective had still not been achieved, so in 1985 the Commission brought out its 'White Paper on completing the internal market', setting out a practical timetable for a genuine → single market by 31 December 1992. When the deadline arrived, the four freedoms had largely become a practical reality, with only freedom of movement for persons proving impossible to implement fully within the time frame laid down.

Framework programmes for science and technology: The framework programmes for → research and technological development have been the bedrock of Community research and technology policy since 1984 and are the main instrument by which it is implemented. They set the strategic direction for the objectives, priorities and overall volume of EU research funding. Running for five years, they offer research planners a stable background for developing projects.

Free movement of capital: This is where capital is allowed to move freely between countries with different currencies. Because of the effects on a country's balance of payments and hence on the stability of its currency, there are restrictions on capital

movements between most countries. In 1988 the Council decided that capital movements in the EC Member States should be fully liberalized by 1 July 1990. The Community also aims to liberalize capital movements between the EU and non-member countries as far as possible (→ single market).

Free movement of goods: The free movement of goods is one of the four freedoms essential for the functioning of the common market. Free movement of goods across EU frontiers requires harmonized customs duties and taxes, uniform rules on the protection of health, consumers and the environment, and the removal of all other barriers to trade. With the completion of the → single market, the free movement of goods has largely been achieved. However, some exceptions or transitional arrangements still apply in certain areas. Since 1993 the checks that are still necessary are no longer carried out at the borders but on firms' own premises.

Free trade agreement: An agreement to remove all customs duties and prohibit quantitative restrictions in trade between the signatories. In 1972-73 the European Community concluded agreements of this kind with individual EFTA countries.

Free trade area: A group of two or more customs territories where all customs duties and other measures restricting trade between them have been removed. Unlike in a customs union, where the States concerned set up a common external customs tariff, countries in a free trade area retain their own national customs duties in trade with third countries. Examples of free trade areas are EFTA in Europe and NAFTA in North America.

Freedom of establishment: Freedom of establishment is the right of EU citizens to establish themselves in another Member State to run a business, farm or work in a self-employed capacity (Articles 52-58 of the EC Treaty). Although restrictions on freedom of establishment have been forbidden since 1 January 1970, they still exist in practice in the shape of the differences between national rules governing trades and professions and between their qualification requirements. By the end of 1992 most of these barriers had been removed through harmonization and mutual recognition of vocational qualifications and diplomas (→ single market).

Freedom of movement for persons: Workers and self-employed people from EU countries have the right to work and live in any other EU Member State and to receive the welfare benefits available there on the same terms as local workers, without any discrimination on the grounds of nationality (Article 48 of the EC Treaty). With the completion of the → single market, Union citizens can live, work and spend their retirement anywhere they like in the European Union. However, national welfare systems are still the preserve of the Member States themselves and so to prevent abuse, the right to freedom of movement does not yet apply to those dependent on State assistance. The principle of non-discrimination for EU citizens includes the unrestricted right of entry into any Member State.

GATT: There are currently 123 signatories to the General Agreement on Tariffs and Trade, together accounting for 90% of world trade. GATT's purpose is to work for the dismantling of trade barriers. After six rounds of multilateral negotiations, agreement was reached at the Tokyo Round to dismantle non-tariff barriers. In 1986 the Uruguay Round opened, with negotiations extending beyond the removal of trade barriers and distortions to cover new topics such as trade in services, trade-related investment issues and better arrangements for the protection of intellectual property. After years of talks the Uruguay Round ended on 15 December 1993. Responsibility for dealing with trade issues has now passed from GATT to the new World Trade Organization (WTO), which started work at the beginning of 1995.

Growth initiative: At their meeting in Edinburgh in December 1992, the Heads of State or Government agreed a growth initiative for the coming years to revive the European economy by providing increased funding for infrastructure developments. The initiative included setting up a temporary lending facility worth ECU 8 billion, managed by the European Investment Bank, and a European Investment Fund worth ECU 2 billion to provide guarantees for private and public investments. Altogether this should encourage investments totalling over ECU 30 billion. Combined with the newly created Cohesion Fund and national measures, this economic recovery programme is intended to generate healthy growth, help create lasting jobs and boost Europe's competitiveness.

Hague Congress: The Hague Congress of May 1948, organized by an international committee of movements for European unity, brought together some 750 politicians from almost every country in Europe. The call for a united, democratic Europe issued by the Congress in its final resolutions found a wide echo and gave the impetus for launching negotiations that led to the founding of the Council of Europe a year later. The resolutions also called for a European Convention on Human Rights (later drawn up by the Council of Europe), a European Court of Human Rights and a European Parliamentary Assembly, all of which came into being.

Hague Summit: The 1969 Hague Summit marked a milestone in the history of European integration. The Heads of State or Government of the six EC Member States set out their declared aims for the further development of the Community. This included the decision on enlargement northwards and the first steps towards → economic and monetary union, bringing the members of the Community closer together economically and politically.

Harmonization: Coordination or alignment of Member States' economic policy measures and legal and administrative rules in order to prevent disruption of the common market.

Harmonization of customs legislation: It was essential for the EC to harmonize customs legislation in order to ensure that the common customs tariff would be applied uniformly after the establishment of the customs union. This involved bringing in a customs code and new, common rules to keep out third-country products that infringe industrial property rights (trade marks, etc.).

Helios II: This is a programme designed to integrate people with disabilities into social and economic life. The Helios II programme (1993-96) helps to increase the pooling of experience by organizing seminars, fact-finding trips and work experience, all of which are set up around different topics every year. Working together with NGOs, the Commission part-finances activities in the fields of medical rehabilitation, integration into general and vocational education systems and the independence of people with disabilities (⇒Horizon, Eurathlon (Sport for the disabled)).

For further information, contact:
European Commission, DG V/E.3, Rue de la Loi 200, B-1049 Brussels, Tel.: (322) 296 05 61

Horizon: This programme addresses the needs of anybody particularly subject to prejudice when seeking work. This includes people with disabilities, the long-term unemployed, drug addicts, immigrants and the homeless. The programme supports measures aimed at improving the quality of the training of the target group together with activities directly leading to the creation of jobs for that group (⇒Helios, Youthstart, NOW).

For further information, contact:
European Commission, DG V/B.4, Rue de la Loi 200, B-1049 Brussels, Tel.: (322) 295 28 70

Info 92: Info 92 is one of over 40 databases set up by the EU. It contains constantly updated information about the single market and can be accessed by various means, including via modem (for a fee).

Infringement proceedings: Infringement proceedings are brought before the → European Court of Justice to decide on alleged infringements of the Treaties by the Member States. Where an infringement is thought to have been committed, proceedings may be brought either by one of the Member States or by the Commission (Articles 169, 170 of the EC Treaty). The Treaty on European Union gave the Court of Justice the new power to impose penalties on the Member States if they fail to comply with its judgments (Article 171).

Interreg: Interreg is a Community initiative for border regions that grants assistance for cross-border cooperation on schemes such as infrastructure projects, cooperation between public utilities, joint ventures by businesses and cooperation on environmental protection.

Intervention prices: Under the common agricultural policy, prices for the main farm products are only allowed to fall within a certain range to a fixed lower limit, known as the intervention price. When prices fall below that level, national intervention agencies have to buy up products at the intervention price (there is no ceiling on quantity), so giving producers a guaranteed price (→ agricultural policy).

Jean Monnet project: This project promotes the teaching of the process of European integration, providing financial assistance for the setting up of permanent education structures in the fields of EC law, European economy, politics and history by means of chairs at universities and other higher education establishments inside and outside the Community. In addition to the Jean Monnet chairs, projects, courses and studies related to integration are supported and doctoral grants are awarded.

For further information, contact:
European Commission, DG X/C.6, Jacqueline Lastenouse Bury,
Rue de la Loi 200, B-1049 Brussels, Tel.: (322) 299 94 53

JESSI (Joint European Submicron Silicon): JESSI is a Eureka research project running until 1997 that involves various research institutes and companies from France, the United Kingdon, Italy, the Netherlands and Germany. The aim of the project, which has a budget of ECU 3.8 billion, is to extend integrated-circuit chip technology.

JET (Joint European Torus): JET is the largest experimental project in the controlled thermonuclear fusion research and training programme.

Joint action: Joint action is the means by which the EU Member States seek to defend their interests under the new → common foreign and security policy brought in by the Treaty on European Union (Article J.3). The Council, acting by unanimous decision, defines the scope and objectives of joint action and the means, procedures and conditions for implementing it. In the views they express and the action they take, the Member States are then bound to uphold the positions agreed, so ensuring that the Union can act as a cohesive force.

Joint Research Centre (JRC): The Member States of Euratom established the JRC in 1957 for research on the peaceful uses of nuclear energy. There are eight separate institutes at Ispra (Italy), Geel (Belgium), Karlsruhe (Germany), Petten (Netherlands), and Seville (Spain). In addition a large-scale facility for experimental work on thermonuclear fusion (JET) was set up in Culham (United Kingdom) in 1983. The JRC carries out research under the EU programmes, with the focus on industrial technology, environmental protection, energy and standardization. The JRC's budget amounts to ECU 900 million (1995-99).

JOULE: JOULE (Joint opportunities for unconventional or long-term energy supply) is a research and development programme on non-nuclear energy and rational energy use. Earmarked funding for 1994-98 totals ECU 967 million.

Kaleidoscope: Initiated in 1990, the Kaleidoscope programme primarily aims to disseminate and raise awareness of culture and to promote artistic and cultural cooperation between experts. It comprises three actions supporting three types of project: artistic and cultural events with a European dimension; the encouragement of artistic and cultural creation (vocational training or continuing education measures); the promotion of cultural cooperation through networks (the exchange of information between cultural establishments in Europe) (⇒Ariane).

For further information, contact:
European Commission, DG X/D.1, Rue de la Loi 200, B-1049 Brussels , Tel.: (322) 299 94 19

Leader: A Community initiative for rural development under the Structural Funds. Leader offers assistance for the economic development of rural communities in the regions where structures are weakest. The main focus is on organizing rural development, helping people to gain new qualifications, promoting rural tourism, supporting small but innovative firms and promoting high-value farm products. The second stage of the initiative (1994-99) has a budget of ECU 1.4 billion.

Leonardo da Vinci: Since 1995 the Community programmes for vocational training have been grouped, extended or continued under the heading of the Leonardo da Vinci programme (→ education and youth). Leonardo, with a proposed budget of ECU 620 million (1995-99), will replace the following programmes (among others) as they run out: Comett (cooperation on training and further training between universities and industry), PETRA (initial vocational training), FORCE (further vocational training) and Eurotecnet (innovation in teaching methods).

Liberalization: The removal of existing national restrictions on the movement of goods, services, payments and capital across frontiers, impeding free competition between States.

Besides the EU, where liberalization between its members has gone farthest, a number of other international organizations are seeking to promote liberalization, in particular GATT, the OECD and the International Monetary Fund (IMF).

LIFE: On 18 May 1992 a regulation was adopted creating a single instrument (LIFE) to finance environmental operations, incorporating all the existing ones (GUA, Medspa, Norspa, ACNAT). LIFE finances priority environmental measures both in the Community and under international cooperation schemes. Altogether ECU 400 million is earmarked for the period 1991-95 (→ environment).

Lingua: An EU programme to promote foreign language teaching and learning. The aim is to improve communication within the European Union. Support covers only the languages of the EU Member States, especially the less widely used ones.

Lomé Convention: The Lomé Conventions are multilateral trade and development agreements between the EU and the 70 ACP countries. They give the ACP countries associated status with the EU, offering them not only financial assistance but also substantial trading advantages on exports to the EU. The Conventions are the heart of the EU's → development policy. Lomé I was concluded in 1975, running for five years; it was followed by Lomé II (1980), Lomé III (1985) and finally Lomé IV in 1990, which will run for 10 years, with a budget of ECU 13.2 billion over the first five years. The main focus of the Convention is the long-term development of the countries involved. Lomé IV also incorporates agreements for the protection of human rights and the development of democracy.

Luxembourg compromise: → Council of the European Union.

Majority voting: Many of the decisions taken by the Council of the European Union are adopted unanimously. But to prevent progress in the Community from being blocked by specific interests, the Treaties of Rome also provided for simple or qualified majority voting. However, after the Luxembourg compromise – and until the Single European Act came into force – most decisions were taken by unanimous vote. Since then, majority voting has been explicitly required for decisions on the single market (with only a few exceptions) and is regularly used in practice. The areas where qualified majority voting is used were subsequently extended further by the Treaty on European Union (→ decision-making procedures).

Marshall Plan: Scheme announced by US Secretary of State George C. Marshall in 1947 to rebuild the European economy after the Second World War (European recovery programme). Up to 1952 some USD14 billion was made available to 18 countries in Western Europe in the form of credits, non-repayable loans, material and food aid. The Marshall Plan played a key part in rebuilding the economy in Western Europe, and especially in West Germany. In political terms it was complementary to the American policy of containing Communist influence.

MED: This programme promotes local cooperation with Mediterranean third countries, whereby the EU goes beyond the traditional framework, financing measures to help set up companies in the Mediterranean area (MED-Invest), regional projects to improve infrastructure (MED-Urbs), cooperation measures between universities and in the field of research (MED-Campus and MED-Avicenne) and cooperation in matters relating to the media (MED-Media) ($\Rightarrow$ECIP).

MEDIA (Measures to encourage the development of the audiovisual industry): A programme to develop the audiovisual industry in the European Union and establish competitive structures. It grants assistance for the training and further training of workers in the film industry, for the development of film projects and for Europe-wide distribution of programmes ($\rightarrow$ media policy).

Merger control: In September 1990 a 'Regulation on the control of concentrations between undertakings' came into force, under which proposed cross-border mergers involving firms with a combined worldwide turnover of more than ECU 5 billion (initially) are subject to approval by the Commission. The aim is to avoid excessive concentrations of power in individual sectors of the economy. Mergers below the threshold still come under national law.

Merger Treaty: The Merger Treaty of 8 April 1965 ('Treaty establishing a single Council and a single Commission of the European Communities') set up joint institutions for the European Atomic Energy Community, the European Coal and Steel Community and the European Economic Community. It came into force on 1 July 1967. The European Parliament and the European Court of Justice, however, had been joint institutions of all three Communities from the outset when the EEC and Euratom were founded.

Messina Conference: At a conference in Messina on 1 and 2 June 1955, the six Foreign Ministers of the ECSC decided to begin negotiations on integration along the lines of the European Coal and Steel Community in other areas. The outcome was the Treaties of Rome founding the EEC and Euratom, which were signed on 25 March 1957.

Monitor: Monitor is a Community R&TD programme on strategic analysis, forecasting and evaluation. It involves action under three headings: SAST – strategic analysis of the impact of developments in $\rightarrow$ science and technology; FAST – long-term forecasting and assessment of the interaction between science, technology, the economy and society; Spear – the methodology and effectiveness of assessing research and development in social and economic terms.

Most-favoured nation clause: A country granting another most-favoured nation status undertakes to accord it all the most favourable trading terms which it offers to others. This principle is a basic element of the GATT and other trade agreements.

Mutual recognition: This involves the Member States recognizing each other's different rules or qualifications as equivalent if they fulfil the same purpose. Under this principle the Court of Justice ruled in the *Cassis de Dijon* case that a product lawfully produced and marketed in one Member State can be sold throughout the Community. In the effort to achieve the goal of a single market, mutual recognition is a flexible alternative to the rather cumbersome and bureaucratic process of harmonization.

Net contributor/beneficiary: Although the EU is financed from its own resources to further broader European aims, the difference between what a country pays into the EU budget and what it gets back has been a frequent source of concern to politicians. Since the common agricultural policy still swallows up a large portion of the EU budget, the countries that are major farm producers benefit the most. As an industrial country, Germany is the largest net contributor – according to estimates it paid some ECU 25 billion more into the budget in 1994 than it received back; but as a major exporter it is also one of those that benefit most from the common market.

New Community Instrument (NCI): The NCI is one of the financial instruments used by the Community. To help achieve its structural policy goals the Community raises loans, which it then on-lends, in close cooperation with the EIB, to finance investments in energy, regional development, industrial restructuring and adaptation and measures to boost economic growth.

Non-discrimination principle: No discrimination is allowed on the basis of nationality in the areas covered by the EC Treaty. As an extension of the freedom of establishment it is a fundamental prerequisite for creating a single market. In addition it strengthens the sense of equality and belonging that is important for establishing a European identity.

NOW: The Community initiative for the promotion of equal opportunities for women in the field of employment and vocational training (formerly New opportunities for women programme) aims to facilitate women's entry into working life. More than just helping women to escape from unemployment, it is intended to improve their access to industries with a promising future and leading positions. This is why management training qualifies for support, as does the setting up of small and medium-size companies or cooperatives and the training of counselling personnel. Particular focus is placed on transnational activities. A total of ECU 470 million has been allocated to NOW for 1994-99 (⇒Horizon).

For further information, contact:
European Commission, DG V/B.4, Rue de la Loi 200, B-1049 Brussels, Tel.: (322) 296 31 14

Obstacles to trade Regulation: The new Regulation of December 1994 covering obstacles to trade enables EU industries and companies and the Member States to demand action by the EU to ensure observance of international trade regulations should third countries introduce or continue to apply obstacles to trade. The term illicit trade practices, on which the New commercial policy instrument (NCPI), the predecessor of this Regulation, was based, was replaced by obstacles to trade.

OECD: Founded in 1961, the OECD (Organization for Economic Cooperation and Development) fosters international cooperation between industrialized countries with free market economies. Its main aim is to coordinate economic, trade and development policy. All the EU countries are members of the 24-strong OECD.

Official languages of the EU: Under a unanimously agreed Council Regulation, the EU now has 11 official languages, all with equal status: Danish, Dutch, English, Finnish, French, German, Greek, Italian, Portuguese, Spanish and Swedish. None of the member countries wishes to forgo the use of its own language since this is an issue of considerable symbolic importance. Every official EU act is translated into all the official languages. More than one in five of all EU staff work in the language service. Below ministerial level the working languages are English, French and – increasingly – German. The → European Court of Justice in Luxembourg uses only French.

Ombudsman: Under Article 138e of the EC Treaty the → European Parliament appoints an Ombudsman for the lifetime of the Parliament, to whom any EU citizen can submit a complaint about maladministration in the activities of the Community institutions or bodies. He can conduct inquiries and if the complaint is substantiated, he forwards a report to Parliament and the institution concerned. In July 1995 the Finn, Jacob Magnus Södermann, was appointed to the post. Address: Palais de l'Europe, F-67006 Strasbourg Cedex.

Organization for Security and Cooperation in Europe (OSCE): Since 1 January 1995 the OSCE has been carrying on the work begun in the 1970s by the Conference on Security and Cooperation in Europe (CSCE). The CSCE played an important part in the development of the European policy of *détente*. With the Charter of Paris in 1990 the Conference changed dramatically, acquiring operational functions. The OSCE operates in three 'baskets': security questions in Europe (basket 1); cooperation on economic, scientific, technology and environment matters (basket 2); and cooperation on humanitarian and other matters (basket 3). In all, the OCSE numbers 57 members, including the United States of America and Canada.

Origin rules: As it is often difficult to determine the actual country of origin in the case of goods whose production involves a series of processing stages in different plants, origin rules define which country is to be regarded as the country of origin. Through origin rules the EU is seeking to prevent firms from non-member countries 'circumventing' external frontiers by transferring individual stages of production to the Community.

Own resources: Until 1970 Community spending was financed entirely by contributions from the Member States, after which its financing was gradually shifted to own resources. The own resources system gives the EC a measure of financial independence from the Member States, making it easier for it to pursue wider European goals independently. On 1 January 1971 the Member States began paying over revenue from agricultural levies and customs duties to the EC budget (in full since 1975) and since 1979 a portion of the Member States' VAT revenue has also gone into the budget. In 1988 the crisis over the EC's finances was resolved by the European Council's adoption of the decisions proposed in the Delors I package. This introduced a fourth resource consisting of a percentage (calculated annually) of the EC countries' GDP. In December 1992 the Edinburgh European Council agreed a further increase in own resources, raising the GDP percentage from 1.2 to 1.27 until 1999 (Delors II package).

Permanent Representatives Committee (Coreper): The Permanent Representatives Committee reports to the Council. Consisting of representatives from the Member States at ambassador level, or their representatives, it is responsible under Article 151 of the EC Treaty for preparing the work of the Council and for carrying out the tasks assigned to it by the Council. A total of 250 working parties examine the legal instruments to be dealt with and report to Coreper.

Petersberg Declaration: The Petersberg Declaration of 19 June 1992 marked a stage on the road to transforming the Western European Union (WEU) into the defence arm of the European Union and the European pillar of the Atlantic Alliance. The Declaration by the

WEU Council of Ministers included the statement that, besides 'peacekeeping' duties under UN or CSCE/OSCE auspices, the WEU could undertake 'peacemaking' combat tasks in certain circumstances. A planning cell was established to prepare contingency plans for the employment of forces under WEU auspices.

PETRA: PETRA is a Community action programme for the vocational training of young people and their preparation for adult and working life. Under way since 1989, its aim is to enhance the quality of training in the light of the needs of the common market and to ensure high-quality vocational training for young people. A network of training initiatives has been set up for this purpose (→ education and youth).

PHARE: The aid programme for economic restructuring in Eastern Europe was agreed in 1989 by 24 countries (EC, EFTA, USA, Canada, Australia, Turkey, New Zealand, Japan), with the task of coordination being given to the Commission. The PHARE programme consists of many individual projects and operations. The EU and its Member States contribute around 50% of the funding. Aid is granted for measures underpinning the process of economic reform in Eastern Europe. The EU and the PHARE countries draw up annual indicative programmes setting out the basic aims and focus of assistance. Responsibility for implementing the programmes normally rests with the PHARE countries themselves. The basic principle is that aid should primarily go to private enterprise. Under a Council Decision of November 1992 the PHARE programme was integrated into a multiannual strategy linked to the Europe Agreements and other aid operations. The year 1994 saw the implementation of 125 programmes totalling ECU 963.3 million (→ enlargement).

Preferential agreement: An agreement under which each party grants the other preferential treatment in their trade with one another.

Qualified majority: The → Council takes decisions either unanimously or by simple or qualified majority vote. The Single European Act and the Treaty on European Union extended the use of majority voting for decision-making in order to give Community interests greater weight when confronted with national interests. In qualified majority voting under Article 148 of the EC Treaty, Germany, France, the United Kingdom and Italy each have 10 votes, Spain 8, Belgium, the Netherlands, Greece and Portugal 5, Austria and Sweden 4, Denmark, Finland and Ireland 3 and Luxembourg 2. A decision is adopted if it receives at least 62 votes (out of 87). Decisions under the common foreign and security policy require, in addition, the support of at least 10 Member States. At an informal meeting at Ioannina in 1994 the Foreign Ministers agreed that in the event of a very narrow qualified majority they would first make every effort to obtain a larger majority. This compromise settled the dispute about re-weighting the qualified majority after the recent enlargement.

Quotas: Quotas are restrictions on the quantity of imports or exports and are used to regulate supply. Besides imposing quotas on goods, another way of restricting trade is to use foreign exchange quotas, limiting the amount of foreign currency available for the purchase of particular types of products.

RACE: RACE (Research and development in advanced communications technologies for Europe) is the EU's most comprehensive programme in the field of telecommunications. One of its foremost aims is to develop broadband communications technologies for the simultaneous transmission of sound, images and data (→ information society).

Regulation: Regulations are the strongest form of Community legislation. They have general application, are binding in their entirety and are directly applicable in all Member States.

SAVE (Special action programme for vigorous energy efficiency): This is a programme designed to promote the better use of EU energy resources while protecting the environment. The main areas of investment are technical studies on the development of standards and technical specifications, measures to promote the development of infrastructure for renewable energy sources, assistance in the creation of information networks in order to improve coordination of the activities of the Community and of individual States and measures to encourage more efficient use of electricity (⇒Thermie II).

For further information, contact:
European Commission, DG XVII/C.2/SAVE, Rue de la Loi 200, B-1049 Brussels,
Tel.: (322) 296 00 23

Schengen Agreement: Concluded in Schengen (Luxembourg) in 1985, this agreement is aimed at the gradual removal of controls at internal frontiers between the Member States. There is also a further agreement on arrangements for processing asylum applications and cross-border cooperation between police forces. The original 1990 target date for opening up the borders for travellers had to be put back several times. Once the 'Schengen Information System' (SIS) had been set up to help in the fight against cross-border crime, the complete removal of border controls was agreed on 26 March 1995 – initially between seven EU countries (Germany, France, Spain, Portugal, Belgium, the Netherlands and Luxembourg). Italy, Greece and Austria will follow later. The United Kingdom, Ireland, Denmark, Sweden and Finland are not party to the Schengen Agreement (→ justice and home affairs).

Schuman Plan: On 9 May 1950 the French Foreign Minister, Robert Schuman, unveiled a plan for limited integration that set in motion the process leading to the creation of the European Coal and Steel Community in 1952. It accommodated a range of different interests. France was concerned to bring the German coal and steel industry under joint control in order to rule out any future prospect of war, while Germany – still with only limited sovereignty – seized the chance to be acknowledged as an equal among the six founder members and to use the opportunity which the scheme presented for reconciliation. To commemorate the occasion, 9 May has been designated Europe Day.

Services: The freedom to provide services is one of the four fundamental freedoms laid down in the EC Treaty (Article 59) and became a practical reality with the introduction of the single market. It enables EU citizens to provide services across national frontiers without any restrictions on the grounds of nationality. 'Services' means any services provided through self-employed, industrial, agricultural or professional activities.

Single European Act: The Single European Act, which was ratified in 1987, supplemented and amended the Treaties of Rome, extending the powers of the Community in several areas and refining decision-making procedures. The introduction of decision-making on the basis of qualified-majority voting under the cooperation procedure was one

A FRONTIER-FREE EUROPE

The Schengen Agreement

No personal controls
at internal borders. Stricter controls at external borders, including ports and airports.

Visa and residence policy
partially harmonized. Uniform visa for all Schengen countries. Common asylum policy.

Cooperation between police forces
'Schengen information system' (SIS) – common computerized investigation and information system. Hot pursuit arrangements to allow police forces to pursue suspects across borders.

 Signatories to Schengen Agreement

Schengen Agreement in force

Cooperation agreement

of the basic necessities for the completion of the → single market. While the single market objective was very much the focus of political attention, the Single Act also provided a legal basis for European political cooperation, which had been developing since 1970. The Maastricht Treaty is a continuation of the deepening process embarked upon with the Single European Act.

Sluice-gate prices: Under the EU farm-price system the sluice-gate price is made up of the cost price of products for processing (eggs, poultry, pork), the agricultural levy and an additional levy. These products enjoy special protection against imports from non-member countries that are priced below cost, in addition to the agricultural levies. The sluice-gate price is calculated on the basis of average production costs on the world market. If import prices are below it, the additional levy is charged to bring them up to the sluice-gate price.

The SME action programme: The action programme for small and medium-sized enterprises (SMEs) is designed to enhance growth, competitiveness and employment. A total of ECU 112.2 million has been allotted to the programme, which comprises pilot projects and subprogrammes relating to partnership, information and finances and is set to run from 1993 to 1999. The European Economic Interest Grouping (EEIG) is closely involved in the implementation of the SME action programme (⇒EEIG, BCC, BC-NET, CSF).

Social Charter: In order to take account of the social dimension of the single market (itself an essentially economic enterprise), on 9 December 1989 the European Council adopted a Community charter of fundamental social rights, setting out minimum standards in a 30-point list. It covers basic rights for all EU citizens as regards freedom of movement, equal treatment, social protection and fair wages. Although the Social Charter is not legally binding, the United Kingdom voted against it (→ social policy).

Social dialogue: Social dialogue is the term used to describe meetings between representatives of management and labour ('the social partners') at European level. It dates back to the mid-1980s, when the European Trade Union Confederation (ETUC), the (UNICE) Union of Industries of the European Community and the European Centre for Public Enterprises (ECPE) began meeting under the chairmanship of the Commission. In the run-up to completion of the single market, the social dialogue was seen as a way of helping to ensure reasonable general conditions.

Socrates: Set up in early 1995, Socrates is an EU programme combining the earlier Erasmus and Lingua education programmes, plus other measures (→ education and youth). The funding available totals ECU 850 million (1995-99), with the focus on three main target areas: (1) measures for higher education (e.g. student exchanges, recognition of studies abroad, European dimension of studies); (2) measures for pre-school, primary and secondary education (e.g. joint school projects, further training for teachers); (3) general measures (e.g. production of teaching materials, further training for language teachers).

Solemn Declaration on European Union: The Solemn Declaration issued by the European Council in Stuttgart in June 1983 marked a major step on the path to European Union. The Declaration reflected the growing desire for foreign policy to be more closely coordinated under European political cooperation. Improved institutional arrangements and cooperation on the approximation of legislation were agreed and concrete goals were spelled out for economic integration in the following years.

Southward enlargement: In the 1970s, Greece (1975), Portugal (1977) and Spain (1977) all applied for membership of the EC following their return to democracy. Southward enlargement is the term used to describe their accession to the Community (Greece in 1981, Portugal and Spain in 1986). The substantial differences in structure and wealth between old and new members posed fresh problems for the EC. Political considerations – the expectation that membership would bolster domestic stability – were the main factor behind approval of their membership applications, despite the concerns about the economic consequences.

Spaak Report: In April 1956 the Spaak Report was presented to the Foreign Ministers of the ECSC countries, recommending the creation of a European Economic Community and a European Atomic Energy Community. At their conference in Messina in 1995 the ministers had asked a committee of experts under the chairmanship of the Belgian Foreign Minister, Paul-Henri Spaak, to examine ways of pursuing economic integration further. The Spaak Report formed the basis for the Treaties of Rome that were signed on 25 March 1957.

Stabex: The Stabex system is one of the cornerstones of the EU's development policy. The EU guarantees the ACP countries minimum levels of earnings for some 40 agricultural products which make up the bulk of their exports. If earnings drop in comparison with the average over the previous years, the Community steps in to meet the deficit with bridging loans or non-repayable credits ($\rightarrow$ development).

Stabilizers: In 1988 the European Council decided to introduce stabilizers in order to curb the growth of farm policy spending. Under the scheme, the guaranteed prices for certain farm products is reduced in the following year if the production ceiling for the previous year is exceeded. This helps to cut back surplus production ($\rightarrow$ agricultural policy).

Standardization: The single market requires the introduction of European standards in place of the existing national standards. Under the EU harmonization directives, the European standards organizations CEN and Cenelec are developing European standards. Common standards will eliminate a wide range of barriers to trade.

Structural Funds: The EU's Structural Funds are administered by the Commission to finance Community structural aid. They comprise the Guidance Section of the EAGGF for agriculture, the Regional Fund for structural aid under the regional policy, the Social Fund for social policy measures, and the new Financial Instrument for Fisheries (FIFG). The Cohesion Fund created in 1993 also serves to further the Community's structural policy objectives. Financial support from the Structural Funds mainly goes to the poorer regions to strengthen the Union's economic and social cohesion so that the challenges of the single market can be met right across the EU. Action is focused on six main objectives. The lion's share goes towards Objective 1 (development and structural adjustment of regions lagging behind). Altogether the budget of the Structural Funds has quadrupled in the last few years, totalling more than ECU 161 billion for the period 1993-99.

Subsidiarity principle: The Treaty on European Union introduced the principle of subsidiarity into the EC Treaty (Article 3b). This means that the Community may take action in areas which do not fall within its exclusive competence 'only if and in so far as the objectives of the proposed action cannot be sufficiently achieved by the Member States and can therefore, by reason of the scale or effects of the proposed action, be better achieved by the Community'.

Subsidy: Subsidies are aids granted to businesses by the public authorities for specific economic policy purposes in the form of direct financial support or tax concessions and the like. For example, subsidies may be granted to keep a business or even an entire sector going, to help companies adjust to changed circumstances, to boost productivity and growth in business and industry. Subsidies that distort competition are prohibited in the EU. Exceptions are permitted where the subsidies are aimed at social, structural and regional improvements. Since subsidies are an obstacle to free trade, efforts are under way, for instance through GATT, to dismantle them altogether.

Sugar Protocol: The Sugar Protocol is an addition to the Lomé Convention under the EU's → development policy. To help secure the earnings of developing countries that are mainly dependent on agriculture, the Union guarantees to buy up an agreed amount of cane sugar annually at EU prices, which are substantially higher than world market prices.

Sysmin: This is a system designed to stabilize the ACP countries' earnings from mining. Among other things, they are granted special loans under Sysmin to finance specific mining projects. In the event of a fall in raw mineral production or exports owing to technical or political difficulties, these aid measures are intended to help maintain the profitability of mining and so prevent a decline in export earnings in this sector.

TACIS: TACIS (Technical assistance to the Commonwealth of Independent State and Georgia) is an EU aid programme set up in 1990 to provide technical assistance for the independent States of the former Soviet Union and Mongolia.

Tariff quotas: Introducing tariff quotas is a way of allowing imports of limited quantities of particular goods duty-free or at reduced rates. By using tariff quotas, the EU or individual Member States are able to ensure supplies of essential goods without reducing their customs protection beyond the amount covered by the quota.

Tax harmonization: Differing tax rates pose an obstacle to the → single market. The EC Treaty provides for the harmonization of indirect taxation (Article 99). This would involve removing all tax borders within the Community, the effects of which have had to be offset to avoid competitive distortions. The most notable example is VAT: the closer the Member States' VAT rates are, the smaller the amount of compensation required. In the field of direct taxation, harmonization of direct taxes on businesses will create a level competitive playing field for all. But tax harmonization involves appreciable restrictions on national sovereignty and has therefore always met with considerable resistance. In October 1992 the Council adopted directives on the approximation of VAT and excise duty rates, in preparation for the removal of border controls on private travel. Under the tax compromise, it is planned to go over to the country-of-origin principle for commercial trade in 1997. Until then the controls that are still needed because of differing tax rates in the Member States have switched from the borders to firms themselves.

Telematics applications: The EU's telematics applications research programme incorporates the AIM, DELTA, DRIVE and Eurotra programmes. The aim is to build the foundations for the gradual introduction of networked European communications technologies in administration, transport, health care, education, libraries and linguistics.

Tempus: Tempus is the Trans-European mobility scheme for university studies. In response to the opening up of Central and Eastern Europe, the EU sought to cater for the specific needs of the countries concerned by setting up the Tempus programme, which operates along the same lines as the existing Community programmes on education and training, and a European foundation for vocational training. Tempus gives financial assistance for joint projects arranged by organizations from EU countries with partners from Central and East European countries. Originally it covered Hungary, Poland, Czechoslovakia and its successor States, the former Yugoslavia and Bulgaria. The programme concentrates primarily on specialist areas of particular importance for the process of economic and socio-political change in Central and Eastern Europe. The second stage of the programme (1994-98) also covers the States of the former Soviet Union under the TACIS programme.

Thermie II: This programme offers financial support to projects on the demonstration of innovative energy technologies. The projects are supposed to test on a real-life scale the ability to function of the new techniques and technologies which have passed the research stage but which it is difficult to implement owing to the fact that there are greater economic risks involved than in the case of traditional projects (⇒SAVE).

For further information, contact:
European Commission, DG XVII, (Energy), Demonstration projects, energy savings and alternative energies, Rue de la Loi 200, B-1049 Brussels, Tel.: (322) 296 04 36

Threshold price: Threshold prices are the minimum prices for imports of farm products into the EU. Imports that are cheaper are brought up to the threshold price by imposing levies and customs duties. The aim is to protect European farmers from cheaper competitors abroad.

Trade barriers: The removal of customs duties and quantitative restrictions in trade between the EC Member States was a major step towards creating a → single market. But free trade can also be hampered by other obstacles (what are known as 'non-tariff barriers'). These include charges on imports and technical barriers due to differences between countries' laws or quality standards (for foodstuffs or medicines, for instance). By harmonizing, standardizing and approximating their laws, the Member States had largely succeeded in removing all remaining barriers to trade by the time the single market came into operation at the end of 1992.

Trans-European networks: In order to exploit the full potential of the → single market, the Community is contributing towards the development of trans-European networks (Articles 129b-129d of the EC Treaty), that is cross-frontier infrastructures in the field of transport, energy, telecommunications and the environment. Measures taken must promote the interoperability of national networks and access to them. In 1994 the European Council decided to provide support for 14 priority transport projects and 10 energy projects.

Treaties of Rome: The Treaties of Rome are the treaties establishing the European Economic Community (EEC) and the European Atomic Energy Community (EAEC/Euratom) plus additional protocols. They were signed on 25 March 1957 by Belgium, Germany, France, Italy, Luxembourg and the Netherlands. The EEC and Euratom, together with the

European Coal and Steel Community (ECSC), which had been set up some years earlier, make up the European Communities. The most important of the treaties is the EEC Treaty (renamed EC Treaty in 1993), the preamble of which sets out the principal goals (these include an ever closer union among the peoples of Europe, economic and social progress of the member countries, constant improvement of living and working conditions, the preservation of peace and liberty). The Treaties of Rome entered into force on 1 January 1958 (→ treaties).

Trevi Group (Terrorisme, radicalisme, extrémisme, violence internationale): This is the name given to informal cooperation between the EU Ministers for Home Affairs and Justice to combat international terrorism and drug trafficking. It was set up in 1975 and has been operational since 1976. The Ministers responsible for internal security in the Community meet at this level twice a year to discuss cooperation and joint strategies. The Trevi Group also cooperates with non-member countries. Cooperation between the Member States on → justice and home affairs is regulated by Article K of the Treaty on European Union.

UNICE: (Union des confédérations de l'industrie et des employeurs d'Europe – Union of Industries of the European Community). Founded in 1959, UNICE represents the interests of member confederations from the EU and EFTA. It coordinates their positions on European issues and puts across their views, especially to the European institutions. Address: 4a Rue Joseph II, boîte 4, B-1040 Brussels.

Union citizenship: Under Article 8 of the EC Treaty everyone who is a national of an EU Member State is also a Union citizen. Union citizens enjoy the following rights: to move and reside freely in the EU; to vote and stand as candidates in municipal and European elections wherever they reside; to receive protection from the diplomatic and consular authorities of other Member States in third countries; and, to petition the European Parliament. In addition Parliament appoints an Ombudsman to consider complaints by Union citizens about the Community administration.

Western European Union (WEU): In 1954, the Western European Union developed from the Brussels Treaty which had been signed in 1948 as a defensive alliance against Germany. Its primary role is to guarantee mutual assistance in the case of an attack on Europe and to maintain peace and security within Europe. For a long time the WEU was viewed as NATO's weak arm despite the fact that the links between the signatories go far beyond NATO agreements. The WEU is currently undergoing a revival as a consequence of the discussions about a European pillar in defence policy and a declaration on WEU in the Maastricht Treaty providing for the gradual development of WEU as the defence component of the European Union.

White Paper: A White Paper is an official set of proposals in a particular policy area. A Green Paper, by contrast, merely sets out a range of ideas that are intended as a basis for discussion on the way to reaching a decision.

White Paper on completing the internal market: This White Paper was published by the Commission and formally approved by the European Council in 1985. It listed 282 proposals and measures to eliminate the practical, technical and tax barriers standing in the way of the → single (or internal) market. Each year the Commission submits a report to the Council and the European Parliament on the measures that have been implemented. By 1 January 1993 around 95% of the measures listed in the White Paper had been adopted.

White Paper on growth, competitiveness and employment: Published by the European Commission in December 1993, this White Paper set out a series of strategic proposals aimed, among other things, at reducing the high level of unemployment in the European Union. It called for market-oriented economic policies, improved infrastructures through the creation of trans-European networks and employment policy measures that were to be implemented mainly by the Member States themselves. The Commission hopes that this will make it possible to halve unemployment by the end of the century.

World Trade Organization (WTO): After the Uruguay Round of GATT negotiations ended, a new independent World Trade Organization was set up in 1995, to which all the existing GATT members belong. The WTO's tasks include fostering trade relations between its members and serving as a forum for future multilateral trade negotiations.

Youth for Europe: Youth for Europe III is an action programme to encourage youth exchanges in the European Union. The third stage (1995-99) involves continuation of the existing Youth for Europe programme and also incorporates projects under the PETRA and Tempus programmes. Run on a decentralized basis by individual national agencies, over the next five years the programme will cover more than 400 000 young people between the ages of 15 and 25, including young people from countries outside the EU (→ education and youth). Address: United Kingdom: British Council, Youth Exchange Centre, 10 Spring Gardens, London SW1A 2BN, Tel. (0171) 389 4030; Ireland: Léargas, 1st floor, Avoca House, 189-193 Parnell Street, Dublin 1, Tel. (01) 873 14 11.

Youth for Europe III: The object of this action programme is to promote youth exchanges in the EU, Iceland, Norway and Liechtenstein. Aimed at teenagers and young adults between the ages of 15 and 25, it gives those interested assistance in preparing an international youth exchange as well as financial support. Training programmes for youth group leaders and organizers are also available (⇒Horizon, Youthstart, Eurathlon).

For further information, contact:
Ireland: Lé argas, 1st Floor, Avoca House, 189-193 Parnell Street, Dublin 1,
Tel.: (01) 873 14 11

UK: British Council, Youth Exchange Centre, 10 Spring Gardens, London, SW1A 2BN,
Tel.: (0171) 389 4030

Youthstart: Youthstart is an important instrument in the fight against unemployment among young people. Aimed at young people under the age of 20, its aim is to ensure a minimum level of training and qualifications throughout the EU, to create links between training and the labour market, to promote independent counselling and to make available supporting infrastructure (⇒Youth for Europe, Horizon).

For further information, contact:
European Commission, DG V/B.4, Rue de la Loi 200, B-1049 Brussels, Tel.: (322) 299 40 73.

A chronology of
European integration

A chronology of European integration

by Michael Matern

19 September 1946	Speaking in Zurich, Winston Churchill calls for a United States of Europe.
8 to 10 May 1948	Coordinating committee for European unity organizes Hague Congress. In its resolutions the Congress calls for a united democratic Europe and the creation of the Council of Europe.
5 May 1949	Council of Europe set up in London, to be based in Strasbourg.
9 May 1950	French Foreign Minister Robert Schuman proposes creation of European Coal and Steel Community (ECSC).
24 October 1950	French Prime Minister René Pleven puts forward plan to create an integrated European army.
18 April 1951	Belgium, the Federal Republic of Germany, France, Italy, Luxembourg and the Netherlands ('the Six') sign Treaty establishing European Coal and Steel Community (Treaty of Paris).
27 May 1952	The Six sign Treaty to establish European Defence Community (EDC). However, French National Assembly refuses to ratify it in 1954.
10 August 1952	The High Authority, ECSC executive institution, starts work under Presidency of Jean Monnet.
10 September 1952	Foreign Ministers of the Six ask ECSC Common Assembly to draft Treaty establishing European Political Community (EPC). Presented on 10 March 1953.
10 February 1953	Common market established for coal, iron ore and scrap.
1 May 1953	Common market established for steel.
30 August 1954	Treaty to establish EDC and therefore EPC rejected by French National Assembly.
1 and 2 June 1955	Foreign Ministers of the Six, meeting in Messina, agree to move ahead with integration. Intergovernmental committee set up, chaired by Paul-Henri Spaak.
25 March 1957	In Rome the Six sign Treaties setting up European Economic Community (EEC) and Euratom (Treaty of Rome).
1 January 1958	Treaty of Rome comes into effect. Walter Hallstein is first President of the EEC Commission, Louis Armand first President of Euratom Commission.
1 January 1959	Customs duties within the EEC reduced by 10%.
21 July 1959	Seven Member States of the Organization for European Economic Cooperation (OEEC), Austria, Denmark, Norway, Portugal, Sweden, Switzerland and United Kingdom agree to set up EFTA (European Free Trade Association). Treaty comes into force on 3 May 1960.

1 January 1961	National duties of EEC States partially aligned for first time. Goal is a single external tariff.
10 February 1961	Heads of State or Government agree closer political cooperation. Committee of officials chaired by Christian Fouchet to draw up a plan.
9 July 1961	EEC-Greece Association Agreement signed.
31 July 1961	Ireland applies to join EEC.
9 August 1961	United Kingdom applies to join EEC.
10 August 1961	Denmark applies to join EEC.
8 November 1961	Accession negotiations open with United Kingdom.
14 January 1962	Council adopts first four regulations for a common market in agriculture, first financial regulation and regulation governing competition.
17 April 1962	Negotiations on political union abandoned because no agreement reached on Fouchet committee proposals.
30 April 1962	Norway applies to join EEC.
14 January 1963	French President de Gaulle vetoes British membership.
22 January 1963	France and Federal Republic of Germany sign Treaty of Friendship and Cooperation in Paris (Elysée Treaty).
29 January 1963	Accession negotiations with United Kingdom broken off.
20 July 1963	Association Convention between EEC and 17 African States and Madagascar signed in Yaoundé (Yaoundé Convention).
12 September 1963	EEC-Turkey Association Agreement signed.
8 April 1965	Treaty signed merging Executives of the three European Communities (ECSC, EEC, Euratom).
10 May 1967	United Kingdom makes second application for EEC membership. Ireland also makes second application.
11 May 1967	Denmark makes second application for EEC membership.
1 July 1967	Merger Treaty of 8 April 1965 enters into force. Jean Rey is first Commission President for all three Communities (ECSC, EEC, Euratom).
24 July 1967	Norway makes second application for membership.
28 July 1967	Sweden applies for membership.
1 July 1968	Customs union completed and common external tariff established.
29 July 1968	Freedom of movement guaranteed for workers within the Community in order to establish common labour market.
18 December 1968	Commission presents 'Mansholt Plan' for reform of agriculture in the Community to Council.
4 March 1969	EC signs Association Agreement with Tunisia and Morocco.
29 July 1969	Second Yaoundé Convention signed. It comes into force on 1 January 1971.
1 and 2 December 1969	Heads of State or Government meet in The Hague to discuss completion of single market, greater integration and enlargement of the EC. They agree to phase in economic and monetary union (EMU) by 1980, to speed up integration and cooperation on political matters. They also agree to open negotiations with Denmark, Ireland, Norway and the United Kingdom.

19–22 December 1969	Council agrees a financial arrangement for agriculture, to allocate EC its own resources and to strengthen European Parliament's budgetary powers.
1 January 1970	Responsibility for external trade policy passes from Member States to EC.
21 April 1970	Council decides that from 1975 EC will receive its own resources.
30 June 1970	Second round of negotiations with Denmark, Ireland, Norway and the United Kingdom opens in Luxembourg
2 July 1970	Franco M. Malfatti becomes President of European Commission.
8 October 1970	Werner Plan on phased attainment of economic and monetary union, named after Luxembourg's Prime Minister, is presented to the Council and Commission.
27 October 1970	Foreign Ministers, meeting in Luxembourg, present Davignon Report on European political cooperation (EPC) to Heads of State or Government.
5 December 1970	EC-Malta Association Agreement signed.
1 July 1971	Community agrees 'system of generalized preferences' in trade with 91 developing countries.
22 January 1972	Treaties signed concerning accession of Denmark, Ireland, Norway and the United Kingdom to the European Communities.
21 March 1972	Currency 'snake' introduced: Governments of Member States and Council agree to let the exchange rate of Member States' currencies fluctuate by no more than 2.25%.
22 March 1972	Sicco Mansholt becomes President of European Commission.
10 May 1972	In a referendum Ireland votes to join EC.
13 July 1972	House of Commons approves UK accession to EC.
22 July 1972	Free trade agreements signed with the EFTA States which did not apply to join EC (Austria, Iceland, Portugal, Sweden and Switzerland).
25 September 1972	In a referendum Norway rejects EC membership.
2 October 1972	In a referendum Denmark votes to join EC.
19 and 20 October 1972	Heads of State or Government of the enlarged Community agree to transform EC into a European Union and adopt new timetable for EMU.
19 December 1972	EC-Cyprus Association Agreement signed.
1 January 1973	EC formally enlarged to nine members. EC granted sole responsibility for common trade policy.
11 and 12 March 1973	Ireland, Italy and United Kingdom leave currency 'snake'. Finance Ministers decide joint float against dollar with fixed exchange rates.
14 May 1973	Norway signs free trade agreement with EC.
23 July 1973	Foreign Ministers present second report on EPC (Copenhagen Report).
26–27 July 1973	Ministerial conference held in Brussels between EC and 46 African, Caribbean and Pacific states (ACP States) on establishing relations.
5 October 1973	Finland signs free trade agreement with EC.
21 January 1974	Employment and Social Affairs Ministers adopt the Community social action programme whereby EC becomes active in three

areas: employment issues; harmonization of living and working conditions; and, participation by both sides of industry in EC social and economic policy decisions.

9 and 10 December 1974	In Paris Heads of State or Government agree to meet regularly as European Council.
28 February 1975	EC and 46 ACP States sign first Lomé Convention granting financial and technical assistance and trade concessions.
10–11 March 1975	In Dublin Heads of State or Government meet for first time as European Council.
18 March 1975	Council of Ministers agrees to set up European Regional Development Fund.
11 May 1975	EC and Israel sign cooperation agreement.
5 June 1975	In a referendum United Kingdom votes to stay in EC.
12 June 1975	Greece applies to join EC.
16 September 1975	Official relations established between EC and China.
1 and 2 December 1975	Rome European Council agrees to introduce a European passport and to participate in North-South dialogue.
16 February 1976	Council for Mutual Economic Assistance (CMEA) proposes agreement between its members and EC.
27 July 1976	Accession negotiations open with Greece.
20 December 1976	Roy Jenkins becomes President of European Commission.
28 March 1977	Portugal applies to join EC.
1 July 1977	Customs duties between nine EC members completely removed.
28 July 1977	Spain applies to join EC.
6 and 7 July 1978	Bremen European Council approves plan to set up European Monetary System (EMS) and European monetary unit (Ecu).
5 September 1978	EC countries start negotiations on common fisheries policy.
17 October 1978	Accession negotiations open with Portugal.
5 February 1979	Accession negotiations open with Spain.
13 March 1979	EMS takes effect retrospectively from 1 January 1979.
28 May 1979	Acts relating to Greece's accession signed in Athens.
7 and 10 June 1979	First elections to European Parliament by direct universal suffrage held in the nine Member States.
17 and 20 July 1979	First session of directly elected Parliament in Strasbourg. Simone Veil elected first President of Parliament.
31 October 1979	Second Lomé Convention signed by EC and 58 ACP States in Lomé.
7 and 8 March 1980	Community signs cooperation agreement with ASEAN States.
2 April 1980	Community signs cooperation agreement with Yugoslavia.
12 and 13 June 1980	Venice European Council issues statement on Middle East conflict.
28 July 1980	EC signs cooperation agreement with Romania.
6 October 1980	Commission declares state of manifest crisis in steel industry and requests Council approval for the introduction of production quotas.
1 January 1981	Greece becomes 10th Member State.
6 and 20 January 1981	German and Italian Foreign Ministers propose strengthening EPC (Colombo/Genscher initiative).
6 January 1981	Gaston Thorn becomes President of European Commission.

13 October 1981	At European Council meeting in London, Foreign Ministers approve London report on procedural improvements for EPC.
4 January 1982	Foreign Ministers condemn imposition of martial law at special conference on situation in Poland.
19 February 1982	Pieter Dankert elected second President of Parliament since introduction of European elections.
23 February 1982	In a referendum Greenland votes to leave EC.
30 June 1982	Joint declaration by Parliament, Council and Commission on measures to improve budgetary procedures.
25 January 1983	After six years' negotiation Member States agree common fisheries policy.
17 to 19 June 1983	European Council signs Solemn Declaration on European Union in Stuttgart.
14 February 1984	Parliament approves draft Treaty on European Union as drawn up by Institutional Affairs Committee under Altiero Spinelli.
14 to 17 June 1984	Second direct elections to European Parliament.
25 and 26 June 1984	Fontainebleau European Council makes progress in important areas: agreement to set up Dooge committee on institutional affairs and Adonnino committee on 'a people's Europe'.
24 July 1984	Pierre Pfimlin elected third President of Parliament since introduction of European elections.
26 September 1984	Commercial and economic cooperation agreement initialled by China and EC.
8 December 1984	Third Lomé Convention signed by EC and 65 ACP States.
7 January 1985	Jacques Delors becomes President of EC Commission.
29 and 30 March 1985	Brussels European Council agrees integrated Mediterranean programme removing all remaining obstacles to Spanish and Portuguese accession.
12 June 1985	Instruments of accession of Spain and Portugal signed.
14 June 1985	Commission presents White Paper on completion of single market.
28 and 29 June 1985	Milan European Council reaches majority decision to convene Intergovernmental Conference to amend Treaty of Rome in accordance with Article 236 of the EEC Treaty.
2 and 3 December 1985	Luxembourg European Council agrees institutional reform extending Community responsibilities and legal framework for cooperation on foreign policy. Treaty amendments brought together in Single European Act.
1 January 1986	Spain and Portugal join Community, bringing membership to 12.
17 and 28 February 1986	Single European Act signed by Governments of the 12 Member States.
1 January 1987	EPC secretariat set up in Brussels.
20 January 1987	Sir Henry Plumb elected fourth President of Parliament since introduction of European elections.
14 April 1987	Turkey applies to join EC.
1 July 1987	Single European Act enters into force.
11 and 12 February 1988	Brussels European Council agrees to 'Delors I package' reforming financial system and common agricultural policy and doubling EC Structural Funds.

29 March 1988	Commission presents Cecchini report ('The Cost of non-Europe') quantifying the advantages of a single market.
26 September 1988	Commercial and economic cooperation agreement signed by Hungary and EC.
15 to 18 June 1989	Third direct elections to European Parliament.
26 and 27 June 1989	Madrid European Council agrees to convene Intergovernmental Conference in line with 'Delors Plan', drawn up by governors of central banks under Commission President Delors, providing for creation of EMU in three stages.
29 June 1989	Spain joins EMS.
17 July 1989	Austria applies to join EC.
26 July 1989	Enrico Barón Crespo elected fifth President of Parliament since introduction of European elections.
19 September 1989	Commercial and economic cooperation agreement signed by Poland and EC.
15 December 1989	Fourth Lomé Convention signed by EC and 68 ACP States.
19 December 1989	Start of negotiations between EC and EFTA countries on strengthening cooperation and forming European Economic Area (EEA).
9 May 1990	Trade and cooperation agreement signed by Bulgaria and EC.
19 June 1990	Second Schengen Agreement signed in Luxembourg.
25 and 26 June 1990	Dublin European Council agrees to convene an Intergovernmental Conference on EMU and another on political union.
1 July 1990	Stage I of EMU begins.
4 July 1990	Cyprus applies to join EC.
16 July 1990	Malta applies to join EC.
21 August 1990	Commission adopts package of measures for integrating German Democratic Republic to EC.
3 October 1990	Treaty between Federal Republic of Germany and German Democratic Republic enters into force unifying Germany. The five new *Länder* are part of EC.
8 October 1990	United Kingdom becomes 10th member of EMS.
29 March 1991	Members of Schengen Agreement and Poland agree abolition of visa requirement, which takes effect on 8 April 1991.
24 June 1991	Finance Ministers achieve breakthrough on harmonizing VAT and excise duties on alcohol, tobacco and mineral oil. From 1993 standard rate of VAT should be no less than 15%.
25 June 1991	Spain and Portugal join Schengen Agreement.
1 July 1991	Sweden applies to join EC.
9 and 10 December 1991	European Council Summit in Maastricht. Heads of State or Government reach agreement on draft Treaty on European Union.
16 December 1991	Europe Agreements signed by EC and Poland, Hungary and Czechoslovakia in Brussels.
13 January 1992	Egon Klepsch (PPE) elected sixth President of Parliament since introduction of European elections.
7 February 1992	Maastricht Treaty on European Union signed.
18 March 1992	Finland applies to join EC.
5 April 1992	Portuguese escudo joins EMS.

2 May 1992	In Porto EC and EFTA Foreign Ministers sign agreement establishing European economic area (EEA).
20 May 1992	Switzerland applies to join EC.
2 June 1992	In a referendum 50.7% of Danes vote against ratification of Union Treaty.
20 September 1992	In a referendum 51.05% of French vote in favour of ratification of Union Treaty.
25 November 1992	Norway applies to join EC.
6 December 1992	In a referendum Switzerland votes against EEA agreement.
11 and 12 December 1992	Edinburgh European Council accepts Danish wish to opt out of a single currency and common defence policy in the European Union. It endorses Delors II package on financial arrangements for EC until 1999 and growth initiative.
22 December 1992	Europe Agreement signed by EC and Bulgaria in Brussels.
1 January 1993	Single market largely completed.
12 January 1993	Iceland ratifies EEA Treaty. Except for Switzerland, all EFTA States have done so.
1 February 1993	Europe Agreement signed by EC and Romania.
17 March 1993	Additional protocol enables EC and EFTA to permit EEA Treaty to enter into force following withdrawal of Switzerland.
18 May 1993	Following acceptance of Denmark's opt-outs, 56.8% of Danes vote in favour of Union Treaty in second referendum.
2 August 1993	Following upheavals within EMS, Economics and Finance Ministers temporarily widen ERM currency bands from 2.25 to 15%.
4 October 1993	Renegotiated Europe Agreement signed by EC and successor States of Czechoslovakia.
12 October 1993	German Constitutional Court rules in favour of Treaty on European Union. Ratification now completed in all Member States.
29 October 1993	At special summit in Brussels European Union Heads of State or Government agree location of new EU institutions. European Monetary Institute to be in Frankfurt, Europol in the Netherlands and European Environment Agency in Denmark.
1 November 1993	Treaty on European Union enters into force.
10 and 11 December 1993	Economic situation in European Union is main topic of Brussels European Council meeting. Commission President Delors presents White Paper on growth, competitiveness and employment.
1 January 1994	Stage II of economic and monetary union begins.
16 March 1994	Accession negotiations concluded with Norway, after Austria, Finland and Sweden.
1 April 1994	Hungary applies to join EU.
8 April 1994	Poland applies to join EU.
9 to 12 June 1994	Fourth direct elections to European Parliament.
12 June 1994	In a referendum 66.4% of Austrians vote in favour of joining EU.
24 and 25 June 1994	At European Council meeting in Corfu EU and Russia sign partnership agreement.
19 July 1994	Klaus Hänsch (PSE) elected seventh President of Parliament since introduction of European elections.
16 October 1994	In a referendum 57% of Finns vote in favour of joining EU.

13 November 1994	52.2% of Swedes vote in favour of joining EU.
27 and 28 November 1994	52.2% of Norwegians vote against joining EU.
9 and 10 December 1994	Essen European Council agrees strategy to bring Central and East European States closer to EU and approves Commission's new Mediterranean strategy.
1 January 1995	Austria, Finland and Sweden join EU.
9 January 1995	Austria joins EMS.
19 January 1995	After fierce debate European Parliament approves new European Commission.
23 January 1995	Commission begins its five-year term under President Santer.
26 March 1995	Schengen Agreement enters into force. No more passport controls between Benelux countries, France, Germany, Portugal and Spain.
12 June 1995	EU signs Association Agreements with Estonia, Latvia and Lithuania.
22 June 1995	Romania applies to join EU.
26 and 27 June 1995	Cannes European Council gives mandate to reflection group to prepare 1996 Intergovernmental Conference on revision of Treaty on European Union.
27 June 1995	Slovak Republic applies to join EU.
18 July 1995	EU signs first Association Agreement with Tunisia as part of new Mediterranean policy.
17 September 1995	Sweden holds European Parliament elections for first time.
27 October 1995	Latvia applies to join EU.
20 November 1995	EU signs Association Agreement with Israel.
27 and 28 November 1995	At Euro-Mediterranean Conference in Barcelona EU agrees long-term partnership with North African and Middle East States. One aim is Europe-Mediterranean free-trade area by 2010.
28 November 1995	Estonia applies to join EU.
2 December 1995	New transatlantic agenda signed in Madrid. European Union and USA declare willingness to develop trade and work together closely to resolve international problems.
8 December 1995	Lithuania applies to join EU.
14 December 1995	Bulgaria applies to join EU.
15 and 16 December 1995	Madrid European Council decides on euro as name for future European currency. Timetable for introduction of EMU to remain unaltered. From 2002 Euro is to be sole legal tender for EMU Members. Free-trade agreement signed with Mercosur States.
1 January 1996	Customs union between EU and Turkey enters into force.
17 January 1996	Czech Republic applies to join EU.
29 February 1996	Russia becomes 39th member of Council of Europe.
27 March 1996	After British scientists prove that BSE (bovine spongiform encephalopathy) can be transmitted to humans through consumption of beef, European Commission imposes worldwide export ban on British beef and beef products.
29 March 1996	Intergovernmental Conference on revision of Maastricht Treaty formally opens in Turin. Within 12 months proposals are to be developed on justice and home affairs, closeness to people,

	openness, improving institutional effectiveness and foreign policy decision-making structures.
3 June 1996	EU Employment and Social Affairs Ministers adopt common position with view to adopting Directive on posting of workers. Employees sent by their companies to other EU countries must be employed under conditions applying in host country.
10 June 1996	Slovenia applies to join EU.
20 June 1996	EU Energy Ministers agree Regulation to liberalize energy market within the EU.
21 and 22 June 1996	Florence European Council adopts Europol Convention.
13 October 1996	Austria holds European Parliament elections for first time.
14 October 1996	Finland joins EMS.
20 October 1996	Finland holds European Parliament elections for first time.
6 November 1996	Croatia becomes 40th member of Council of Europe.
24 November 1996	Italy rejoins the EMS exchange rate mechanism
13 and 14 December 1996	The European Council in Dublin agrees a stability and growth pact for the economic and monetary union and the future euro notes are presented to the public. The European leaders commit themselves to fighting international crime.

List of authors

Sven Behrendt – Centre for Applied Policy Research, University of Munich.

Udo Diedrichs – Institut für politische Wissenschaft und Europäische Fragen (Institute of Political Science and European Affairs), University of Cologne.

Dr Christian Engel – Staatskanzlei des Landes Nordrhein-Westfalen (Chancellery of North-Rhine Westphalia), Düsseldorf.

Dr Jürgen Erdmenger – European Commission, Directorate-General for Transport, Brussels.

Dr Fritz Franzmeyer – Deutsches Institut für Wirtschaftsforschung (German Institute for Economic Research), Berlin.

Dr Eckart Gaddum – ZDF-Landesstudio (Regional centre of second German national television channel), Thüringen.

Prof. Erwin Häckel – Deutsche Gesellschaft für Auswärtige Politik (German Foreign Policy Society), Bonn.

Olaf Hillenbrand – Centre for Applied Policy Research, University of Munich.

Josef Janning – Centre for Applied Policy Research, University of Munich.

Bernd Janssen (†) – European Education Centre, Bonn.

Dr Mathias Jopp – Institut für Europäische Politik (Institute of European Politics), Bonn.

Henry Krägenau – HWWA-Institut für Wirtschaftsforschung (HWWA Institute for Economic Research), Hamburg.

Dr Thomas Läufer – Deutscher Bundestag, Speaker's office, Bonn.

Barbara Lippert – Institut für Europäische Politik (Institute of European Politics), Bonn.

Michael Matern – Landeszentrale für politische Bildung Rheinland-Pfalz (Rhineland-Palatinate Office for Political Education), Mainz.

Andreas Maurer – Institut für Europäische Politik (Institute of European Politics), Bonn.

Patrick Meyer – Centre for Applied Policy Research, University of Munich.

Prof. Jörg Monar – Centre for Federal Studies, University of Leicester.

Dr Melanie Piepenschneider – Konrad Adenauer Foundation, St Augustin.

Dr Elfriede Regelsberger – Institut für Europäische Politik (Institute of European Politics), Bonn.

Dieter Rometsch – Institut für Europäische Politik (Institute of European Politics), Bonn.

Reinhard Rupprecht – Bundesministerium des Innern, Abteilung Innere Sicherheit, (Ministry of the Interior, Internal Security Department).

Nicole Schley – Centre for Applied Policy Research, University of Munich.

Dr Peter-W. Schlüter – European Monetary Institute, Frankfurt am Main.

Ralf Schmitt – Badisches Tagblatt, Wirtschaftsredaktion (Baden daily newspaper, economy section), Baden-Baden.

Dr Otto Schmuck – Rhineland Palatinate representation to the Federal Government, Bonn.

Kristin Schreiber – European Commission, Directorate-General for Industry, Brussels.

Dr Bernhard Seidel – Deutsches Institut für Wirtschaftsforschung (German Institute for Economic Research), Berlin.

Jürgen Turek – Centre for Applied Policy Research, University of Munich.

Prof. Winfried von Urff – Department of Agricultural Policy, University of Munich-Weihenstephan.

Prof. Wolfgang Wessels – Department of Political Science and European Affairs, University of Cologne.

Prof. Werner Weidenfeld – Geschwister-Scholl-Institut für Politische Wissenschaft (Geschwister-Scholl Institute of Political Science), University of Munich.

Anita Wolf-Niedermaier – Graduiertenkolleg des Mannheimer Zentrums für Europäische Sozialforschung (Research school of the Mannheim European Social Research Centre).

Editor: **Nicole Schley** – Centre for Applied Policy Research, University of Munich.

List of abbreviations

ACP	African, Caribbean and Pacific countries parties to the Lomé Agreement
ASEAN	Association of South-East Asian Nations
Benelux	Economic Union of Belgium, Luxembourg and the Netherlands
CAP	Common agricultural policy
CCT	Common Customs Tariff
Cedefop	European Centre for the Development of Vocational Training
CEN	European Committee for Standardization
Cenelec	European Committee for Electrotechnical Standardization
CFSP	Common foreign and security policy
Comett	Community programme in education and training for technology
COPA	Committee of Agricultural Organizations in the European Community
Coreper	Permanent Representatives Committee
COST	European Cooperation on Scientific and Technical Research
CSF	Community support framework
EAGGF	European Agricultural Guidance and Guarantee Fund
EBRD	European Bank for Reconstruction and Development
EC	European Community
ECB	European Central Bank
ECJ	European Court of Justice
Ecofin Council	Council of Ministers for Economic and Financial Affairs
ECSC	European Coal and Steel Community
ECU	European currency unit
EDF	European Development Fund
EEA	European Economic Area
EEC	European Economic Community
EFTA	European Free Trade Association
EIB	European Investment Bank
EMCF	European Monetary Cooperation Fund
EMI	European Monetary Institute
EMS	European Monetary System
EMU	Economic and monetary union
Envireg	Programme for regional environment measures
EP	European Parliament
EPC	European political cooperation
Erasmus	European Community action scheme for the mobility of university students
ERDF	European Regional Development Fund
ESA	European Space Agency
ESC	Economic and Social Committee
ESF	European Social Fund

Esprit	European strategic programme for research and development in information technologies
ETUC	European Trade Union Confederation
EU	European Union
Euratom	European Atomic Energy Community (EAEC)
Eureka	European Research Coordination Agency
Europol	European Police Office
FIFG	Financial Instrument for Fisheries Guidance
GATT	General Agreement on Tariffs and Trade
GDP	Gross domestic product
GNP	Gross national product
HDTV	High-definition television
Interreg	Community initiative for border areas
JET	Joint European Torus – research project on controlled thermonuclear fusion
JRC	Joint Research Centre
Leonardo	Reshaped PETRA programme
Lingua	Programme to promote training in foreign languages in the European Community
MEDIA	Measures to encourage the development of the audiovisual production industry
NCI	New Community Instrument (borrowing and lending facility to promote investment)
NET	Next European Torus (nuclear fusion project)
OSCE	Organization for Security and Cooperation in Europe
PETRA	Action programme for the vocational training of young people and their preparation for adult and working life
PHARE	Poland and Hungary: aid for economic restructuring
RACE	Research and development in advanced communications technologies for Europe
SIS	Schengen information system
SME	Small and medium-sized enterprises
Socrates	Reshaped Erasmus programme
Sprint	Strategic programme for innovation and technology transfer
TACIS	Technical assistance to the Commonwealth of Independent States and Georgia
TARIC	Integrated customs tariff of the European Communities
Tempus	Trans-European mobility scheme for university studies
TREVI	Terrorism, radicalism, extremism, vandalism international
UNICE	Union of Industries of the European Community
UNO	United Nations Organization
WEU	Western European Union
WTO	World Trade Organization

European Commission
Institut für Europäische Politik

Europe from A to Z
Guide to European integration

Luxembourg: Office for Official Publications of the European Communities, 1997
266 pp. — 16.2 x 22.9 cm.

European Documentation series — 1997

ISBN 92-827-9419-9

Europe from A to Z is for all readers looking for quick and
comprehensive answers about the main themes, concepts and facts
surrounding European union.
It answers any questions you might have in plain language and makes
Europe readily understandable.

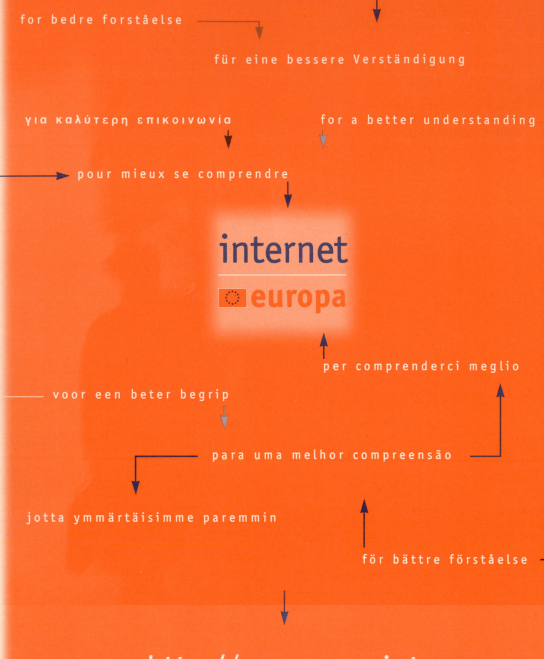

http://europa.eu.int